Som

Hope for Our Time

SUNY Series in Judaica
Hermeneutics, Mysticism, and Religion

———————————

Michael Fishbane, Robert Goldberg, and Arthur Green
EDITORS

Hope for Our Time

Key Trends in the Thought of Martin Buber

Avraham Shapira

translated by
Jeffrey M. Green

STATE UNIVERSITY OF NEW YORK PRESS

Published by
State University of New York Press

Printed in the United States of America

For information, address the State University of New York Press,
State University Plaza, Albany, NY 12246

Marketing by Nancy Farrell
Production by Bernadine Dawes

Library of Congress Cataloging-in-Publication Data

Shapira, Avraham, 1935–
    [Mivnim du 'aliyim be-haguto shel M.M. Buber. English]
    Hopes for our time : key trends in the thought of Martin Buber /
Avraham Shapira : translated by Jeffrey M. Green.
        p.   cm. — (SUNY series in Judaica)
    Includes bibliographical references and index.
    ISBN 0-7914-4125-3 (hc : alk. paper). — ISBN 0-7914-4126-1 (pb :
alk. paper)
    1. Buber, Martin, 1878–1965. 2. Philosophy, Modern—20th century.
3. Philosophy, Jewish. I. Title. II. Series.
B3213.B84S4813   1999
296.3'092—dc21   98-54462
                                                                  CIP

1   2   3   4   5   6   7   8   9   10

Contents

Preface

This book is dedicated to the memory of Professor Alexander Altmann, one of the guiding spirits of contemporary Jewish studies—teacher, rabbi, scholar, and man of letters. I enjoyed the privilege of extended personal contact with him from the late 1970s until the last months of his life, in Spring 1987. We conducted lengthy conversations, both at his home in Newton Centre, near Boston, and during each of his numerous visits to Israel; in between, we maintained contact by writing. We discussed at length the dilemmas of Jewish existence in our time in America and Israel, the issue of tolerance and the Jewish tradition, and the "problem of man" in this age.

We spoke more than a little on the special place held by Martin Buber among the giants of the creative Jewish spirit in the twentieth century. During the course of my lengthy meetings with Professor Altmann at his home during the beginning of 1982, I discussed with him the attempt in my doctoral dissertation to identify basic dual structures in the thought of Martin Buber. If I may say so, he responded with deep interest, which he expressed thereafter in a number of personal letters. Following the submission of the dissertation and its approval by the Senate of Tel-Aviv University, he wrote, in an evaluation of my work dated 6 September 1984:

> . . . I wish to comment on Avraham Shapira's recently completed work, "Dual Structures in the Thought of Martin Buber." . . . It is the ripe fruit of intensive and penetrating occupation with Buber's

thought by a writer of note who was personally close to Buber and wrote what amounts to a most intimate spiritual biography of the man. Never before has the totality of Buber's vast oeuvre been analyzed so thoroughly and with a comparable degree of genuine understanding. Shapira's novel approach traces Buber's spiritual development to the reality of inner experiences and, at the same time, makes the important discovery that there are certain dualistic "structures" that determine throughout the mold of his thinking. It is the carefully documented presentation of these structures that constitutes the core of the book and furnishes the key with which to unlock the world of Buberian thought. Many areas of Buber's work—his anthropology, educational theory, and political notions, among others—are illumined by the new approach. The organic unity of Buber's achievement emerges in full clarity. I am convinced that this extraordinary piece of work by Avraham Shapira will usher in a new wave of heightened interest in the abiding significance of Martin Buber and thereby deepen our awareness of the spiritual issues we have to face on many fronts. . . .

It was Professor Altmann who encouraged me to rework this dissertation in book form. Most of the chapters of the present work are based upon it. Sadly, I am unable to share with him my joy in the completion of this project.

This book is associated with Professor Altmann's name through additional threads. The scholars who accepted it for publication by SUNY Press, Professors Michael Fishbane and Arthur Green, were both disciples of Professor Altmann. A shared relation to Buber's universe formed the background for my meeting with my friend and colleague, Professor Paul Mendes-Flohr, likewise a student of Professor Altmann, who continues in his path. My discussions with Mendes-Flohr regarding Buber's thought are reflected in the present book, which likewise contains references to the original writings of this friend. I conducted fruitful conversations concerning the issues discussed in this book with Professor Gilya Gerda Schmidt of the University of Tennessee, Knoxville. Her professional advice and insights assisted me in the shaping of the book; she also served as editor of the final manuscript.

The careful and devoted work of the book's translator, Dr. Jeffrey Green, left its mark upon this English version. Rabbi Tamar Kolberg carefully read the manuscript of the translation; her extensive knowledge and the fineness of her distinctions assisted me greatly. The late Raphael Buber, the eldest son of Martin Buber and the guardian of his spiritual legacy, was a partner in spirit and a personal friend. He passed away at a ripe old age in December 1990. The lively interest that he always displayed in my work on Buber's thought, including the subject of the present book, was of great significance to me. I cherish his memory.

Finally, my beloved wife Iris and our children Yaniv, Sivan, and Yonat were active partners in the shaping of this work. If my spiritual and scholarly work has borne fruit, it is thanks to them.

To all these, my gratitude from the depths of my heart.

AVRAHAM SHAPIRA
TEL AVIV UNIVERSITY

INTRODUCTION

The writing of Mordecai Martin Buber (1878–1965) comprises nearly sixty-five years of creativity. His bibliography includes hundreds of entries, and his works have been translated into twenty-three languages, including Finnish and Japanese. He was immersed in several cultural realms, some reaching far beyond the Jewish and Western worlds. Buber himself shows awareness of this quality of his writings by referring to them as "mein Geistergarten" (my garden of spirits).[1] He was a polymath whose encyclopedic knowledge was placed at the service of his worldviews.[2] The expression of these views rather than the mere extent of his knowledge made him one of the few universal men of the twentieth century.

The many-sidedness of his creativity over long, productive years and the admirable breadth of the knowledge and cultural heritages with which he grappled make it difficult to present an exhaustive account of his spiritual endeavors.

Many species are planted in his "garden of spirits." Multiple disciplines are represented there, as well as varied modes of expression (from systematic philosophical exposition to fiction and poetry). It may well be asked whether it is possible to locate guidelines or underlying structures that bind together all of this wide-ranging material. And another question: Is it possible to discuss each of the branches of his enterprise by itself? More than forty years of thought and research are concentrated in certain areas of this life work, such as his Hasidic writings, his Bible projects, and others. Is it possible to combine all of these in a unified ensemble? And, if this is indeed possible, what is the nature of this unity?

The following study treats these questions regarding the formation of Buber's work in its entirety.

POLAR DUALITY

The circumstances of Buber's life introduced him into various cultural environments. From childhood he experienced tensions between opposing tendencies within the Jewish world as well as those between it and the surrounding cultures (Polish-Christian, German, general European). From the beginning of the second decade of his life, and more strongly as a young man, he was subject to divergent tendencies that brought him to a mode of experience that he called a "vortex," and "Olam-ha-Tohu" (the World of Confusion), as he says some twenty-five years afterward in *My Way to Hasidism* (1917). As a young man, while studying at the university, these existential oppositions grew stronger in several respects. At this time he became intensely involved with German culture.

He was struggling with the polarity of "Judaism" versus "Mankind," and "East" versus "West," and he was involved with mystical aestheticism and the Zionist movement. He did not wish to ignore the components of the landscape of his childhood or to repress the spiritual tendencies to which he clung. Hence his being was torn between the contradictory elements of realms that were far removed from each other. He called for "no blurring and neutralization of opposites" (as he wrote in a letter to G. Landauer, dated 18 March 1913). The existential duality that characterized Buber was embodied in ways of conceiving and thinking based principally on *polarity*. For him this meant the refusal to view opposing (and even contradictory) realms as dichotomies, that is, as mutually exclusive; instead, he saw them as conditioned upon each other. For him polarity is primarily a living, existential experience, from which are derived his hermeneutic methods and philosophical discourse. As this polarity developed within him, he consolidated on its basis an approach to creation, to man, to nature, and to history. The first process of consolidation appears in his writings from 1910 to 1913. Afterward, he viewed polarity as "the source and significance of all things of the spirit."³ All the spiritual transformations and developments after that time never abandoned the rootedness of this approach. His writings always embody tensions between ways of thinking that are difficult to reconcile with each other. He seeks to relate them to each other and to deduce "the unity of the life of the spirit" from them.

POWERS AND FORMS

Buber's focusing on "lived experience" and personal creativity has been discussed more than once in the scholarly literature about him. These features were already central in the presentation of his ideas in his articles written in the early years of the twentieth century; at this time he also rejected "pure conceptualism" and the elements that organize a systematic order.

Buber strove from the beginning of his career to develop "a new language" embodied in "color." Pictorial and colorful "vision" was identified in his early view with "inebriating suggestion" and with ecstasy. The affirmation of "color" arose with the rejection of "form." "Reality," he stated, "places the obstacles of form and boundary in the artist's path." The colorful is dynamic, whereas "form" is static, lacking vitality. "Form separates, color unites." In his writings, "the colorist hymn" is contrasted with abstract thinking ("cognitive phenomenon") and viewed as the opposite pole of organizing patterns, methods, and structural formation.⁴ But, at the same time, he is not content with experiential-mystical subjectivism; the visual image ("nature") and the conceptual abstraction ("form") are often joined together in his thought in unarticulated complementarity. It is concealed but decipherable: "that which one locks, the other opens." As Heine wrote, "Art and philosophy—the image and the concept—the Greeks separated them. Their combination in religion predated their 'duality.'"⁵ And this may be seen as characterizing the combination (which is not a mixture) of opposites within Buber's personal "religion."

Throughout his life, Buber repeatedly glorifies "the infinite ethos of the moment."⁶ For him the transitory situations of the stream of life receive a particular gravity of their own. He appears to be consistent in his desire to see "Eternity" in the "Moment" in the areas of thought and faith, in political and social questions, and in entirely personal situations. At the same time, from the beginning of his path as a thinker, he was not content with the "Moment," but placed it within the horizon of "Eternity."[7]

In his own words, Buber knows only "the plenty of every passing hour with the demand and responsibility in it." He refers to his writings as testimony to "experience." He claims repeatedly that he has no "doctrine," that "no system accords with what he has to say." But as early as his writings of 1901, he acknowledged the need for a theoretical stratum beyond the subjective-experiential level. Buber presented these two strata as the dualities of "Love – Consciousness," "Intuition – Science," "Color – Form." He came to admit the cognitive necessity of abstract concepts, which served as spiritual anchors and helped to prevent a lapse into chaotic amorphism.

Upon the matrix of these early gropings Buber went on to develop dual structures during the first decade of the twentieth century, and by means of them he conceptualized the relation between the foregoing two strata. The most important duality is embodied in his book, *Daniel* (1913), in the structure of Realization *(Verwirklichung)* – Orientation *(Orientierung)*. From these leads a developmental line, to which he himself points, toward the I-Thou – I-it structure. Its most significant implications are discussed in *I and Thou* (1923), the outstanding systematic expression of the dialogical axis of his thought.

The aspiration to salvation that marked Buber's spiritual world was expressed not only in yearnings for unity in the areas of the individual and his society and nation, but also in orientation toward redemption in the end of days, and this aspiration was interwoven in his thought until his old age. His messianic faith nourishes inexhaustible hope for peace in the world and for its perfection in the kingdom of God. Conceptual duality gives rise to his hope for salvation: "The uncleanness of the creature and its need for redemption are one; that God dwells in it and that God wills to redeem it, these two are one."[8] Personal redemption, the attainment of "peace of the soul," is what makes possible the continued and constant struggle whose aim is "peace of the world," the restoration of the kingdom of God.[9] "The world in which we live—a world filled with burning contradictions," he says, is also filled "with yearning for salvation."[10]

Unity, the horizon where the existential cleavages in disintegrating reality are bound together, is not attainable in historical reality. The overcoming of divisions has the status of the object of yearning. It is identified with "the messianic world." "Unity" and "redemption" in the Jewish, historical sense are the same thing in Buber's writings.

The unificatory concepts that he advocates are not single units that are all of a piece. They are founded on perceptions of duality. Thus, for example, he interprets the biblical concept of "wisdom" as the combination of principle and action, the spirit of reality; for him, the unity embodied in this concept results from the joining together of opposites. He contrasts it with the Greek concept that refers to wisdom for its own sake, which is the product of a culture built on a duality that separates thought from action.[11] Perhaps in this, too, there is reflected an existence marked by opposites, by existential cleavages, and that yearns for what is beyond them.

A comprehensive view of Buber's writings shows that rather than calling for a unity that joins polar opposites, he points out the dynamic tension between them. The assumption of "primal tension with one another which is fought out and resolved in the world process"[12] permeates his thinking throughout his life. Lacking unity as a concrete possibility, it was necessary to find conceptual crystallizations and organizing elements for his thought.

THE "MYSTICAL" STAGE AND THE "DIALOGICAL" STAGE

In this context one should point out the distinction, which was significant for Buber himself and is accepted by some Buber scholars, between the early "mystical" stage and the "dialogical" stage in his spiritual biography. My study shows that these are not completely separate stages—though he presented them that way. The second stage is imbued with the tension of struggle against the earlier one, and extensions of the earlier stage have a significant effect on the latter one, though most of these are hidden or latent. There is also a transitional phase between the two stages. Buber refers to the transition itself as "a conversion" or "a transformation." His allusions to this event do not, however, afford a complete picture. A special chapter of this study is dedicated to an examination of Buber's "conversion" and its significance in his world.

Though following the appearance of *I and Thou* Buber gave a dialogical character to his writings in every field, both the tendencies and patterns of his thought were firmly established before the "conversion" took place. Following the "conversion," his thinking had new contents and emphases, but a continuity existed with his previous thought patterns. During the "dialogical" stage, then, more of a change occurred in the emphases of his conceptual vocabulary than the basic tendencies that nourished it.

The dialogical aspect of his thought is based on the assumption that "in everything the principle of polar duality rules."[13] The examination of his polar approach in chapter 1 shows that its application is more comprehensive than that of its dialogical underpinning.

THE CHARACTER AND PURPOSE OF HIS CONCEPTS

Certain concepts central in Buber's thought were formed in the early years of the twentieth century. It may be said that his most outstanding concepts took the place of tenets of faith, principles, commandments—which are conspicuous by their absence in his worldview. This holds true in particular regarding his articles on Zionism and Judaism.

These concepts are also present intensively, with changes in meaning or emphasis, in his writings following his shift from mysticism to dialogue. Then their "purpose" becomes clearer—singly as well as in the structures in which they function. They are meant to serve as signposts on the "way" (the concept "way" is also embodied in Buber's writings by the terms "direction" and "vocation") in the processes of self-examination of the individual and the community. It is a "decision" that will lead to "fulfillment," which is identified with a "life of dialogue." His concepts are meant to serve as shared ideas, which every individual forms in his unique, personal way. My study shows that Buber's value concepts fill a function that he assigns to "spirit" and "spiritual power": to be "an authority above life in the present," maintaining a reciprocal relationship with it. As such, his concepts function as "central points" or foci in his work. They are not formulated as abstract philosophical concepts, but rather as the fulfillment of value imperatives that are imbued with the drive to be implemented.[14]

In Buber's thought, from its beginnings to its final expression, there is a pronounced tendency to avoid making its conceptual foci explicit. His concepts are mainly planted within contexts of discussion without explaining their connotations. Very often they are merely implied in his discussion; that is, they function without being indicated by a linguistic sign.

This tendency can also be noted with regard to the structures within which the concepts are embedded. These structures are more a hidden or implicit infrastructure than an explicit or declared presence in his writings.

All the areas of Buber's spiritual enterprise are interconnected; a single worldview is expressed in them. This worldview pervades not only his books and articles but also his notes about people, his short essays, the introductions that he wrote to the works of others, and his poetry. A unity of approach characterizes the entirety of his work; Buber was good at mastering the conceptual mechanisms of all the scholarly disciplines with which he dealt; and he understood them according to his own hermeneutics. These central axes in his thought are embodied in his distinct concepts with their structural crystallizations. The same concepts, though in various representational guises, exist in every area of his work. Understanding of the context in which his concepts are found in a given work often requires reference to the context of the discussion in another work (where that concept is also central). "Words of Torah need each other, for what one locks, another opens."[15]

Although value concepts are occasionally presented singly in Buber's writings, they have no independent status in isolation. Most of them also, and perhaps primarily, constitute members in dual structures, and they function as such even when they are not mentioned together with the other member concept of the structure to which they belong. The proper understanding of the value significances that he attributes to his concepts, of their connotations, is only possible when one knows their place in the structures of which they are components. Even when he refers to a concept by itself, ultimately it does not exist for him independently. Frequently the reader, even the experienced reader, of Buber's writings encounters difficulties in understanding the context of a discussion and even of an article or book by itself. Revelation and concealment, explicitness and implicitness, accessibility and obscurity— all these derive not only from his use of language but also from the organic character of his thought: like a living organism, every chapter or component of his thought is not an independent unit at all, but rather a member in a unified totality. "The words of Torah are poor in their place but rich elsewhere."[16]

Against the background of this understanding of the character of Buber's concepts, it is possible to become familiar with the quality of the conceptual structures in which they are embedded.

THE ESSENCE OF HIS STRUCTURES

Buber's concepts and their dual combinations give his worldview "directions" (a term that he himself uses) that provide an armature for every area of his thought. At the same time as *he strives to reject systems and principles of thought, he builds a sort of antisystematic system* on their basis, a system that is implicit in his writings in every field. The present study seeks to locate Buber's conceptual structures, to trace the history of their development, and thus to provide keys to Buber's view in its entirety.

While his concepts do sometimes appear singly, the proper understanding of their significance is impossible without knowledge of their place in the dual structures where they function as members. Every structure is based on an abstraction of the multitude of phenomena in reality, on the one hand, and concrete expressions are derived from it in the world of his experience, on the other.

It appears possible to characterize the particular combinations of the central structures in Buber's thought as what he calls a utopian aspiration, "the organic wholeness" of "the new society": "the combination of magnetic centers of action which are interconnected."[17] He terms this ensemble a "dual system," and this term can also be applied to his antisystematic system.

In the present study, four central structures have been located, which constitute patterns of thought transcending any particular area or period in Buber's work:

- Distance – Relation
- Vortex – Direction
- Moment – Eternity
- I-It – I-Thou

Individual chapters are devoted to the first three pairs. The fourth structure, which is the only one with which Buber scholarship has dealt from various points of view, is discussed in several of the foundational chapters of this study.

In the spiritual climate in which Buber's world was formed, the subjective point of departure, anchored in inner consciousness, determined his relationship toward the surrounding world. On the basis of the duality of "inwardness" and "outwardness" he brought out and consolidated two of the central structures of his thought: "Distance – Relation" and "Vortex – Direction."

The first of these was formed on the axis of the structure "experience – existence." The first member of this pair epitomized the source of primary creativity, the individual's drive to self-fulfillment. During Buber's "mystical stage" he emphasized "experience," and frequently representations of it not only comprised the inner point of departure of his works but also its purpose. In 1918–21 this structural pattern was infused with new contents, principally with Zionist-social connotations. By means of it the associated duality of "creativity" and "communion" (or "community") was expressed, but not in conceptual terms that represented it as a consolidated structure.

In 1925 Buber developed a new crystallization of this structure, the members of which were now the "instinct of origination" and the "instinct of communion" (dialogical). He continued to shape it, starting in the 1940s, as the focus of his philosophical anthropology. I call these embodiments, which are based on instincts, "Buber's Doctrine of Positive Instincts." His anthropology can be interpreted by means of two positive instincts, that of "creativity" and that of "communication," and it is presented as an ethic of self-realization, consistent with his dialogical approach. Another outgrowth of this structure is embodied in the duality of which one member is individualization (the formation of the personality) and the other is mutuality. Beginning in the early 1950s Buber came to call it "Distance – Relation." One manifestation of this structure is represented in his expression: "peace of the soul—peace of the world."

In the "Vortex – Direction" structure, the first member represents spiritual chaos or the aimless and turbulent inner urge to power, while the second member represents personal control, path, direction. Buber's concept "decision" points to the transcendence of inner chaos toward "direction," and it comprised an important focus in his worldview from somewhat before 1910. Beginning at that time, he started to identify the members of the structure under discussion with the duality of evil and good. In this identification lies the root of the ideas developed almost forty years later in his anthropological work, *Images of Good and Evil* (1952), into which the varied representations of the "Vortex – Direction" structure flow once again and are reiterated.

Buber uses this structure, among other things, to express his approach to the contrast between "happiness and tribulation, or order and turmoil," as well as the contrast between "truth and lie," and "justice and wrong." From Buber's very earliest references to the aimless urge to power, to the vortex, he does not relate to it entirely negatively but states that *from it* must be found the channel of realization and direction. This idea of "the redemption of the sparks" is later developed by emphasizing that the instinctive urge to power is not a negative evil so long as it is connected to a creative direction; good requires overcoming, choice. The source of evil is in passivity and the lack of "decision." ᴰᴿ ᴾᴼᵂᴱᴿ ᶜᵒʳʳᵘᵖᵗˢ

Buber's refusal to be content with the instant, with the momentariness of the moment, in the experience of transitory self-realization, is also what brought him, at the beginning of his career, to trace structural outlines in which "eternity" is placed on the horizon of "the moment." In his mystical stage, two contradictory tendencies were embodied by means of this structure:

- reaching past the present and the "historical" toward the "monumental" or the "eternal" (which is not to be identified with a transcendental approach)
- yearning for mystical unification with the cosmos (the infinity of the universe).

From the first harbingers of Buber's dialogical conception, a new relation toward "eternity" is expressed by means of displays of this structure, and this came to be identified with the divine and with the God of Israel. But not only the dimension of faith in his dialogical philosophy is represented by means of this structure. Within the variety of its manifestations there are also many in which this dimension is obscured or does not appear at all.

Buber was far from intending that his structures should combine together into a system or structure with static principles. Each of the structures from among those indicated above forms an existential ap-

proach to a transitory situation at the same time as a view beyond it;
in each of them emphasis is placed on the processes within the "lived
moment" that is accompanied by perspective:

> • One who concentrates on his individual experience, the
> "Distance," which is the area of individualization, must, ac-
> cording to Buber, remember that the formation of the person-
> ality is not a goal in itself but rather a prelude to a life of
> "Relation," a dialogical existence.
> • One who is subject to the "Vortex" of his inner life should
> seek its hidden horizon, the "Direction" for which he must strive.
> • The person living for the "Moment" must be guided by
> orientation toward "Eternity."
> • A person involved in a dialogical experience must recall
> that human life is impossible without the reality of the "I-It"
> relationship.

Each of Buber's structures contains at least one member concept
that embodies a desired goal. Mainly he refers not to an ideal existence but to an attainable reality. That visionary horizon is imbued
with power summoning and hastening its realization. It portrays the
individual and society toward which one strives. Hence, understand-
ably, each of these structures is based on breaking through the confines of the individual himself. Each of them is imbued with a point of
view and a relation to human life and social existence.

All of Buber's structures were developed in accordance with the
positive or negative value with which he endowed them. This is what
determines the character of their members and the nature of the relations between them. They represent and express *dynamic* life processes
with their complexity and multiplicity of meaning, and therefore it is
impossible to examine them according to systematic, philosophical
criteria. Each of Buber's structures has its own typology, which can be
clarified by locating the relations between its members.

Members of some of the structures overlap or are even identical,
and these should be mentioned. The concept embodying dialogue, for
example, serves as a member in three of his structures. Its representations and the emphases in its expression vary according to the character
of the structure of which it is a component. Its embodiments are "I-
Thou," "Direction," and "Relation." It is also present to a significant

degree in the member "Moment." The assumption implied in many of the contexts of discussion in which the concept "Moment" appears is that this is an existential situation that is concretized in dialogical life.

There are a number of parallel or overlapping dimensions between the structures "Distance – Relation" and "Vortex – Direction." The point of departure and the first stage in the process of representing both of them are the inner world of the individual: in one it is "Distance" or "the Creative Instinct," and in the second it is "Vortex" or "Chaos." In both of these structures, this first stage constitutes the ground for the growth and formation of the second stage. The first member of "Vortex – Direction" expresses a value that is negative or liable to be negative if one does not transcend it. Both "Relation" and "Direction" represent the desired human condition, the "Fulfillment of Man" in a "dialogical existence."

The structures "Distance – Relation" and "Vortex – Direction" are bounded within the world of man, in inner human and interhuman processes. But the other two, "Moment – Eternity" and "I-Thou – I-It," possess a dimension of dialogue with "the eternal Thou," or with the "Eternal."

In the edifice of thought under discussion, these dual structures are given additional tasks beyond appearing within the aforementioned central structures or those derived from them. They have other embodiments, which cannot be identified with the central structures, or else there is a partial overlap between them and other polarities, such as "Personality – Character," "Majority – Many," "Nation – World" (individual – universality), "Mysticism – Dialogue," "Teacher – Leader," "Humanism – Faith," "Revelation – the Eclipse of God," "Belief – Faith (Pistis)," "Community – Collective," "Ought – Is," "Person – Cause," "Conscience – Vocation," "Personal – Historical," "Revolutionary – Soldier," "Goal – Means," "Fate – Choice," "Nation – Land," and "Society – State."

Buber never presents a comprehensive statement of his worldview in any of his central works. In the present study, strata of his thought have been located, the scattered stones of the edifice have been assembled, and the unified, organic tissue buried in his writings has been reconstituted. The search for the embodiment of the concepts of his thought and for the structure that bears it has proven to be the way to locate the trends in the development of his thought.

COMMENTS ON BUBER'S
MEANS OF EXPRESSION

It is often difficult to follow the paths of Buber's thought, to get to the bottom of his ideas. We are dealing here with a creative thinker, a philosopher who was also a poet and an artist with language. Varied linguistic associations unite with his ideational tendencies (together with the concepts that embody them) in the melting pot of his creativity. His thought is not an act of "consciousness of the mind" but rather an expression of the fullness of his world, of "experience" and "mind" in combination. His language is enchanting, even when it is not fully understood.

Buber's style, along with central tendencies of his thought, was formed in the spirit of the fin de siècle. In his language resonate the styles of Rilke, Stefan George, Richard Beer-Hofmann, and others. The spirit of Vienna in that era marked Buber's style for many years.

From the beginning of his path as a thinker, during his early twenties, Buber showed poetic tendencies. As a young man he wrote poems but generally did not publish them; he continued to write poetry on various occasions in adulthood, including in his old age.[1] But his uniqueness as a linguistic artist is expressed not only in his poems and literary works (central to which is his Hasidic novel, *For the Sake of Heaven*), but also in his articles, essays, philosophical writings, and even in his letters.

Buber did not always manage to unite content and form in his works, nor were his artistic-stylistic drives always consistent with his value goals. Sometimes it was not the form that prevailed, but rather mystical yearnings that imbue his work with atmospheric charm: at such times their hypnotic dimension is liable to shunt aside his dialogical intentions. Occasionally the stylistic magic of his writings seizes the reader but does not actually address his intelligence. And sometimes, by contrast, his *artistic* side combines with his *philosophizing* side, thereby overwhelming the responsibility of the *educator and teacher* that he wished to fulfill. He strove to combine these three dimensions: that of the *artist*, the *thinker*, and the *man of social responsibility*. Principally he desired the fusion of "creativity" and "consciousness." "The growth of the form and the growth of consciousness," he said, "are both guided within human experience as potentialities. The form grows, as it were, from itself. I once saw a clay cup, the handiwork of an ancient Japanese ceramicist, and I marveled, for it looked like the handiwork of nature; delicate traces of fingers were visible on the clay, and the impression made was that the creative power of nature had only passed through the hand of man and used it for its action. Thus artistic, ideational, and social forms are born in the womb of our soul, but, as it were, not from our seed."[2] These three dimensions—*the artistic, the ideational, and the social*—are meant to be indissolubly combined. This applies both to written and oral works. Buber's radiant or hypnotic, enchanting, power is mainly attributed to his public appearances in the first decades of the century (in Germany and to some degree in other German-speaking countries). Gershom Scholem's testimony, which combines closeness and critical distance, is reliable:

> Here is Buber's voice, a voice speaking from the "Three Early Addresses on Judaism" from 1909–1910 and from his first books on Hasidism. That voice aroused an enormous echo within us: it promised something, it enchanted, it demanded. . . . Our raw and anarchical sentiment was enthralled by the call, for with all the beauty and the flow of the balanced and rich sentences, it also contained more than a little anarchy and "the abyss calling to the abyss."[3]

The question of the rational understanding of Buber's writing also applied to his oral presentations and continued to apply during the decades following his departure from Germany. He did not visit the United States until 1951. Walter Kaufmann recounts that at that time Buber gave long lectures, often from a written text, which most of the audience was unable to understand. I heard responses in a similar spirit from people who recall Buber's impressive lecture to a packed house in Carnegie Hall in New York in 1951. One person who attended told me that he managed to find a place in the crowded hall but didn't understand a word of the lecture. This difficulty did not arise, however, in Buber's personal conversations or when he was addressing small groups in his home.[4]

Sometimes his linguistic artistry serves him faithfully. But sometimes he is captured by the charms of his own linguistic ability. And occasionally his language also functions as a sort of "game" of revelation and concealment, revealing a handbreadth and concealing two. Although Buber reveals his experiences in the furnace of his spiritual life to his readership, he also seems to erect barriers between himself and those who peruse his writings. And there are additional difficulties, for which he is not immediately responsible, which the experienced reader needs to overcome.[5] Yet Buber is a master architect. Almost all of his writings, short or long, have an architectonic structure, the masterwork of a wise man who, with his heaven-sent talent, controls and shapes his work as a structured mosaic. The didactic dimension that is something conspicuous in his writings may put readers off rather than attract them. But if we manage to overcome these obstacles, we will become aware of the inner truths that sustain his work, and we will see the stature of a spiritual giant engaged in a mighty struggle with himself. We are dealing here with "an unusual personality, drawing upon the mighty forces of its subjective faith, sometimes rising up to an exalted discovery of objective certainty. A rare personality stands within the storms of this most perturbed period—as though s/he cannot overcome it."[6]

1
POLAR DUALITY

EXISTENTIAL DUALITY AND ITS EXPRESSIONS

In his childhood and youth, Buber lived in several different cultural worlds simultaneously, worlds that were in fact rather distant from each other. From the end of the nineteenth century until he began his university studies in Vienna, he lived in the spirit of fin-de-siècle doubt, constantly struggling with tensions that riddled his world.[1] He wrestled with the shreds of his own torn Jewish world, with the tensions between his origins and German culture, and also with conflicting tendencies within his aim of fitting into German culture. The flame of these inner struggles is discernible through the conceptual distinctions contained in his early writings. The rifts within his Jewish identity are embodied in several intertwining dualities:

- Hasidism versus Haskalah
- Eastern European *Yiddishkait* versus emancipated liberalism
- Life in the diaspora versus the visions of Zionism

Buber conceived these and similar oppositions not simply as spiritual and cultural tensions, but primarily as inner splits. "We have become aware of a deep schism in our existence," he wrote, in the first-person plural, as though testifying as a witness.[2] He gave sharper and more revealing expression to this feeling about the world in saying

17

of the "Yehudi" that "he experiences it in his inmost self, as a duality
of his I."[3]

As noted above, Buber also experienced spiritual struggles transcending questions of Judaism and the Jews. Between the turn of the
century and the beginning of World War I he drew upon realms that
were very distant, perhaps even cut off from each other: Far Eastern
and Christian mystical doctrines and western philosophy, particularly
that of the nineteenth and early twentieth centuries. Several of the foci
of his spiritual leanings came directly out of his affinities with German
folk ideology and from his being anchored in the organic-developmental approach.[4]

Beyond the existential and spiritual tensions mentioned above, an
additional contradiction stands out, pervading both the shreds of his
Jewish world and also his quests within other cultures. This was the
duality of decline versus rebirth, the destruction of the world of the
past together with the drive for renewal.[5] In an early article written
about his friend Gustav Landauer, a man who shared his spirit, Buber
expressed the inner struggles comprised by that contradiction:

> Consciousness that every true action is rooted in the deepest
> doubt, that every true creation is based on the most radical nega-
> tion, that every pure affirmation of the world derives from the final
> despair—all of this has been hinted by philosophers and mystics of
> all ages. However none of them ever acquired, [like Landauer,] that
> awareness of our immediate feeling of life, nor did they make it
> flourish. With no one else can such impressive and varied forms of
> this basic motif be found. However only rarely does the entire per-
> sonality itself become the expression of that message; for Landauer
> never tires of probing examples and doubting answers, undermin-
> ing certitudes, but, each time, knowing how to raise up a new pic-
> ture of the world in place of the old model; instead of the old an-
> swer, giving a new metaphor of the world; and he builds a kingdom
> of untrustworthy illusions, playfulness, awareness as creativity, where
> the ground has been completely removed from under our feet.[6]

Here one feels Buber's identification with Landauer's spiritual world,
expressed directly by his use of the first-person plural, thus stressing
Landauer's "awareness of our immediate feeling of life."

Buber struggled with the conflicts in his being and tried to relate
them to each other, both in a personal-existential manner and also
with conceptual efforts to resolve the contradictions. Buber's friend

and partner in his educational and political activities for many years, A. E. Simon, called him "the bridge-builder."[7] But at times Buber freed himself, as it were, from the effort of building bridges—or else he viewed it as irrelevant from the start—and he turned to a spiritual-mystical world, cut off from his Jewish identity, as in *Daniel* (1913).[8]

> This little book is suffused with cultural and literary allusions drawn from East and West. The Greco-classical and the Indian, the pagan-Scandinavian and the Christian worlds meet and are absorbed here. The reader would barely sense that the author is Jewish if he were not to attend the whispered reservation sounded melodiously and objectively by the words "to the Christians." Jacob and Esau, too, are mentioned without identifying them, as a bare illustration and as an aside. In this book, Buber is seen embarking on his long journey through the world of universal human thought.[9]

Buber also entertained yearnings for mystic fusion in entirely personal existence, "entry" to which was acquired by denying common human reality and rational-scientific ways of thinking.[10]

Resonances of western cultures in all their strata and hues are present in his work, side by side with manifestations of the Far East. One must ask what part of all the cultural abundance that is woven into the various areas of his writings also became a dominant part of his spiritual world. The question also arises as to the limit of his ability to digest and fuse opposing, sometimes even mutually contradictory, cultural worlds.

Buber's sense of living in a polar world, as expressed in the 1904 article previously cited, finds direct extension in a letter he sent to Max Brod many years later, on 12 December 1926, where he confesses that he is divided between standing on the edge of an abyss and extricating himself from it. In that letter, too, Buber reveals himself by means of reference to the intricacies in Franz Kafka's *The Trial*:

> Throughout I have read this book as touching upon myself most profoundly, and even in the passages where it oppressed and stunned me, my trust in it was unaffected, and I never reflected that perhaps something should or could be different than what it is. . . . . The meaninglessness with which we are dealing here is counted a producer of meaning until the last moment. But as we deal with it and are entangled in the thickets of concrete anti-meaning, is it not precisely there and precisely in that way that we, with cruel dedication,

from time to time, though we refuse to admit it, become aware of a meaning which is shown to be not at all like ours, though it is addressed to us and makes its way upward through all the pollution to the walls of our hearts. And at the last moment, the correct moment, does the meaning nevertheless reach them and conquer them? And now, take these words as though your ears were his.[11]

Whereas the 1904 article on Landauer reveals a utopian affirmation of life arising on the horizon of existential despair, the letter to Max Brod, which depicts being on the threshold of destruction, reflects no focus of light, positiveness, or faith—but rather only a constant struggle with the lack of meaning. The occurrence to which he testifies is not a unique event but rather one that is repeated, as he says, "from time to time." One may place these two revealing expressions in the background of a passage ostensibly devoted to portraying Rabbi Naftali of Roptchitz but actually expressing, though implicitly and in disguise, the feelings about the world of their author, Martin Buber:

We hardly know of another zaddik whose soul harbored such a mass of contradictions as did that of Rabbi Naftali of Roptchitz. But if we consider them all together, they are by no means formless and chaotic, but give the picture of a real human figure. He introduces into the hasidic world a type not uncommon among the distinguished intellectuals of the modern era: a mixture of irony and yearning, skepticism and belief, ambition and humility.

From his youth on, he was given to jests, many of them bitter, and to all manner of pranks including some that were really malicious. In his youth, he reflected on his own endowments with extreme pride, in his age with doubts verging on despair. He once observed that his teacher Rabbi Mendel of Rymanov was holy and knew nothing of cleverness, and added: "So how can he understand what I am like?"[12]

One who knows of Buber's traumatic experiences and the tragic spiritual struggles that marked his intellectual biography through his testimony in writing,[13] and who also knew him personally and held long conversations with him, cannot but sense his own features in the description of this Hasidic master. In the foregoing lines a dual structure predominates, a turbulence in direction that commenced in Buber's youth with his aspiration to overcome the "world of confusion" and break out of inner chaos towards a "direction" or "way." Manifestations of this structure appear in different guises in Buber's thought over more than a generation.[14] Here, in depicting Rabbi Naftali of Roptchitz, we find an exceptional example of it: in opposition to turbulence ("formless and chaotic") Buber does not posit a "direction," as he usually does, but rather a turbulence that has the form of "a real human figure." Here we no longer have the aspiration to transcend turbulence but rather an expression of awareness of the need to resolve the "mass of contradictions" so that they will not be chaotic. There is no single path from the mass of contradictions to a state of clarity. One must know how to struggle with them and how constantly to raise a form up out of the turbulence.

It seems to me that this is an expression of personal lucidity, the fruit of years of experience; this is the wisdom of old men who know "the limits of advice," the boundaries of human ability, acknowledging that "man's purpose in the world is to fight that stranger [Satan] to his last breath upon earth, and to introduce him from time to time to the very Being of the Holy One, Blessed be He."[15] Among the contradictions Buber mentions here are those between skepticism and faith and between great pride and doubts bordering on despair. These enable us to trace a direct line from the expressions of the secrets of his worldview in the article of 1904 through his letter of 1926 and on to the passage under discussion here. A broader understanding of this passage demands that it be seen in the context of Buber's interpretations of the figure of Rabbi Naftali of Roptchitz in *For the Sake of Heaven*. He took several traits of that personality from the world of Hasidism and others from his own personality in the spirit of the process that typified his own spiritual biography.[16]

The foci of Buber's thought cannot be separated from his biography. His worldview is inseparable from his experiences.[17] The structure of his ideas was consolidated, as noted above, with the absorption of various currents of thought and influences, which did not erase his rootedness in the spiritual possessions of his people but merely shunted it aside, for a short time. He wanted to digest opposing sources of sustenance with the power of his spirit, and at times his spiritual pendulum swung to one pole and stayed there for a while. However, at bottom he strove to create a synthesis marked with the stamp of his own personal "direction."

Below I shall try to clarify the features common to many of the types of duality in his writing.

WHAT IS POLAR DUALITY?

*There is no need to speak at length of the essential duality in the
Jewish psyche. Duality as a basic characteristic of the Jewish nation
has been noted by a number of scholars of our national character.
This duality is seen as the source of our calamity and our great
poverty, and also as the source of our wealth and strength. Duality:
that is, the rule of two characteristics in the soul of the nation,
contradicting each other and vying against each other. This duality
turns the soul of the nation into the battlefield of a never-ending war.
This war wears us down; the two elements fight with each other and
oppose each other and obscure each other. Thus they weaken and
obscure the face of the nation. On the other hand these contrasting
elements enrich our national character. They do not let us slumber.
The opposing powers are fertile in their union, making the nation
many-faceted and variegated.*
                     —H. N. Bialik, "On Duality in Israel" (1922)

The foregoing discussion has already shown that Buber's struggles with
various kinds of duality were marked by a tendency toward resolving
contradictions, bridging chasms, and bringing together distant extremes; he simultaneously wrestled with various polarities and also
related them to each other.

The dual approach was the foundation of Buber's thought from
its earliest expressions. An early lecture given to a Berlin circle in 1900,
never published during his lifetime, already had its base in dual distinctions.[18] Here the duality was between the "old community" and
the "new community." The former is expressed, according to Buber,
in utilitarianism and coercion, while the latter is directed towards creativity and freedom.[19] This lecture also discusses the conflict between
external social arrangements in a modern city and "inner form" (which
will give birth to the "new community").[20] At twenty-two Buber spoke
in this lecture of "the harmony of opposites" which exist beside each
other within the interior of the individual. That harmony will permit
"the joining of forces for unity in life."[21] Buber was referring to the
duality of inner versus outer, the outer being identified with the "new
society." He also emphasized the object of his yearnings by means of a
second duality, that of life and fellowship as two sides of a single entity.[22] All these pairs of opposites represented various and contrasting
versions of the concept of what is and what ought to be. The mystic
and utopian regime for which he yearned was embodied in his notion
of the "new community."

Between the time when he gave the lecture mentioned above and afterwards, when he proposed a worldview combining examples of the dualistic approach to man in the world, Buber consolidated his thinking and conceptions. He expressed his new view in an article ostensibly devoted to discussing the work of the Jewish artist Lesser Uri.[23] This discussion is based on pairs of related principles or situations, such as "form" and "color,"[24] "inner" and "outer," and "personal" and "historical."[25] He also spoke of "the moment" versus "eternity," "the historical" versus "the monumental,"[26] isolation versus human settlement,[27] destiny versus choice,[28] and life versus idea.[29] This list does not exhaust all the examples of duality in "Lesser Uri." The effort emerging in this article to build a dualistic picture of the world was not unique. It was deepened in Buber's subsequent writings in the first decade of the twentieth century, in which the vital foundations for the later consolidation of his thought were laid.[30]

The formation of one of the types of duality in "Lesser Uri" enabled Buber to establish a general principle: that since the time of Adam and Eve "everything is a miracle and everything is necessity,"[31] and neither of these two realms is possible without the other. "Everything touches upon everything else, awakens and develops everything else . . . everything because of its fellow and within its fellow"—either as an "eternal war" or as "eternal brotherhood."[32] In these formulations, which point toward a fundamental duality, the parts of which are related to each other, there are indications of the kind of duality that was to occupy a central place in Buber's thought. His letters from 1910 to 1913 show repeated efforts to characterize his dualistic world view in the spirit of the foregoing formulations, observing the contrasts within the world and the pairs of opposites that abounded in his spirit as a kind of division in which the parts are not cut off from each other and do not contradict each other. He called this duality "Polaritaet" (polarity).

The phenomenon of polarity entails the existence or manifestation of two contrary principles at once, influencing each other and reacting to each other and also conditioning each other.[33] The opposite of polarity is dichotomy—division into two mutually exclusive members that negate each other.[34]

In principle, one may say that Buber's formulations of the essence of polarity apply beyond the context in which they were originally presented. This assumption also applies to his interpretation of the essence of polarity in the early speeches on Judaism:

It is a fundamental psychological fact that the multiplicity of man's soul appears to him, recurrently, as a dualism. . . . Man experiences the fullness of his reality and his potentiality as a living substance that gravitates toward two poles; he experiences his inner progress as a journey from crossroads to crossroads. No matter what changing meaning-contents *(Inhalte)* or names the two opposites of man's inner striving may have, no matter whether the choice at the crossroads is perceived as a personal decision, an eternal necessity, or even a matter of chance, the basic form itself remains unchanged. One of the essential, determining facts of human life (perhaps even the most essential), it conveys the awesomeness of the primal dualism, and with it the source and significance of all things of the spirit.[35]

It would seem that this was the purport of the sentence that he placed in parenthesis in a personal letter to his friend Gustav Landauer, dated 10 October 1910: "I am now, as I never have been, full of a goal [*Ziel*] and full of alienation [*Entfremdung*] at the same time."[36]

In another letter, dated 20 May 1912, Buber once again presented polarity as an essential and primary characteristic of the world. There he speaks of "the act of polar becoming that is eternally renewed" and that marks the spiritual activity of mankind, which is *single.* "The polar nature of thought," Buber states, "is a primary fact of the spirit."[37]

Polarity occupied an important place in his philosophical-mystical work of 1913, *Daniel.* There it is illuminated from various viewpoints in the fourth and fifth dialogues, "On Polarity" and "On Unity."[38] In the context of these dialogues there is, among other things, reference to what Buber calls "the primordial dualism itself."[39] They state prominently that truly to experience the world means to experience the dualities permeating the tension between spirit and matter, form and material, existence and becoming, intelligence and will, the positive and the negative element.[40] In order fully to grasp Buber's underlying ideas in *Daniel,* they must be extracted from the mystical poetry of his language.

In his correspondence, Buber referred to the contents of *Daniel,* and he himself clearly summarized the central conception of polar duality that he presented in it. One of his correspondents was Gustav Landauer. The background of their exchange of letters is as follows: in 1913 a German publication devoted a special issue to Buber, who was then only thirty-five years old but already well known beyond the circle of those who heard his lectures.[41] Prominent in that issue of the magazine was a comprehensive article by G. Landauer that made reference to Buber's remarks on the basic duality of feminine and masculine as expressed in the recently published *Daniel*.[42] The issue that concerned Landauer was the importance of the feminine element for the recovery of the declining cultural life of Europe. Buber, finding that his friend had not properly grasped his approach in this matter, responded in a letter dated 18 March 1913. Landauer answered Buber's letter the following day, reiterating his position.[43] Buber presented the duality of female and male in the context of "the tensions which are spoken of in the last dialogue of *Daniel*," and on that basis he presented the main points of his conception of polarity. He does not conceive of the duality (which, in his opinion, is found everywhere) as something that splits experience into two different and separate worlds, but rather as a cause of tension between its contrasting elements. The elements upon which he concentrates in his letter—the feminine and the masculine—are conceived as polar opposites; each of them must find its "opposite pole so that from the two of them the unity of the spiritual life may be created." He emphasizes that it is not his intention "to blur the contrasts and neutralize them."[44]

The themes of the fourth and fifth dialogues in *Daniel*, "On Polarity" and "On Unity," are interconnected. The main idea at base of both the dialogues is set forth in the aforementioned letter. He wished to live simultaneously (to use names of essays by Ahad Ha-Am) "At Both Extremes," to experience the polarity of being "Between the Realms." He did not view the contrasting realms in life as different and separate from each other, but rather he wished to *relate* them to one another, postulating that "in the spirit this tension is intermingled."[45]

A fitting supplement to the foregoing letter is found in another one written to Sh. H. Bergmann on 7 May 1913, which dealt with the subject of "Realisierung" (realization or fulfillment) in *Daniel*. In this context he added, almost incidentally:

> By the way: it was said that before the creation of the world there existed only the Creator and His Name—that, it appears to me, is because unity, which is not conceived of as a goal but as a source, can no longer be grasped as pure unity, since we are not capable of grasping this entire act of creation except in polarization, as an expression of immanent duality.[46]

In contrast to the unity of the life of the spirit expressed in Buber's letter to Landauer, the letter to Bergmann brings out the problematic nature of "unity beyond all duality," that is, the unity of God.

Buber's view of the essence of polar duality appears to be that it is not a static situation. It is a living experience that changes in form and is subject to dynamic processes, in which there are contradictions. Buber was aware of self-contradictions as early as the first decade of the century (in a source to which we have already referred): "Judaism is not simple and unequivocal, but permeated by contrasts. It is a polar phenomenon."[47] These basic assumptions nourish later presentations of his conception. Thus, for example, in the context of a discussion of culture, he states that "it is impossible to grasp its essence without a grasp of its contradictions." These are active within "several kinds of duality which are found in every cultural process." "True culture" is, for Buber, "the active unity of the spirit" in every area of life. It is an essence "which is produced by a *polar* process."[48] The consistency of law and system in philosophy and science is incompatible with the desire for unity. This desire is organic by its very nature and arises out of a reality, at the basis of which are interrelated dual divisions.[49]

POLARITY AND RELATION: POLARITY THAT TRANSCENDS DIALOGICAL THINKING

Buber tells of the deep change that took place in his path, "an overturning of the heart," as he calls it, following which he departed from a mystical, personal existentialism in the direction of dialogue: from being swallowed up in a "fullness without obligations" to a "dialogical life of relatedness, involvement, and responsibility."[50] One might suppose that this turning point brought about the formation of the unified direction that supplanted duality in his view of the world; however, we must determine whether the patterns of duality, especially that of polar duality, did continue to play a central role in his writings even after World War I, when that "overturning of the heart" took place.[51]

Sh. H. Bergmann was among those who noted the continued presence of duality in Buber's thought. As early as the 1930s he wrote an article pointing out the connection between the expressions of inner duality in Judaism and the aspiration for unity, as found in Buber's "Judaism and Humanity" (1910), and the duality and unity at the basis of his "I and Thou." Buber's gaze is directed particularly at the *relation* underlying dialogue: "the duality of I and Thou is the essence of the world. This is not actually duality, but rather unity; the two axes of this unity, the I and the Thou, are merely the two columns spanned by the arch. *The inwardness of the world is relatedness.*"[52]

Many years later Bergmann developed and sharpened this viewpoint in his introductory essay to his Hebrew volume, *Besod Siach*, in which he points once again to the basic approach common to both the early "Speeches" on Judaism and to Buber's philosophy of dialogue. Now he states clearly, however, that in its various stages this duality is based on polarity. In Buber's speeches given in the years around 1910, Bergmann finds an expression of the existential situation which also characterized him as a child of that time. The main feature of this existential situation was the attraction "to two opposite poles" and also the aspiration "to build a bridge" between them. "The polarity of existence and the joining together of the poles" are, in Bergmann's opinion, the main subject in Buber's dialogical thinking.[53]

Bergmann's comments do not exhaust all the kinds of polarities at the foundation of Buber's dialogical thought.[54] Its underpinning is a dual structure, the two facets of which are "the world of relationships" (the I-Thou relation) and the "world of otherness" (the I-It relation).[55] Polarity characterizes not only the I-Thou duality that builds up the "world of relationships," but also the relationship between the "world of relationships" and "the world of otherness." Moreover, in his portrayal of this structure in his writing Buber traces dual conceptual schemas, interpreting one facet as being embodied in the essence of dialogue with its opposite member, while at the same time they are also in polarity with each other. Such dual schemas are freedom and determinism,[56] community and collectivity,[57] religiosity and philosophy.[58] Each of these dualities has variant forms in Buber's writings, taking on the form appropriate to the contexts in which each appears. Thus, for example, the schema of freedom and determinism also appears as prophecy and destiny (and/or prophecy and apocalypse).[59]

Buber sometimes tends to express a general rule by concentrating on one of its representations. As an example of that, here are his statements in "The Faith of Israel" regarding the polarity of freedom and determinism:

> It is only when reality is turned into logic and A and non-A dare no longer dwell together that we get determinism and indeterminism, a doctrine of predestination and a doctrine of freedom, each excluding

the other. According to the logical conception of truth only one of
two contraries can be true, but in the reality of life as one lives it
they are inseparable. The person who makes a decision knows that
his deciding is no self-delusion; the person who has acted knows
that he was and is in the hand of God. The unity of the contraries is
the mystery at the innermost core of the dialogue.[60]

These statements may be applied not only to the various guises of the
foregoing polarity but also to the types of polarity connected with
Buber's dialogical philosophy. In his opinion it is impossible to live in
only one reality, whether it is a dialogical reality or a reality characterized by the I-It relationship. These two modes of existence are not
mutually exclusive and are not isolated from each other. They are related to each other. At the same time he gives primary preference to a
life of relationship.

Having noted the aspects of polar duality emerging from his dialogical thought, we must inquire whether all manifestations of polar
duality in his writings can be included within his dialogics. I shall try
to respond to this question through the examination of two complementary declarations of faith, in the combination of which I find the
principle of Buber's conception of polarity. I refer to passages that
stand by themselves and that were interpolated into his writings. One
of them was written in the late 1940s and the second a few years
afterwards. In both passages the story of creation in the Bible serves as
a platform for the presentation of the duality in which the orders of
nature join together with the world of history, as well as for expressions of this duality in human existence. In the context of the first
passage our unredeemed world is presented as based from the start on
"the double nature and the double fate of man":

> The Book of Genesis begins with two accounts of the creation which,
> no matter when and how the one or the other originated, comple-
> ment one another perfectly, like nature and mind, and like man's
> sense of living at the fringe of the cosmos as a latecomer, and man's
> sense of being at home in the center of his world, as one of its first-
> born. The first account of the creation ends with a double blessing:
> a blessing upon the first human beings and a blessing upon the Sab-
> bath. The second account ends with a double curse: a curse upon
> the first human beings, and a curse upon the ground. Between the
> two stands sin. The blessing inaugurates natural man, the curse in-
> augurates historical man, and both together inaugurate the double
> nature and the double destiny of man.[61]

The kinds of duality mentioned in the second passage are presented as pairs of polarities, and a generalization is also made according to which the principle of polar duality permeates everything:

> The Torah, the teaching of Israel, is a teaching of distinction. As the creation is founded on distinction: in space—between the higher and the lower waters, in time—between day and night and so forth, and at the end of creation stands man, he too divided into man and woman, so man is bidden by revelation to distinguish: between God and idols, between true and false prophets, between pure and impure, between good and evil, between sacred and profane; in sum, between that which conforms to God and that which does not conform to Him. There is no place for an indeterminate multiplicity. . . . But in contrast to the cosmic divisions, which embrace both poles with the same affirmation, the divisions of revelation are either armed with the strongest accents of Yes and No, of pleasing to God and condemned by Him, as is the case with the "ethical" distinction between good and bad, or the perfection concentrates itself at the one end and leaves a wide room for all that is outside of it, as is the case with "cultic" distinction between sacred and profane. And the destiny of man, his destiny in the most exact sense of the term, that of the individual and that of the totality, depends upon the right distinction. In the sphere of the holy this finds expression in the tradition that whoever comes into unauthorized contact with its symbols has forfeited his life, in the realm of good and evil it finds expression in the message that God has placed before his people "life and good and death and evil." Here the structures of creation, to which life and death belong, are mixed with the structures of revelation.[62]

The duality of nature and history, which Buber took from romanticism,[63] is presented directly in the passage from "Abraham's Mission," and in the second cited passage it is represented in the phrases "the structures of creation" and "the structures of revelation." By means of biblical exegesis he spreads out the full extent of the polar duality that he finds everywhere. Here polar distinctions in the Torah of Israel are brought out rather than the unity of opposites within creation as emphasized in biblical monotheism.

In the passage from "The Faith of Israel" quoted above the characteristics of polar duality are presented as being in accord with Buber's general outlook: the presentation of "a thing and its opposite" at the same time and their relation to each other. It also shows a negative attitude toward dichotomies. However, at the same time, it does place emphasis on dialogics (unlike the paragraphs quoted above from "The Mission of Abraham" and *The Origin and Meaning of Hasidism*).

Buber's dialogical thought, with all its ramifications and all its importance in his world, is ultimately an aspect—though a central one—of his dualistic view of the world. The dialogical aspects of this approach do not encompass or exhaust it. Buber's polar duality has important expressions that transcend the application of his dialogical faith.

In the various stages of his writing he repeatedly emphasizes "direction" and "path."[64] But he did not ultimately believe in an unequivocal, unidirectional path, and he discovered an ability to penetrate the reasons for a contrary view and even to identify with it. He had a tendency, though it was not emphasized or made much of, to *experience* the polar duality of paths. This emerges, among other things, as we follow the pendulum swings of his attitudes towards Herzl, which vacillated between opposition and admiration.

Buber's contacts with Herzl date back to 1899, when Buber invited him to come and give a lecture to the Leipzig Zionist Federation. Their joint efforts in the Zionist movement began when Herzl invited Buber, who was twenty-three, to edit *Die Welt*, the central organ of the World Zionist Organization.[65] Buber's youthful admiration for Herzl could not blunt the edge of his approach to Zionism, which, from the start, was at the opposite pole to that of the prophet and father of the Jewish State.

In the months immediately following Herzl's death in 1904 Buber published three articles dealing with Herzl. Subsequently he pondered over his image for decades.

The earliest of these articles, "Theodor Herzl," was published a month after Herzl's death and was apparently meant to be a eulogy, though written with critical distance. Buber, then twenty-six, torn between the contradictions of his world, saw things, both near and far, in their perspective. He emphasized the various aspects of the dualities that, in his opinion, characterized Herzl's being. He opened by mentioning that in late 1895 and early 1896 two of Herzl's books appeared, *Das Palais Bourbon* and *Der Judenstaat*, "which are in strange contrast to each other, but not in opposition."[66] In reviewing these books Buber struggles with the conception of Zionism found in *Der Judenstaat*, "where the persecution of the Jews became the Jewish question, and the common enemy became the basis of Jewish nationalism."[67] He also noted that Herzl's book "can make an idea into a program, make a movement into a party, and arouse the masses."[68] As his article continued Buber pointed out three paradoxes that typified seven years of activity on the part of the journalist who became an active Zionist leader after the First Zionist Congress:

1. the paradox of a decidedly western individual at the head of a movement rooted entirely in the East;
2. the contradiction between Herzl's disdain for politics and his yearnings for great action and the daily activity of the Zionist movement;
3. the paradox of a statesman without a state, active among states and heads of state.[69]

Herzl died, states Buber, "without being conscious of the tragic paradoxes which he bore in his soul." The article ends with praise for the purity and faith of the man who "left even his opponents with a picture of a sunny and harmonious phenomenon." However this praise was tempered with a critical note; Herzl is presented as "a poet whom his nation's fate turned into a hero."[70]

A different point of view guided the second article, entitled "Herzl and History," which Buber published about a month afterwards.[71] A residue of depression from Buber's relations with Herzl seeped into this article. In it Buber continued an argument which he had had with Herzl in his lifetime. At the same time he never tired of praising and extolling his opponent. He even spoke of Herzl's conception of Zionism in an essentially favorable light, without bringing out the points of criticism that were included in his first article. Remarks on Herzl's personality stand out in this article, though they were not presented centrally. The relationship that united the man and his actions was emphasized: "Herzl, in his entire essence, had to make himself and his movement into one thing. That was the source of his great power. He believed in himself not as someone believing in a *person* but as a believer in a *cause*." The unity of Herzl the man and his activity is also implicit in sentences like the following: "Above all Herzl's personality stands before one who surveys [it] in the light of history"; 'he was the lord of a sick nation': he unconsciously forged an image for his nation which the nation called by its own name." The article ends with words that cannot be outdone: "a figure without the shadow of a flaw, with the pure outlines of a genius, a brow radiant with messianic light—the highest grace."

These outlines provided the basis for the exaltation of the figure of Herzl in an article written six years later, "He and We."[72] Whereas the first of Buber's articles about Herzl ("Theodor Herzl") called attention to the tragic paradoxes in his world, here Buber did not attribute these existential oppositions to the subject of his article but rather to the Jews of the diaspora of his time—presenting himself as one of them:

> Judaism is given to us in problematic fashion; since our own inner being is given to us in problematic fashion; because existence is given to us in the form of a problem. This is the great, tragic Jewish inheritance: the problematic essence, the diaspora form of inner duality.[73]

This way of being was epitomized in what he called there "the great paradox of being." In this article the lines formerly used to depict Herzl were now used by Buber to represent his own world. At that time the contrasts that typified his existential situation aroused longings within him to transcend duality. Along with that inner duality he had then presented a second duality, that between what is and what ought to be—the object of one's longings; the latter duality is embodied in the title of his article: "He and We."

Buber presents "activism" in contrast to the "problems" of the diaspora Jew: "[T]he man whose foundation is activism was given an inner life in the form of a full measure of urges, which he grasps in order to use them"; existence is given to him "in the form of a full measure of reality, which corrects his form and then waits for him to correct its form." In contrast, "the man of problems was given an existence in the form of a full measure of contradictions, demanding reparation by him and finding their reparation only in what is beyond nature and not in experiential reality."[74] Diaspora Jews, with whom Buber identifies himself, must overcome "all the sin," "all the inner restraints," and "first overcome thousands of despairs"[75] in order to achieve the dimension of unity.[75] Herzl, by contrast, is viewed as a unified man "by his very nature,"[76] and in his being the antithesis of the diaspora Jew he is an object of esteem.

"He and We" is contemporary with Buber's early speeches on Judaism, and the existential situation that was their background also resonates in it. There is a special affinity between it and the second of the two aforementioned lectures, "Judaism and Mankind,"[77] in which

Herzl is presented as the embodiment of the desired mankind: "a pure power, unity, greatness."[78] The significance of these traits for Buber emerges from his discussion of the character of the "Jewish movement" in the beginning of the very same article. Buber is wary of ideologies whose human subject is not kept in view, of a "program" based on the masses, in whom the "human visage" disappears. His dream is directed towards a "task" based on "people's humanity."[79] As in the article discussed above, "Herzl and History," here too Herzl is taken as expressing the palpable unity of the individual and his enterprise, and here that means the combination of idea and action: "Theodor Herzl is a leader for active life." The "task," "life," and "the human visage" here are placed on the same footing. It is not clear whether Buber also intended to imply that Herzl looked to individuals in their individuality, to "people's humanity," and paid heed to them,

Many years later, in "The Cause and the Person," the duality between "man" and "idea" or "enterprise" that is presented in several guises in "Herzl and History" and "He and We" was given the form of a dual structure, the poles of which are "cause" and "person."[80] That article takes an ambivalent attitude towards Herzl, at the basis of which is a distinction between the man and his conception of Zionism. Not only that, his relation to the "person" is no longer toward an elevated, unified figure. Buber also says of himself that even at the time of the Sixth Zionist Congress in 1903 he had a mixed attitude toward the personality of "his leader and guide." Until then Buber's critical attitude towards Herzl's conception of Zionism had been related to the content of that conception and distinct from his personal attitude towards Herzl.[81]

Even with the passage of several decades Buber did not acquire an unequivocal perspective upon his adversary. Another aspect of his ambivalent relationship towards Herzl appears, after many years, in an article in honor of the eightieth anniversary of the Zionist leader's birth in response to the question: "What would Herzl say if he were still alive?"[82] In Buber's opinion Herzl was a "magnanimous and wide-ranging liberal," and, as such, he strove "to supply the existing forces with the possible action in the given conditions of life." But such a view is not consistent, according to Buber, with Zionism, "the meaning of which is the desire fundamentally to change the conditions of the people's life, in such a way that by means of that change the primordial essence of the nation will break through the shell of its degeneration."[83]

Hence his conclusion was that, because Herzl was Zionist, "a new soul entered him. But he did not give it all the room it demanded." That soul is a kind of "primordial essence that is different from the ordinary sphere, which should have been allowed to break through the shell."[84] Buber assumes that Herzl never learned to heed the voices of his hidden interior, his primordial Jewish soul, in which the source of his Zionism received its thrust. He brought up the question: "And would Herzl have heard, if he had remained alive, what the second soul demanded of him, the additional soul, which was truly nothing but the primordial soul?" His answer, with which the article ends, is unequivocal: "I am certain that if Herzl had passed through our experiences with us, he would have recognized that no mere plan can make us truly into one nation, but merely the spirit, which is one. And at that moment, when Herzl acknowledged that, his Zionist soul would have overcome his liberal soul. . . . When I imagine Herzl to myself as an old man, I know that at this time he would not have been with those who are in the habit of speaking in his name, but rather with the faction which is gradually coming into being."[85]

Herzl the liberal, we are told in the body of the argument, saw Zionism as "a tarred road paved between a bad present and its improved continuation." Buber, the utopian, imagines it as "a cord strung between the secret of the distant past and the secret of the near or far future."[86] He "knows" that Herzl, in his alertness to the stirrings and imperatives of his "primordial soul," would also have seen that if he still had been alive.

Beyond the condemnation of what Buber saw as the outward aspect of Herzl's world, there is hidden a struggle against the leading tendencies of the Zionist movement; he wishes to free Herzl's path from identification with political Zionism, with which he had had a basic disagreement for many years.

Various manifestations of duality of the soul, which are aspects of a single basic approach, appear in Buber's writings of the 1940s; it is the duality of the "visible I," which guides the steps of most people, versus "the hidden self of the personality," which must be laid bare, fostered, and allowed to flourish.

Our survey of Buber's attitudes toward Herzl shows the polar shifts that took place in it over four decades. One cannot point to a straight line of development in that attitude. From emphasis upon the contradictions in Herzl's being, of which Buber had to take note in the article written soon after his death, the pendulum swings to the pole of praise and admiration just a month afterwards (in "Herzl and History"). Thence a direct line leads to a unified view of Herzl, full of respect and admiration, in 1910. That attitude deteriorated over the years, and in 1940 Buber saw Herzl as the figure of his own world: as having two souls, as living an existence of opposites, of which he was not aware in his short life. His ideological grappling with Herzl continued, finally concluding in two chapters of *On Zion*.[87]

The contradictions between Herzl's visage in Buber's articles from various times illustrate conflicting tendencies and inner struggles within the person doing the describing. Two of the articles devoted to Herzl, "He and We" and "The Cause and the Person," even permit Buber, as we have seen, to testify directly about the inner rift within his world.

It is fitting that the manifestations of duality in Buber's attitude toward Herzl's world should be placed in the background of his becoming acquainted with the mighty battle between the two roots of the soul (including the worldviews that derive from them). This battle provides the focus for a kind of novel that Buber wrote based on the world of Hasidism. The occasion upon which Buber expressed the assumption that two souls were vying within the author of *The Jewish State* would seem to be no coincidence. If Herzl had still been alive, it would have been his eightieth birthday. At that time Buber was involved in a stormy crisis of inner duality corresponding to ideological duality, expressed in *For the Sake of Heaven*, a work based both on historical events and on the spiritual struggles within the Hasidic movement in the eighteenth and first half of the nineteenth centuries. The aforementioned article was published a short time before Buber started serializing many of the chapters of this book in the daily press.

Two central figures vie with each other on the stage of that work and represent diametrically opposed views of the world: "the Seer of Lublin" and "the Holy Yehudi." The tension of the contrasts between them had preoccupied Buber intensely, as he reports, as early as the last year of World War I. At about that time he began a novel focused on the relations between those two men, but that project ended twice in failure, and he abandoned it, returning to it at the beginning of World War II.[88]

The Seer was a withdrawn man, tending to melancholy and removing himself from mundane affairs. He was taken up with his mystical visions. The "Yehudi," in contrast, was characterized by humane

understanding and sensitivity toward his fellow man. As early as 1922
Buber wrote, "Anyone dealing with this issue [of their relations] finds
that his foot has trod upon tragic soil." Even then he saw that the
relation between the Seer and the Yehudi was a combination of inclination *(Neigung)* and opposition *(Gegensatz)*.[89] This gives us a key to
understanding a work that he pieced together two decades afterwards.

The paths of religious faith and behavior exemplified by these two
spiritual leaders are not mutually exclusive. They do penetrate each
other to some extent. The Seer viewed the Yehudi as compensating for
his own shortcomings, and the Yehudi could not free himself from an
inner bond with his master, the Seer. This polar duality, which was
depicted on the basis of Hasidic sources, reflects a mighty battle in
Buber's own inner world between his spiritual drives, including his
tendency toward mysticism, and the dialogic experience here on this
earth. His conscious leaning was towards identification with the Yehudi,
but at the same time a hidden affinity with the Seer bubbles up in his
work. He struggles with these two poles—his two paths—at the same
time. I have already noted the significant place in *For the Sake of Heaven*
that is given to Rabbi Naftali of Roptchitz. The contrasts from which
his portrait is drawn are a reflection of the contradictory strains that
were combined in Buber's own spiritual world.[90]

In this context we cannot discuss the other characters of this work,
which express the inner recesses of its creator's world. "None of Buber's
books is as personal as those about Hasidism," noted Gershom
Scholem.[91] Perhaps we might extend that statement and view *For the
Sake of Heaven* as the most personal and confessional of all of Buber's
writings. In any event, Buber's testimony regarding the radical contrast expressed in this work are an indication of his general view of the
world:

> What I had to try to do was to penetrate to the kernel from both
> sides. This attempt could succeed only if I placed myself in the ser-
> vice of neither of the two tendencies. My only admissible point of
> view was that of the tragic writer who must delineate conflicting
> forces, each in its own nature, and whose antithesis is not between a
> "good" and an "evil" will, but lies within the cruel antithesis of
> existence itself.[92]

These words are echoed in an earlier statement about the tragic inability "to be, . . . in an inner sense, the representative of *one* side," which

appears in "The Cause and the Person," just as they are consistent with his statements about polar duality permeating everything.

We have already seen that it is impossible to make his duality consistent with systematic philosophical systems. Moreover, Buber does not accept the pairs of philosophical concepts traditionally used in ethics and aesthetics: good and evil, beautiful and ugly. His view removes them from the confines of an abstract, theoretical discussion and roots them "here in the earth," in the reality of mundane life. "Behind" these he places parallel pairs of concepts (which are familiar to us from his writings), exemplifying his value concept by means of them:

> Behind the common pairs of opposing concepts, good and evil, beautiful and ugly, there stand others. . . . Behind good and evil as criteria of the ethical stand direction and absence of direction.[93]

Between the members of these pairs there is no relation, nor is there polar tension. These conceptual schemes permit a unidirectional relation beginning with the negative concept and heading towards the positive concept: "The negative concept is immediately bound to the positive, being the emptiness to its fullness, the chaos to its cosmos."[94] The negative member exemplifies a potentiality that contains a drive to realization. The movement of coming into being that begins in that member is essentially drawn out in the realization of the "vocation" of each and every individual; on the basis of this model, two of the central structures of his writings are intensified: vortex versus directionality, and distance versus relation.[95]

In his writing it is also possible to locate a few objects of discussion to which unity is attributed. These too are not grasped as unified in every respect, but as the fusion of pairs of opposites. When Buber discusses the portrait of any figure, manifestations of duality occupy an important place in his discussion; at times he juxtaposes the figure with its opposite or places it in contexts of duality within the figure's worldview, and sometimes he lays bare oppositions or inner struggles in the figure's life. The earliest of his writings about Aharon David Gordon, in whom he saw "the teacher of truth," places him in opposition to most of the wordy preachers of the generation. In that sketch he also presents Gordon as combining the duality of working the land and looking at the stars in the heavens.[96] That combined duality of

earth and stars also provides the basis of the expression of unequivocal admiration found in another article, written two years later in
memory of Gordon.[97] In the chapter on Gordon in *On Zion*, where
Gordon is presented as a unique, exalted personality ("We have found
none other like him," Buber writes), the whole discussion is based on
pairs of opposites: "social phenomena" versus "natural phenomena,"
the bearing of suffering versus freedom, Henry David Thoreau and
Walt Whitman, on the one hand, and Gordon on the other.[98] Buber's
other portraits and discussions of the character of people's paths are
also based on dualities.[99] There seems to be only one work in all of
Buber's writings that is based on unity (the fusion of various tendencies), and not on duality—and that is his portrait of Arthur Ruppin.[100]

DUALITY AND THE YEARNING FOR UNITY

In Buber's early writings, expressions of a fragmented existence and
the contradictions that divide him[101] are found alongside definite yearnings for unity and redemption. From the end of the first decade in the
twentieth century he articulated a yearning to combine the present
moment with history and the personal-experiential with the eternal.
The ego's striving to be redeemed from its inner contradictions was presented in these works in close connection with messianic ideas. This is
how he formulated these matters in one of his early lectures on Judaism:

> It is this striving for unity that has made the Jew creative. Striving to
> evolve unity out of the divisions of his I, he conceived the idea of the
> unitary God. Striving to evolve unity out of the division of the hu-
> man community, he conceived the idea of universal justice. Striving
> to evolve unity out of the division of the world, he created the Mes-
> sianic Ideal, which later, again under the guiding participation of
> Jews, was reduced in scope, made finite, and called socialism.[102]

The yearning for inner unity of the character was presented at the end of
this article in the context of his hopes for a renewal of Judaism that
would permit it to fulfill its unifying mission in human society in
general.[103]

It is no coincidence that this speech itself is also the first instance
in which Buber presented a condensed formulation of his polar conception.[104] There was tension in his soul between visionary pathos and

gloomy realism stamped with the dimension of tragedy: he expressed a strong urge for unity, and, at the same time, he pointed out "the primal dualism, . . . the source and significance of all things of the spirit."[105] In another article from that period he brings out the yearnings of the "diaspora Jew" (Buber's contemporary) for unity, yearnings that make him "a man of problems." He has "a way to overcome his problematic nature" and, at the same time, "he cannot undo his inner dualism." He can only "raise himself up above it and attain that unity of the powers of the soul which become prepared to receive *enlightenment;* enlightenment, which teaches a person enterprise and action."[106] Here he presents a combination of optimistic affirmation of life and sober acknowledgment of the limits of the uprooted Jews' ability to free themselves completely from the duality that clings to them.

It is interesting that even the God of Israel, the embodiment of unity and its source, was involved in Buber's polar image of the world and its expressions in those years:

> We are incapable of grasping this whole creative act except as *polarity*, as an expression of immanent duality. It is extremely important that God, who, in the eyes of prophetic man, is a unity beyond all duality, is found, in fact, again and again, involved in duality, because the transcendence of human existence, in which man lives by a conception of himself, is repeatedly soiled by giving an image to that existence.[107]

Later, however, in the dialogue stage of his spiritual biography, this conception changes: the good becomes identified with personal "vocation," with self-realization,[108] and the "unity of God" is grasped as dwelling "above good," that is, beyond human application:[109] "The unity of God is not the Good; it is the Supergood."

At an early stage in his spiritual path Buber came to know only one self-realizing unity, which is decidedly a mystical unity. He was drawn to it with one aspect of his thinking, which was hardly connected to the expressions of his Judaism; the chapter "Ecstasy and Expression," which introduces his *Ecstatic Confessions,* opens with an indication of ecstasy as an expression of unity: "[T]he man who lives it," he says there, "turns into a unity untouched within by any duality."[110] Plurality *(Vielheit)* and Duality *(Zweiheit)* are viewed as the opposite of Unity *(Einheit),* to which he attributes, in the non-Jewish manifestations of his spiritual world, an entirely personal meaning; it is identified with the ground of being *(der Grund des Erlebnisses)* of the man "without borders" *(unbegrenzte)*.[111]

The same line is continued in his *Daniel*, the last chapter of which ("On Unity") expresses a yearning for personal unity to be acquired by means of a fusing of polar oppositions.[112] Buber did not know unity as a reality of life. It remains merely a desired realm and a constant challenge. He once again expressed his inability actually to attain the object of his yearning: "Einheit ist das, was ewig wird" (Unity is that which is constantly becoming).[113]

That primary quality of his yearnings also echoes in Buber's tone from the year when World War I ended. His statement is unequivocal: "Unified, unifying, total man, free in God, is the goal of mankind's longing."[114] But these remarks do not fit in with the spirit that imbues the pages of *Daniel*. For he is no longer interested in the individuality of the individual but rather in the individual Jew as a member of his people and as a Zionist. From this point of view, "Herut," the article just quoted, is consistent with the early speeches on Judaism. But the spiritual conception in it is different from that which is embodied in them. It already contains expressions of the dialogical worldview.[115]

Expressions of unity based on the assumptions of Buber's dialogical thinking are few in comparison to the tendencies that stood out in his writings of the first fifteen years of the century. The object of his striving is no longer inner unity itself nor yet unity with the world—as in the manifestations of his mystical thinking with which we are acquainted. Now "the being which has become one can no longer understand itself on this side of individuation nor indeed on this side of the 'I and Thou.'"[116] He did not refer to the unity that does away with the independent essence of the participants in an I-Thou relationship, but rather to the becoming that takes place *between them*. Of love, however, which he sees as a high level of dialogue, he says that "it does not invalidate the 'I'; on the contrary, it binds the 'I' more closely to the 'Thou.'"[117]

The constant drive toward unity is not to be interpreted only by means of the suppositions of his dialogics. It is primary and more comprehensive than they are. Furthermore, the dimensions of the unity that are not connected in their expression to the system of Buberian dialogical thinking are not meant to form a combination in which the independent actuality of its components no longer exists. Buber does not argue for a priori unity but for unity that is achieved—the creation of which is a daily struggle.

2
THE CAUSE AND THE PERSON:
Destiny and Vocation

*The main entree into a thinker's works is not through the content of
his thought, but through its path and method; and nothing permits
us to understand that path and method better than knowledge of the
way he himself understood them, although occasionally we must
determine whether or not he understands them correctly.*
                    —Buber, "Bergson and Intuition" (1944)

Buber's worldview was formed as a direct outgrowth of his biographical experiences, and he wanted it to be understood and regarded that
way. In particular he applied that approach to the trends of his own
thought after the powerful upheaval that took place in his life during
World War I, a process that he calls "a conversion."[1] From then until
his last days, his writings embodied various aspects of his longing to
live a life of dialogue; from 1918, his spiritual biography is characterized by a dialogue voicing tension between what "is" and what "ought
to be," between "destiny" and "vocation."

Scholars and critics of Buber who were his contemporaries, dealing with his works as they were being created, did not find it easy, or
perhaps possible, to observe him from a distance. Buber's forceful personality and the glory of his name illuminated his writings, if not more
than that. Only a few of those students of his work, notably Sh. H.
Bergmann and G. Scholem, pointed out this problem. The former noted
it emphatically in personal letters as well as viva voce (I have letters
that he wrote to me in the 1960s and early 1970s in which he expresses it), and that problem is also brought out in his studies of Buber's

41

thought. The earliest is his "Three Addresses on Judaism" (in Hebrew), published in *HaShiloach*, January-June 1912. That article deals with the well-known addresses Buber delivered in Prague (1909–11).

In the opening passage of one of Bergmann's later articles about the Buberian philosophy of dialogue, he returns to those early addresses, stating: "Anyone who heard those speeches . . . can never forget them and will never forget them till his dying day."[2]

G. Scholem, who became acquainted with Buber's teachings as a young man, testifies to the connection between his "person" and his "cause" (the "writer" and the "writing," in his words), regarding the nature of Buber's influence. At the same time, he makes us aware of the importance of that bond as the basis for understanding Buber's attitudes. Speaking with some reservations about Buber's first two books, *The Tales of Rabbi Nachman* (1906) and *The Legend of the Baal-Shem* (1908), he adds:

> But I recall how fascinating they were in our youth, and how much they did at the time to fire our hearts and bring them closer to the treasures of Judaism. That combination of objective content and the extremely personal interpretation which Buber gave to that content, was marvelously complete. The boundaries between them were not visible—nor did we seek them. A particular inspiration was manifest here, and that inspiration produced a kind of marvelous unity between the writer and the writing.[3]

In addition to that personal account one should add Scholem's statement at the beginning of his comprehensive study of Buber's view of Judaism: "Buber, who attributes such great importance to the mutual relations between spiritual life and the particular, personal element, cannot be discussed without that element."[4]

The foci of Buber's thought and the twists and turns of his intellectual biography[5] are mutually interdependent. To demonstrate the tensions of the affinities between them, Buber developed a conceptual scheme based on two axes: "cause" and "person."

The "cause" for him is a person's works, his vocation, the object of his study or action, a "doctrine" that binds together a movement or society.

By "person" he means the living, concrete individual, the one behind the abstractions and generalizations that make an individual anonymous. The relation between these two axes concerned Buber

THE CAUSE AND THE PERSON: DESTINY AND VOCATION

from the time he was a young man, and he gave various expressions to it in his writings.

Any investigation of Buber's worldview must necessarily swing like a pendulum between those two value concepts.

In a work composed in 1901, the duality with which we are dealing was formulated using the terms "scientific knowledge" and "love."[6] A few years afterwards, in one of the two articles Buber wrote about Herzl, the duality is already structured on the armature of "person" and "work." He states that Herzl "believed in himself not as though he believed in a *person*, but rather as though believing in a *work*."[7] From then on his attitude towards Herzl was predicated on that duality between personal traits and a path, a duality combining "great power, unity, greatness"—terms he applied to Herzl—and "a plan, a method, a work," distinguishing his Zionist vision.[8]

Deviation from that dual tendency is found in an article written late in World War I, where it is stated that true and worthy "personages and personalities are those who place themselves . . . beneath the heavenly dome of their *cause*."[9] Here the man is subordinated in service to his work (whereas in general Buber gives priority to the person).

Not until the beginning of the 1930s did Buber develop the structure of significances that are presented as the axes or limbs of "cause" and "person." That took place when he recalled an event he had witnessed at the Sixth Zionist Congress in 1903: from the platform of that congress Herzl launched a coarse attack against Davis Trietsch (a friend of Buber's who shared his approach). Buber was appalled. "Greatly moved," he hurried up to Herzl in the company of Berthold Feiwel, to make him see that his accusations were unfounded. Herzl admitted that his attack, apparently addressed to the issues, was actually motivated personally: "I would have taken [Davis Trietsch] to task in a wholly different way!" he exclaimed. "Wholly differently! But there before the platform, directly opposite me, a girl—his fiancée, I have heard—placed herself; there she stood, her eyes flashing at me. A wonderful person, I tell you! I could not do it!"[10]

The article in which that event is recounted gives Buber an opportunity to present his approach, based on a critical attitude toward principles and methods, emphasizing the personality that realizes them.[11] The mark made by Herzl's attack on Trietsch was significant in Buber's life beyond the change it occasioned in his attitude towards "his leader and guide." It forced him to confront an ambiguous situation with no way out, one that he describes as an experience of the tragic basis of life. In describing the events following the meeting of the congress at which Herzl spoke, twenty-five years later he spoke of his reaction at that time with the vividness of actual experience:

> It became at once compellingly clear to me that here it was impossible to remain inwardly the representative of *one* side . . . I was twenty-four years of age and this was perhaps the first time that I set foot on the soil of tragedy where there is no longer such a thing as being in the right.[12]

That situation, in which an instinctual urge overcame the objective considerations of a great leader, gave further strength to Buber's decidedly personal approach. He asks

> whether there might not yet be another reality, different from that of obvious world history—a reality hidden and powerless because it has not come into power; whether there might not be, therefore, men with a mission who have not been called to power and yet are, in essence, men who have been summoned; whether excessive significance has not perhaps been ascribed to the circumstances that separate the one class of men from the other; whether success is the only criterion; . . . whether there does not exist a "dark" *charisma*. The man who acts in history does not allow himself to be overwhelmed by such questions, for if he did so, he would have to despair, and to withdraw. But the moments in which they touch him are the truly religious moments of his life.[13]

The reality in which he believes and in the light of which he walks, "different from that of obvious world history," is one which seeks to regard political events with human vision. Some of the "heroes" of his work *Gog and Magog* are conceived in the spirit dictated by that reality, and within them Buber finds a reflection of the path he chose for himself. One such is R. Simcha Bunim of Parsischa. "It was useless to try to discuss political events with him. He sought at once to translate them into human terms. It was as though he were intent upon scraping off from the simple wooden substance of our life a coat of paint and to do it immediately and thoroughly."[14] In Buber's opinion, "Torah," ideology, and political views all are likely to have valuational and existential significance if they are interpreted personally.

He voiced a strong expression of that hermeneutic approach in the course of a conversation held with the historian Ben-Zion Dinur during a visit to Palestine in 1936. They discussed the "use of sources as a means of historical exposition." According to Dinur's memoirs, Buber said that "every historian has his own view of the past, and in the fullness of that personal vision lies his ability to mold the past in his own figure and image." Similarly, he expressed apprehension at the excessive use of sources by the historian; for therein lay a sort of "resignation of the 'person' for the sake of the 'cause.' . . . And we must," he argued, "especially at this time, be wary of actions not directed at the person, since the 'cause' seems more important to those who 'act' sometimes unconsciously, without even being aware."[15]

Once in a great while the polar tension between "cause" and "person" falls away, becoming rather two "emphatic trends"[16] attributed to the same essence. Buber holds that those two foci can be joined and united. The concept of unity was already the object of Buber's yearnings at an early stage of his thought and was emphasized in his "early addresses" on Jewish matters.[17] However, in his extensive writings, one finds but few expressions of that unity coming into being. Here is one such expression, directed towards the unification of a person with his lifework:

> In the human realm no sight is more beautiful than a man who identifies with his lifework to such a degree that his subjective and objective considerations are no longer separate, but both are conjoined; person and cause are merely two aspects of the same reality. That is not simply a subjective phenomenon based upon the man's emotions and will, but we acknowledge that the mixture contains a kind of objective essence, destiny and vocation. It would seem that a man is summoned by that essence for the sake of the vocation incumbent upon him, and the identification which he makes is merely an expression of this being called; we may take a similar view of a function imposed upon him by human groups and their institutions, for the sake of which this identification is made, regarding it as an expression of the summons of which human beings, groups, and institutions act as agents.[18]

Such a person was, in Buber's opinion, Arthur Ruppin, who "bound himself to the task [of settling Palestine] entrusted to him, till he became totally one with it." The identification of a man with his work is uncommon. Destiny places many impediments—external constraints and inner reluctance—in the path of one who wishes to fulfill his vocation. "And when the sign of destiny is stamped on a man's forehead, it is not always visible to the earthly authorities, nor do they help him accomplish it; and it sometimes happens that, although they do their part, the man who is summoned tragically blinds his own heart, remaining with his forces scattered and too lazy truly to accept his vocation, that is to say, with true identification." This identification of the vision or work with a man who bears it takes place when "a man's talents do not use his function in order to act but rather faithfully serve the function. Something which has to be done, which wants to be done, uses the man to be done by him. The man has no desire but to be at the disposition of that cause."[19]

That structure, the limbs of which are "cause" and "person," should be helpful in understanding the relation between Buber the man and Buber the philosopher. He was prey to tension, particularly in his dialogical writings, between his philosophical aspirations (the desire to be accepted as a philosopher) and his rejection of philosophy (both as an abstract study and as a system). On the one hand, he had the pretension, after World War I, to work out his own system of thought. In a letter to Sh. H. Bergmann dated 21 January 1919, he says he is "now working on laying the foundations for a philosophical system (social philosophy and the philosophy of religion). The coming years will be devoted to that system."[20] On the other hand, the very composition of *I and Thou*, the seeds of which are referred to in that letter, implies emphasis on reality brought to life through the denial of dogma, principles, and systematic orders.

He often presents his theoretical work as a personal report; for example, in summarizing his essay "Dialogue," (1932) he states: "I try only to say that there is something, and to indicate how it is made: I simply record."[21] Similarly, in the opening to his later work *Autobiographical Fragments* (1960), he declares: "It cannot be a question here of recounting my personal life (I do not possess the kind of memory necessary for grasping great temporal continuities as such), but solely of rendering an account of some moments that my backward glance lets rise to the surface."[22]

It was important to him to provide philosophical definitions of topics in his writings. Yet at the same time he says, "Once again: I do not philosophize more than I must."[23] That declaration more or less summarizes his approach both in the cited work[24] and in earlier ones.

Philosophical knowledge of man, he claims, is not consistent with the standard methods of philosophical investigation or with scholarship in the humanities in general.

He presents his credo in the opening of "What is Man?" (1938), where it is related to what Buber calls "philosophical anthropology." The latter must refrain from "what may be termed 'dehumanization,'" and its task is to "reach . . . the subject's genuine wholeness, which can become visible only by the contemplation of all its manifold nature," in contrast to "a false unity which has no reality."[25] He regards himself as a philosophical anthropologist, who "does not leave his subjectivity out and does not remain an untouched observer."[26] Buber seeks to bridge the gap between the spirit and reality, a gap about which he frequently warns us.

Embedded in all those assumptions and declarations is the structure of "cause" and "person," which also guides Buber's exegetical approach to Jewish sources.[27] It appears to be implied in the statement: "There was little sense in discussing principles and methods, since, in the final analysis, everything depends not upon them, but upon the person to whom their realization and application is entrusted."[28]

From my discussion up to this point it appears that the duality of "science" and "consciousness" (or "fidelity" and "choice") overlaps that of "cause" and "person." Against that background one should refer back to Buber's declarative testimony regarding his personal method of exegesis:

> Let us assume I am discussing a text from our literature. It has been interpreted countless times and in countless ways. . . . I know that my interpreting, like everyone else's, is conditioned through my being; . . . I guide him who lets himself be guided to the reality of the text. To him whom I teach I make visible the working forces of the text that I have experienced. . . . The facts are there, the faithfulness to them is there; the faithfulness is conditioned, like everything human, and like everything human, of essential importance.[29]

The relation between research and meaning, between "cause" and "person," is based on a personal line of demarcation.

One may distinguish two components here:

1. the personal point of departure, that is, the indissoluble link between the commentator's life and his interpretation;

2. the existential situation of the commentator, which determines both his personal point of departure and what is elicited, what responds to him in the texts being interpreted.

There appear to be two main senses in which Buber's work is a reflection of his life:

    1. as a direct echo (or expression) of his spiritual propensities;
    2. as an expression of the tortuous course of his striving to supply what is lacking.

Both of those senses are bound up in his work. I believe there is a strong affinity between the two and with the aforementioned nexus of problems in his writings, i.e., the "two faces of reality and appearance," or "living by appearances" versus "living by essence," which he viewed as one of the central issues of his dialogical thought.[30] What is desirable, yearned for, sought, in his world, can be identified with the life of dialogue. He holds that the "I-It" relationship can lead only to appearance, whereas the "I-Thou" relationship leads to the essence of existence.[31]

Buber's spiritual biography is a drama with many acts, rich with varied aspects of anguished ambivalence embodied in "the tension between is and ought."[32] His writings reflect the opposing tensions within his existence, along with the effort to emphasize the utopian pole of the axis: "vocation," "the way," "realization"—all expressing the image Buber longed for.

APPENDIX

Buber stated, "I know that my interpreting, like everyone else's, is conditioned through my being," and I have tried to show here that his statement cannot be understood only in its simple meaning. This brings us to the issue of whether "a creator creates in his own image," an issue that has long been a subject of debate in the humanities.

That debate was stimulated by the publication of Ben-Ami Scharfstein's *The Philosophers—Their Lives and the Nature of their Thought*.[33] He argues that there is a strong relationship between a man's life history and his values and concepts, demonstrating his point by reference to the biographies of twenty-two philosophers.

In a critical article in the Hebrew weekly *Koteret Rashit*, Professor Yishayahu Leibowitz disagreed with that approach, and, in response to letters to the editor challenging his opinions, Leibowitz responded by phrasing his views even more sharply:

> To the extent that we know the biographies of great thinkers and creators or even of men who held certain political or social views and introduced something new to human consciousness . . . in most cases we are astounded at our inability to connect those great spiritual works with the conditions of life or the fate of those who created them.[34]

In this context one also ought to present the views of the Israeli novelist A. B. Yehoshua, who concurs with Yishayahu Leibowitz:

> Recently in psychoanalytical research and in research on Kafka [these remarks come from an article on Kafka's "Metamorphosis"] there has been a strong tendency to introduce personalities into works, to the point of totally obscuring boundaries. . . . That extremist biographical approach is inherently dangerous. . . . The act of creation is a chemical interaction or perhaps even a nuclear one between personal, biographical elements and general, cultural substances. . . . So much so that the combination of the elements in the structure of the "personal molecule" changes when it is reshaped in the literary work. Any effort to apply what is brought out in a biography and thus to identify the literary molecule is highly speculative.[35]

As opposed to the biographical trend, which seeks personal testimony in works, he offers an approach according to which "the text alone is the highest, absolute source of authority."

Y. Leibowitz and A. B. Yehoshua would appear to oppose interpreters who seek biography in philosophical works. But Buber himself, with regard to his own thought, makes entirely the opposite demand of his interpreters: he condemns efforts to discuss the creations of his spirit separately from living, personal experience.

Generally a creative person is appalled by psychoanalytical or personal criticism of his works and recoils from it. That, however, is not the case with Buber, who constantly directs his readers and interpreters to bring out the close ties between the "cause" and the "person."

3

A DIVIDED HEART
AND MAN'S DOUBLE

Then he turned to him, asking what he had meant when he said, "We aren't all of a piece." "There are two beings in every one of us," his friend explained.

—Stefan Heym, *Ahasver*

A DIVIDED HEART AND SELF-CONTRADICTION

The division of the self is a fundamental fact of existence in Buber's world. In his writings Buber's struggles with this fact, which take on various guises, echo from the inner core of his being.

An inner being rent by contradictions is often termed a divided heart in Buber's writing. Sometimes he argues for loyalty to but one side of the heart. However, even when he speaks of the "conversion" that he underwent, we find that it did not endow him with a "new heart."[1] The change that he calls a "conversion" did not lead to self-renewal within him, but rather a complication—sometimes tragic—of the struggle between the nature of his heart and the change wrought by "destiny." He speaks revealingly of himself: "I early had a premonition, indeed, no matter how I resisted it, that I was inescapably destined to love the world."[2]

The duality of souls or hearts occupies a central place in his article, "If Herzl Were Still Living" (1940), which I have discussed above in another context.[3] However, Buber's writings contain other, more

51

complex expressions of the problematical existential status of the divided inner being. Two outstanding examples of this appear in sources
with close similarity in structure: "Recollection of a Death" and
"Leopold Krakauer." The first work is devoted to the memory of his
close friend Gustav Landauer,[4] and it is based on two dualities: the
revolutionary and the soldier, and the goal and the way.[5] He writes:

> The true front runs through the licentious soldiery, the true front
> runs through the revolution, the true front runs through the heart of
> the soldier, the true front runs through the heart of the revolution-
> ary. The true front runs through each party and through each adher-
> ent of a party, through each group and through each member of a
> group. On the true front each fights against his fellows and against
> himself, and only through the decisions of these battles is he given
> full power for other decisions.[6]

One senses a decidedly autobiographical tone here, especially in
the final sentence. The models of dual structures underlying "Recollection of a Death" were used fifty years later in a poetical, philosophical article portraying the architect and artist, Leopold Krakauer.
The following lucid and compact passage merits citation in full:

> Leopold Krakauer . . . belonged to no school and emulated no
> style, neither a new nor an old; his own vision inspired in him his
> own language. He was a solitary man; but his solitude was a cre-
> ative and a formative one, indeed, one may say that it was his soli-
> tude that brought him to his work, which we love and with which
> we are familiar as his very own. That happened on the path of a
> meeting which became Krakauer's artistic destiny: that with the land-
> scape of Jerusalem. His solitude met that of the landscape and trans-
> formed itself in it. Only in drawing the Jerusalemite solitude did he
> become the artist that he was.
>   Krakauer carried nothing "from above" into nature. He en-
> tered into the very phenomenon that accosted him, but he did it
> with so powerful a devotion that he was able to grasp it from its
> inwardness, as it were, in the dynamic of its solitude that corre-
> sponded to and answered his own. The inner tension that works out
> of the restless and yet so finished form of the thistle, the great inner
> trembling that is frozen into the limbs of the olive tree as the life
> pain of a man into the lines of his face, yes even the immeasurable
> movement of the smallest little part that hides behind the apparent
> deadness of a heap of stones but that lets something like a strange
> knocking penetrate from itself to us—all that is intensified in

Krakauer's pages to the language of a solitude, a tormented solitude, that is, at the very base of each creature. It is intensified, I say, but this intensification works on us like a discovery. That at times in a drawing of Krakauer's such a tree almost appears to us like a human shape means nothing fantastic; it belongs to the essence of this particular vision of nature.

I am unable to speak of Krakauer as an architect. However regarding one matter I may hint at something related to what I am discussing here. A true artist who engages in two arts does not usually express the same feelings in both, but rather two sides of his being, complementary aspects, each of which acquires a form. Thus we learn from the experience of some of the greatest artists, from Leonardo and Michelangelo to Degas and Matisse. One finds the same thing, I believe, in Krakauer, in his own way, and at his own level. His deep experience with the torments of solitude provide the drive behind his graphic work, and his buildings are based in pining for a life of friendship and warmth of heart. Thus within his soul, as in the souls of many artists and intellectuals today, particularly in this country, we find, side by side, a tendency to sadness and a yearning for the pleasure of friends. Both of these tendencies created works and molded forms, each in its own right.[7]

Leopold Krakauer and Buber were friends. Both were Europeans, both were creative, and both were far from one-dimensional. They both sought an encounter with the Jerusalem landscape and to blend into it. That effort at encounter took place in an anguished solitude that Buber found expressed in Krakauer's work. It should be pointed out that a print by Krakauer hung in a central place in Buber's study in his Jerusalem home (it hung in his son Raphael's house during the latter's lifetime).

The article on Krakauer begins by considering individuality and solitude, "formative" and personal solitude. That solitude was at the core of Krakauer's artistic endeavors, which, as we are told, were predicated upon the duality of solitude. "Artistic destiny" here brought about a dialogical encounter between Krakauer's solitude and that of the Jerusalem landscape. He grasped the dynamic of the inner solitude of nature in Jerusalem, "that corresponded to and answered his own." Buber describes these two solitudes out of identification with them. Under the influence of the grace of the dialogue with the Jerusalem landscape, Krakauer's "solitude transformed itself." The implication here is that he could not step out of his solitude or overcome it. Krakauer, says Buber, "accepted and embraced the nature of Jerusalem, grasp[ing] it from its inwardness, as it were." Ultimately this is not a dialogue in the full sense of the word. The dynamic of the Jerusalem landscape is parallel and responsive to the solitude of the artist who approaches it from the outside. A certain strangeness remains, a hint of distance, and that creates the tension within the encounter. The source of that tension is "a tormented solitude . . . at the very base of each creature." Here we have the duality of solitude both before the encounter through creativity and after it.

Underlying "Krakauer" we find a structural model quite similar to that in "Recollection of a Death." In the earlier article we find tension, not between members of a duality but rather within each member of the duality (in the inner world of the revolutionary). Likewise, here, in "Krakauer," the duality—that of the artist and the Jerusalem landscape—is presented as an inner tension existing within each of the members. This tension is dynamic, the "tormented solitude . . . at the very base" of the artist's being is paralleled (or reflected) in the existence of the subjects of the artist's work in the world of earth, stones, and plants: "The inner tension that works out of the restless and yet so finished form of the thistle, the great inner trembling that is frozen into the limbs of the olive tree, . . . even the immeasurable movement of the smallest little part that hides behind the apparent deadness of a heap of stones." The stirrings of the inwardness of the natural objects appearing in Krakauer's graphics express the stirrings of his own solitude. In the "intensification" of his work, says Buber, the artist is granted a revelation—which is what he calls Krakauer's "peculiar vision of nature," permitting him to raise the outlines of an olive tree's limbs to an expression of a "human shape" whose pain is "frozen . . . into the lines of his face." That description offers another example of Buber's tendency to penetrate to the interior of the two poles of the duality and wrestle with the contraries. He also points directly and clearly at the duality within Krakauer, composed of a graphic drive and an architectural root. The first, he points out, originates in the man's "deep experience" with the torments of solitude, and the second embodies a "yearning for the pleasure of friends," and "pining for a life of friendship and warmth of heart."

The lucid and compact passage just discussed, with its wealth of components (crammed into a single printed page), concludes with emphasis on the unbridgeable duality between the two realms of Krakauer's creativity: "Both of these tendencies created works and molded forms, each in its own right."

In point of fact all the works discussed above—"Conversion," "If Herzl were Alive Today," "Recollection of a Death," and "Krakauer"— refer to the "divided heart," that is, two souls in conflict with each other (or opposed to each other), throbbing within man.

In each of these works different aspects of "self-contradiction" are represented, a Buberian concept that is discussed, though with great compression, in *I and Thou*. Self-contradiction is the opposite of a life of dialogical relationship. Buber views dialogue as the essence of human existence. He identifies it as man's "destiny" and the personal "way" worthy of him. Buber's dialogical thought[8] is one of the main axes of his life work. It is even commonly presented as the center and essence of his views. His systematic work *I and Thou*, which is representative of his dialogical thought, contains a passage—just thirteen lines long—that is devoted to self-contradiction. The first line is a kind of heading: "What is Self-Contradiction?" Buber uses that concept to designate a life of monologue that, in his opinion, contradicts human nature. The end of a monologic life, he claims, is self-immolation. The passage begins, "When man does not test the *a priori* of relations in the world, working out and actualizing the innate You in what he encounters, it turns inside."[9] If the spiritual energy that, in essence, is meant to produce relationships within life is not faithful to the law of its own nature, it cannot struggle against the void, and in any event it is turned inward and acts within the self. "Then it unfolds through the unnatural, impossible object, the I—which is to say that it unfolds where there is no room for it to unfold."[10] At that point man is in conflict with his world, giving rise to self-contradiction. When this development continues and becomes dominant in a man's world, he reaches "the edge of life" and wreaks his own destruction: "What is unfulfilled has escaped into the mad delusion of some fulfillment." That is, a person who does not recognize the self-destruction he causes himself continues to delude himself and "flee" from himself, and he "gropes around in the labyrinth and gets lost even more profoundly."[11] That is a kind of spiritual suicide on the verge of physical suicide.

I know of no description of such a grave and definite outcome for monologic existence elsewhere in Buber's writings.

The passage on self-contradiction concentrates on the extreme stage of the existence of "man for himself," the trackless confusion in which a person reaches a cul-de-sac, namely, self-destruction. But as a background for that stage Buber illustrates degrees of "the I of the ego" that still have something of a return to the dialogical path. The man who "does not believe and encounter" is called by him "the capricious man." An existential situation of that kind can be rectified. It is possible to exchange the "little will," which "is unfree and ruled by things and drives,"[12] for free will and the ability to communicate. The "little will" embodies man's submission to routine, the confusion of spiritual slackness, and the apparently necessary cyclical nature of life.

There is also hope for people who have "some self-contradictions that [people] try to hold back";[13] there is room for a person to struggle with his "little will." If the prisoner does not free himself from his jail, his fellow man may save him from the prison of his confinement within himself. When one's fellow man notes the illusion or self-delusion in which the person before him wraps himself, he can speak with him so as to prove that in this world there is in fact such a thing as a dialogical relationship. "The form that confronts me I cannot experience nor describe, I can only realize it."[14]

Buber holds that our inner rebellion in the presence of a person subject to inner contradiction will impel us to show him "via reality" that there is another path: "How dissonant the I of the ego sounds! When it issues from tragic lips, tense with some self-contradiction that they try to hold back, it can move us to great pity. When it issues from chaotic lips that savagely, heedlessly, unconsciously represent contradictions, it can make us shudder. When the lips are vain and smooth, it sounds embarrassing or disgusting."[15]

Various manifestations of "self-contradiction" are represented in the works of Buber discussed in this chapter. It would seem that he relates the content of this concept to "the God of the sufferers," the God of Job, who "contradicts" (according to Buber) "His revelation by 'hiding His face'" (Job 13:24).[16]

Buber's conception of the divided heart is not necessarily based on a struggle between opposites. Sometimes Buber understands the two polarized paths from within, experiencing them simultaneously. If that were not the case, he would have been incapable of trying "to penetrate to the kernel from both sides." In *For the Sake of Heaven*,[17] Buber declares that he is for one of these paths, that of "Pshysha," and against that of "Lublin." At the very same time, however, he feels that he stands "at a point of very vital oneness with these men," which is to say both with the camp of "the Holy Yehudi of Pshysha" and with "the Seer of Lublin." The struggle between these two alternatives takes place in his own heart: "My heart is at one with those in Israel," he testifies, "who today . . . strive with a striving meant to precede a renewal of the forms of both faith and life. This striving is a continuation of the Hasidic striving."[18]

The duality of doubleness is, as noted, primarily a reality within the human heart: "The rift between those who do violence and those to whom violence is done, the rift between those who are true to God and the apostate element, running not merely through every nation, but also through every group in a nation, and even through every soul."[19] We must note the generality of this statement, according to which the process occurs "in every soul." An existential split, with its roots in inner rifts, is embodied structurally and conceptually in Buber's language throughout more than fifty years of creative activity. We can always go back and discover the "person" behind the "cause" presented in his writing,[20] even in the works from late in his life. That inner duality is also implicit in remarks on the way "genuine poetry" is born;[21] he characterizes the "poet" by saying that within his heart "a dialogue takes place between eternity and the moment," making possible "the coming into being of those very rare impulses which we see fit to call poems."[22] This rare event is the product of "grace," even "divine grace," when the poet "let[s] his heart be the scene of this dialogue." And he, "the poet, is prepared"—in this instance he represents Buber's tragic figure—"to forgive all the sufferings which are liable to come to him" in this dialogue, which is "sometimes very cruel and which takes place within his pained heart." However, is this truly a dialogue, as Buber calls it? For, as he himself adds, only one of the two (necessary for weaving together a dialogue) is open and ready, the human side, whereas the other side, the divine one, is described as "impenetrable darkness." "Such tortures and such grace," Buber states, are found within true poets.[23] I might add in this context that they also characterize the man of faith as Buber conceives of him.[24] The "grace" of which he speaks in "Eternity and the Moment" (as he spoke of it in *I and Thou*) is awaited and yearned for, but it is not at all certain. It does not depend on man's intention or purposive action. The "sufferings," on

the other hand, are a dominant factor in man's internal presence within
Buber's world.

*   *   *

The process of the integration of the personality is meant to begin in the
human heart, or in his soul. Following the Hasidic tradition, Buber calls
it the attainment of "peace of mind."[25] He grasps that beginning as the
start of "the struggle against evil." This struggle "must begin within one's
own soul—all else will follow upon this."[26] He also conceives of the
"inner struggle . . . within the heart of every nation" on the pattern of
this "struggle" and as an organic development following from it.[27]

It would seem that at the basis of the previously mentioned inner
struggles, which are not visible to the eye, lies a struggle within Buber's
heart for the attainment of faith. His God is "the God of the sufferers."[28] Defiance, puzzlement, and questioning of God—even while He
is hidden—begin in the depths of his being. "Within my soul," Buber
says of himself in a conversation about his longing for faith, "one
abyss calls to another."[29] And perhaps these abysses are that of doubt
and despair and that of yearning and desire . . .

The biblical term "a single heart" (Jer. 32:39) refers to a unified
heart, a heart where the rifts have been healed. Perhaps that is the
reason why it appears in Jeremiah along with "one path." These expressions are foreign to Buber's existential condition. The "deep rift"
in his inner being, about which he spoke in his early lectures on Judaism (1909–10), became a model for the formation of a conceptual
structure, and over the years it also became a subject of reflective contemplation. According to his portrayal of this inner split, it affects all
the areas of his life with duality or polar tensions. In his writings contraries constantly press for unity but, without it, continue to vie with
each other. These personal rifts are connected with and conditioned
by "rifts in the heart of the world." That is the spirit in which Buber
interprets the torments of Job, who is actually convinced by the attempts of his three comforters "to mend the rent in his world," for
"this is the rent in the heart of the world."[30]

Thus it would seem that a "dual heart" has the meaning of the
Talmudic expression *shtey levavot* (two hearts) (*Baba Batra* 12; *Tanhuma, Tavo*, 1).

THE DOUBLE

A person's double is someone who resembles him and represents the alter ego within him—whether it is the kernel of his individual personality (which has not been fully realized) or else a suppressed or repressed "other."[31]

The existence of a double indicates a divided or split personality, that a person's visible and public ego is merely one aspect of his world. A person and his double frequently exemplify the duality of external reality versus the true inner nature, hidden from view—that of seeming *(Schein)* versus true being *(Sein)*.

The double, as Jorge Luis Borges has shown, is an "ancient subject." Special terms for the double have been coined in various languages, such as the German "Doppelgänger" and the Latin "alter ego." In Borges's opinion this phantom phenomenon is surely derived from seeing one's reflection in polished metal or water, or simply from memory.[32]

The conception of the psyche represented by the terms "shadow" or "reflection" is held to be widespread in primitive cultures: "Apprehending some danger of the inevitable destruction of the ego, primitive narcissism created the first image of the soul, which is as close a likeness as possible to the physical person, that is, a true double, thus creating a denial of death by doubling the ego in the form of a shadow or reflection."[33]

So we find that the image of a person's shadow representing his double is deeply rooted in man's earliest culture. In Otto Rank's opinion, human development, which gave rise to the concept of guilt, "transformed the concept of the double, which was originally the actual substitute of the ego, and now it became Satan, the opposite of the ego, instead of taking its place."[34]

The purpose of this discussion is not to trace the metamorphoses of the double in literature and art over the generations (it has assumed various guises, one of which, the "mask," is firmly ensconced in the theater and plastic arts). I shall merely make passing reference to the roots of concern with the issue in twentieth-century literature, which reach back into the soil of the romantic period. Romantic writers elaborated various approaches to the divisions in human nature, or "inner plurality," a term that Novalis coined for the simultaneous existence

of two egos within human existence. Novalis himself attributed positive connotations to the concept, founding the ability for the understanding of the self and others upon it. But other German romantic
writers, as well as the great nineteenth-century Russian authors, viewed
that duality as the embodiment of an inner struggle or the tension of
opposites.[35] The image of the double has been rooted in Russian literature since the early nineteenth century, first in the works of Gogol and
later in the novels of Dostoyevsky. Gogol himself was influenced by
German romanticism.

Sometimes the double expresses the demonic antithesis of man's
rational side, that which distinguishes him from the animals. Sometimes, however, it embodies the yearned-for complement of an existing human reality: a feature or aspect that will bring about a way of
mending the personality.

The shadow is a person's double, and not merely his dark side. A
person's shadow is not unequivocal in meaning, nor is it static. "For
we all have many shadows," Ben-Ami Sharfstein reminds us. "I re-
member my shadow, how it grew, changed shape, dimension, and location, and my feeling of power at the possibility of altering it. But in
saying 'many shadows' I do not refer to the dark and flexible forms at
our feet, but rather to our images and voices, our writing, or anything
else that stems from us which can be taken from us" (for example,
"the picture we draw or the voice we record," and also "the smile or
the angry word that detach themselves from us, existing in their own
right").[36]

One of topics that must be treated in a discussion of "man and his
double" or "man and his shadow" is its application to the world of
philosophers and artists. Is an artist's work a mask behind which the
person hides? Or, perhaps, does the work represent its maker's inner
being? On this problematic topic (discussed in the chapter "The Cause
and the Person" and its appendix) Walter Kaufmann responds that
the artist's work exists in its own right no less than his personal behavior, and that both are true. In his opinion the person and his creative
work are of a piece. He does not believe in the duality of self and mask
but holds "we all have many faces." In summing up his trilogy devoted to nine thinkers (Goethe, Kant, Hegel, Nietzsche, Heidegger,
Buber, Freud, Adler, and Jung) he stresses that he did not attempt to
uncover "all their faces." His aim was rather to show a number of
aspects of each of these great intellectuals and to show "how the whole

oeuvre hangs together and how the man and his work are of one piece."[37]

* * *

Buber gave solid literary expression to the motif of the double in "Midnight," the second chapter of *For the Sake of Heaven*, a kind of historical novel based on the Hasidic tradition that concluded Buber's projects in Hasidism. The focus of Buber's book is the intense and prolonged struggle between the path embodied by the personality of the Seer of Lublin and that expressed by the ways of the Holy Yehudi.[38] "Midnight," which, from a literary point of view, can be viewed as an independent work, does not portray the struggle between the Seer and his opponents but rather that between himself and a repressed aspect of his inner being, here represented by the new disciple who arrives in his court.

"Midnight" is introduced by this passage:

> A saying is to be added which the Rabbi [the Seer of Lublin] confided but to a single disciple, who handed it down. "This is a strange matter," said he, "and one that I do not understand. People come to me with mournful hearts and when they leave me their hearts are brightened. Yet I myself am . . ." And here, according to a sound he uttered, it seemed as though he was to say, "heavy of heart." But he caught himself and said instead: "And I myself am dark and do not shine."[39]

The contrast between his behavior as the Seer and the melancholy within his soul greatly concerned the Hasidic traditions and, in their wake, plays a significant role in *For the Sake of Heaven*.

The Seer was considered the leader of his generation at the time of the spread of Hasidism in Poland (1780-1815). With fidelity to the various Hasidic sources, Buber presents him as a gloomy man imprisoned within the creations of his spirit and the dark visions of his soul. His being was given over to visions, to communication with higher worlds; he was certain of his ability to act within the framework of the divine to hasten the advent of the Messiah. This mystic, who wished to bring on the redemption quickly, was at the same time alienated from the human world and not introspective. "Tila," the Seer's second

wife, "requested of her husband immediately after the wedding that
he promise her that in the world of truth she would not be forced to
wait if she needed his help."[40] He tended to plunge into the dark depths
within man, and his own world seemed somber and gloomy to him.
"In his great humility and with a broken heart he informed against
himself: woe to a generation of which I am the leader!"[41] When he was
subject to his "melancholy, . . . he saw no merit or anything good
within himself. He found himself worse than all the creatures in the
world"—to quote words traditionally attributed to him.[42]

His distance from the world of man is also a distance from his
own flesh-and-blood world. It is told that his wife Bila was barren.
The Seer, who was capable of influencing the heavens on behalf of the
whole world, could not pray for her. He had his wife ask "the Yehudi"
to pray for her. In the end she did give birth, but later she again needed
help from "the Yehudi" in similar circumstances, and he replied to
her: "At first I had the degree of sanctity needed to bring the 'Rabbi of
blessed memory' [the Seer] down from beneath the Throne of Honor
to this world and give birth, but now I can no longer do so."[43]

This implies that the Seer's excessive spiritualism prevents him from
having progeny, from becoming a father again. According to a homily
presented in the name of the Seer, "Man is a microcosm, and he has
within him the seeds and all the plants, so why does he not cure himself and combine all these powers, if not for his pride, which is unable
to lower itself to find something so insignificant."[44] Here he condemns
his own fault. Indeed the Seer could not lower himself to human reality "here on the earth and not in the clouds above."

The Seer represents the tendency to seek "Peace of the World," its
perfection and redemption, while skipping the long path that begins
with "perfecting the heart" and the attainment of "Peace of Mind."[45]

Many Hasidic tales depict the antithesis of the path taken by the
Seer. They generally refer to "the Yehudi," to Simcha Bunem of Pshysha,
to Menachem Mendel of Kotzk, and to others, whose path was the
polar opposite of the Seer's. Some stories juxtapose and contrast the
two ways:

> I heard that the Rabbi of Lublin of blessed memory hid himself from
> the world at his high spiritual level so that people would not look at
> him. The rabbi called the Holy Yehudi of blessed memory hid him-
> self with literal interpretations and subtle reasoning which he al-
> ways recited to attract people to him.[46]

The difference between them is presented here as that between someone who immerses himself in individual acts of mysticism, by means of which he "hides himself from the world" and someone involved in the study of Torah in the company of those who come to him, that is, addressing himself to the world of humanity.

A vast abyss extended between the consciousness of sin that characterized the Seer's view of himself and the exalted view held of him by his thousands of disciples and also by those nearest to him. The following story offers an interesting demonstration of this paradox:

> The Rabbi of Lublin, of blessed memory, once said to his eldest son, the holy, righteous Rabbi Israel, of blessed memory, that he would soon call ten men to confess before them. When the holy rabbi did not hurriedly do so, knowing that his father had nothing to confess, he told him, "If you don't go quickly, I shall go outside and confess publicly in the market, and the Name will be disgraced, perish the thought." And he called a quorum of men to him. He confessed that every day he sees every single word of his prayer fly upwards borne by fiery flames. But today he had not seen any words flying up.[47]

This story seems to me to be a combination of an authentic kernel with an apologetic addition by the disciples of the Seer. The main part ends before the content of the confession is detailed. The character of this part of the story is consistent with that of most of the extant stories about the Seer. The content of the confession itself is also consistent with the traditions about the visionary power of the Seer, but it does not fit the implicit message of the first and main part of the story. As for the main part itself, it shows us that even his son, known as "the holy rabbi," was a stranger to his father's spiritual torments, to his struggles with the gloom within him. The main part of the story, quoted above, and the following words attributed to the Seer shed light upon each other:

> All the simple people had experienced an entire return to good; there was no obstacle to redemption within them. The obstacle came from the higher men. By reason of their elevated qualities they could not attain to humility and therefore not to entire conversion.[48]

The polar opposition between the praise for the active power of the rabbi in the divine realm and his humble self-image is insufficient for understanding the complexity and problematic nature of this religious

personality. According to Hasidic traditions there is an additional existential tension in his being: between gloom and self-torment and another
level of his personality. Buber took more than a mere literary interest in
that tension, and it would seem that the first impulses leading him to take
it up and interpret it were autobiographical.[49] "Midnight" is dedicated
to that tension and its embodiment in the man and his double.

The conceptual and literary center of "Midnight" is the Seer's encounter with a new disciple who had come to his House of Study and
whose name (and whose mother's name) was the same as the rabbi's:
"Jaacob Yitzchak, the son of Matel." The plot extends over an entire
year. It begins and ends at midnight, at the midnight lamentation, which
must "be uttered with tears and cries of woe. And so did the Seer utter
it night after night." While he said the customary prayers and studied
the chapters touching on midnight in the *Zohar*, the rabbi was accustomed to sequestering himself with his God and addressing Him in
prayer. One night during the lamentation the rabbi asked for a sign
from heaven as to who was worthy of leading his flock after him. He
was answered, "Jaacob Yitzchak." Since that was his own name he
quickly called out, "Here am I!" Again he asked, and again he received the same answer from heaven, which stunned him. Perhaps he
thought it referred to the Holy Yehudi, whose name was also "Jaacob
Yitzchak." Buber compresses everything the Seer then underwent during that night into two sentences: "Until dawn broke he sat on his low
stool. He heard no more, neither did he ask any more."[50] This sleep-
less night provides the background for what transpired in his House
of Study in the morning. While the rabbi was surrounded by his disciples, a young stranger came running in and asked to be accepted as
his student. In answer to the rabbi's question "Who are you?" the
newcomer answered, "Jaacob Yitzchak, the son of Matel." Thus the
Seer realized that the answer he received from heaven at night did not
refer to his rival, the Holy Yehudi, but rather to his double, in the full
sense of the word. The rabbi was thunderstruck. He "turned pale. For
a little while his eyes underwent a change. . . . But thereupon his glance
became painfully confused; his lids twitched; he drew his spectacles
from his pocket, a thing he did most rarely. He put them on." Trying
to overcome the raging storm in his spirit, he peered at the uninvited
guest through his spectacles, and, having no alternative, he accepted
him as a pupil.[51]

From that day on was a painful period for him. "The new pupil bore himself not otherwise than a creditor might do, who was obliged to take repayment in kind, in board and lodging."[52]

This stranger, outstanding for the intense intelligence of his studies, acted submissively toward the rabbi, yet he also had customs that surprised the rabbi and cast a heavy shadow of painful apprehensions upon him. More than anything the rabbi, who kept an eye on the stranger, was troubled by his requests for private audiences "on the grounds that he needed help against the temptations that beset his soul. He used these hours to tell stories out of his own life. And it seemed to the Rabbi these stories were the events of his own youth, or, rather, the evil distortion and caricature of these."[53]

"In such a wise the year passed" during which the Seer's life was marked by the presence of his double. On the last day, the other Jaacob Yitzchak ben Matel came to the rabbi's room unannounced, asking a question that sounded like an accusation: "When will you announce to them how it is to be with me?" That question was like the one the Seer had asked twice a year previously, after his midnight lamentation. Then he was struck by the lack of an answer from heaven. Now the flesh and blood answer stood before him, imposing itself on the rabbi by its presence. An alter ego is wrested from him, has come to life, and demands its due. The rabbi has no choice but to drive his double away from his court. He isn't satisfied with merely shouting "Go!" He rises to his feet, follows him to the door, and orders, "You are to pack your belongings at once and set forth." When the pupil mutters that he wishes to "say farewell to the comrades," the rabbi projects his own problematic situation upon him and says, "You have no comrades."[54]

This is the psychological, almost modern story that Buber tells us. The framework of the plot is the rabbi's midnight lamentation: the plot opens with a description of the rabbi's brokenheartedness on the night after the pupil's departure, while he was in mystical communion with his Creator: "He sat down on a low stool, so that his knees were high and supported his elbows. His head rested on his hands and he closed his eyes so tight that his lower lids felt the pressure. As always, there appeared first to him a plane or surface of the color of blood; this surface was next rent asunder down its middle; light flooded through, at first with the dull whiteness of milk, then radiant and purer, and at last there was nothing but the whiteness of that light." That act of devotion permits him to address the God revealed to him in his vision, and then he asks, "Why didst Thou do that unto me?"[55]

The stay of the Seer's double also ends in the depths of a night of contemplation, and, once again, in mystical communion with the divinity he asks, "Why didst Thou do this thing to me?"[56] He asks insistently but does not merit a clear answer.

This story of the double is not fictional. With his impressive artistic ability Buber took seeds that he had gathered from Hasidic traditions, nurtured them, and made them flourish. By examining his sources, we gain insight into that artistic ability of his and its connection with the themes of his thinking. The main source recounts:

> Our Rabbi of blessed memory of Lublin said about a year before this event that he had come to this world only because of a man named Jaacob Yitzchak the son of Matel. About a year before the Yehudi of blessed memory came to him a young man came to him whose name was Jaacob Yitzchak the son of Matel, like his own name, and our holy Rabbi of blessed memory was very pleased with him. He kept the boy for about a year and the Hasidim honored the boy very highly after they had heard from the Rabbi of blessed memory that he had only come to this world because of that young man, and when the Holy Yehudi of blessed memory came to him and told him that his name was Jaacob Yitzchak ben Matel, like his own name, our holy Rabbi sent that lad away from him.[57]

Buber inferred the problematic situation that was central to the structure of his version of the story from opaque hints that he found in another Hasidic tale, concerning, as its title says, "The Discovery of our Rabbi the Holy Yehudi of Pshysha and his Drawing Near to the Rabbi of Lublin." This story includes the episode of the Seer's double in a description of the arrival of the Holy Yehudi, accompanied by his Hasidim, the men of Afta, before the Seer of Lublin. On the Sabbath preceding that visit:

> The Rabbi of Lublin told his Hasidim and companions sitting with him at the table, "Behold, I have asked the Holy One Blessed be He, 'Let the Lord of the Spirits of all flesh appoint a person over the entire congregation, let the Holy One Blessed be He show me in my lifetime who will fill my place and guide my holy flock, the holy people of the Children of Israel after me.' And I was answered from heaven that it would be a man who would be with me, and his name would be just like mine, and he would lead the nation of the Lord and show them the path and the holy Torah and the service of the Holy One Blessed be He."

At just that moment the Yehudi and his escorts arrived at his house, and he greeted him very cordially, "and with a joyful heart the holy rabbi, the Yehudi, ran to him. And he greeted him. And he hugged him with both hands and both arms. . . . And he said to him, 'All praise to you and your brave men who have come to me at this time.'" At this point the additional dimension comes in: the double from whom he was rescued, as it were, upon the arrival of the Yehudi (who, according to the story, was meant to be his worthy and expected successor). The Seer goes on to say, right after the salutation cited above, "For if, perish the thought, you hadn't come now and at this moment, who knows what would have happened to me?" Then he speaks of the "dread and great darkness" that had fallen upon him, and this is its meaning:

> For from the heavens it was revealed to me who the man was who would fill my place, that he would guide our holy community in serving Him, may His name be blessed, and that his name would be like mine. This morning a man came to me who was dressed and wrapped in his prayer shawl. And from his aspect he looked like a righteous and saintly man [i.e., he only appeared to be so]. And his name was also like mine, and it occurred to me that he would be the leader of the Jews and the most pious of his generation. Now a great fear and darkness fell upon me. So much so I hadn't the strength to stand on my feet or even to move any limb because of the weakness and distress and the anguish which I had because of this thing.

Apparently the double who pretended to be a righteous and holy man was the man spoken of by the more obscure tradition, which I cited above from *Niflaot Harabi*. The story about the other man, the unworthy double, is patched in, as it were, with the following story, which presents "the Yehudi" as the Seer's successor. Immediately after the quote above, the Seer goes on to praise and extol the Yehudi:

> And now you have consoled me and restored my soul to its tranquility, and to the Lord who has helped me till now. His grace and truth have not left me, and He showed me the man who will be the shepherd, Rock of Israel, who is worthy of that cloak, and whom the crown fits.[58]

In his artistic retelling of the tale Buber brings out a conception combining the hints in *Hitgalut hatzadikim* with the outlines of the portrait of the Seer as depicted in other Hasidic sources. Buber presents the student who is the "creditor," as a reflection of the suppressed side of the Seer's personality.

One of the particular innovations of Hasidism is that it turns the Kabbalistic theosophy of the ARI (Rabbi Isaac Luria) into an anthropology and psychology by directing its gaze at the inner crises of the individual. General ideas became individual values in Hasidism. Gershom Scholem, who points this out,[59] cites Martin Buber's view that Hasidism embodies "the Kabbala become an ethos."[60] That view does not apply to the Seer, who lacked a tendency for introspection, and whose inner vision was directed beyond the human realm. That is the basis of his epithet, the "Seer." With his reproach, "You have no comrades," Buber has the Seer project his own problematic nature upon the student who was removed from his court.

Hasidic sources tend to gloss over the problematic nature of the Seer's personal weakness and to endow his human insensitivity with religious meanings. His estrangement from terrestrial reality is interpreted as the product of his exalted religious mission: "The holy Rabbi of Lublin heard a decree from the heavens: 'Mordecai the son of Gittel, only for the Lord.'"[61] Buber frequently calls attention to the intricacies of the Seer's personality. Thus he has one of his protagonists, a man who had often conversed with the Seer, say the following sentence: "In a case like [that of the Seer] one has almost more dealings with the man's reflection in others than with himself."[62] The implication is that the Seer's double embodies his inner self, and his personality as the leader of his generation is merely a reflection. Buber coined the term "counterpart" (mistranslated as "enemy") for the Seer's double. He has the Seer say: "Why was it that they first sent me that counterpart who called himself Jaacob Yitzchak, the son of Matel, and did not send him [the Yehudi] at once?"[63]

Blinded by loyalty, the Seer's disciples, who witnessed the shock experienced by their master as a result of the presence of the creditor-like pupil, his namesake, in his court, viewed him as an emissary of the Evil One. A conference of the most zealous of them was convened by Rabbi Jehuda Loeb of Zakilkov, "the oldest of the Seer's disciples," to discuss interference with the Holy Yehudi (who was then staying at the Seer's court as a disciple). One follower mentions the stranger who had been a pupil:

Have we not been watching for a whole year what the powers of evil have effected in the way of deceiving the Zaddik? Did not their emissary live and move among us, and did not the Rabbi endure him because, as he himself said to me, he was forced to assume that the horror had been sent from above?[64]

The speaker continues, seeing the Holy Yehudi as continuing in that role: "That onslaught of those powers having failed, they are now weaving a web of finer yarn."[65]

There are parallels between the relationship of the Seer and his double, who was driven out of his court, and his complex relationship with his other namesake, Jaacob Yitzchak of Pshysha, the Holy Yehudi. The relations between these two rabbis is a subject in its own right, demanding a deep independent discussion. Here I can only point out a particular aspect of these relations, which rises out of one context in *For the Sake of Heaven* and may assist us in understanding the parallel: once on the eve of Shavuot guests from other places, including "several Hasidim of Pshysha with their rabbi [the Yehudi] and several Hasidim of Lelov with their rabbi David [who was very close to the Yehudi]," sat at the Seer's table. During the meal Rabbi David noticed that the Seer was immersed in a meditation, the purpose of which was to destroy the Yehudi. The Seer's appearance reminded him "precisely" of the way

a boy had once looked whom he had caught in the act of tearing out the brilliant wings of a butterfly. What had he, David, done on that occasion to prevent the wretched deed? He had uttered the shrill cry of a hawk, for the throat of David could imitate the cries of all the beasts he knew, and the boy had been startled and the cruel hand had been opened and the captive had flown. And on the instant David of Lelov struck his fist upon the Sabbath table. A wine bottle crashed to the floor. The Seer started up. "Who did that?" he asked.[66]

Thus Rabbi David of Lelov interrupted the mystical meditations of the Seer, which had been aimed at the undoing of the Yehudi. Buber's story does not explicitly state the main point but rather is interpreted both by means of the background, which is kept partially hidden, and also by what is told us afterwards. The background of the scene at the rabbi's table, before the Seer's mystical attempt, is a conversation between Rabbi David and the Yehudi, in the course of which the Yehudi said, "The Rabbi is awe-inspiring," and Rabbi David responded, "He is the true human being."⁶⁷ That response does not contradict the Yehudi's statement but rather gives it a different emphasis. Now, on the eve of Shavuot, at the rabbi's table, Rabbi David recalls that conversation. He "observed his teacher from time to time. Nothing that had happened in all the years had changed the attitude to him in his heart. He was often amazed; he never passed judgment. To this day, had they come to him and said, the Seer is awe-inspiring, he would have answered that that was, in fact, the man's true nature. The years, of course, had taught him more concerning the nature of man."⁶⁸ Thus Buber made certain that the awe-inspiring quality of the Seer would echo in our ears before we learned of his dreadful project to cut down "the Yehudi." The rabbi's intention is indicated by the simile of the boy and the butterfly.⁶⁹ After what happened during the meal Rabbi David was asked why he had struck the table, and he answered: "I saw the Rabbi seeking the hall of my friend among the halls of the firmament, in order to rob him of the gifts of the spirit. So I had to shock him and drag him back to earth. I will have sufficed. No man undertakes a thing like that twice."⁷⁰

The Hasidic sources also speak of the Seer's effort to "uproot" his appointed successor, "the Yehudi." Their tale relates to Yom Kippur eve (whereas Buber recounts events of Shavuot eve), but as in Buber's story Rabbi David plays an important part:

Once on Yom Kippur eve the holy rabbi David of Lelov of blessed memory entered the home of the holy rabbi of Lublin of blessed memory. The holy rabbi of Lublin told our master rabbi David that he was meditating on "the Yehudi." He loved him very much and was his companion student, therefore every Yom Kippur he would weep bitterly in his prayer to arouse mercy, and at the end of Yom Kippur our holy rabbi David entered the home of the holy rabbi of Lublin to bless him as was the practice. And when he stepped on the threshold of his home the holy rabbi of Lublin greeted him and told him in these words [translated from Yiddish]: Rabbi David, long may you live, a good week to you, do you know upon whom we meditated on Yom Kippur eve? Our meditations were upon the Holy Yehudi. We wanted to act [cause his death], but from heaven we were answered that we would see the second one in the generation.⁷¹

This would seem to be a widely circulated story, and at the end it says: "It is known throughout the whole world, but told in corrupted form, and this is the true source."

Hasidic literature is rich in demonic elements and tales of horror. Buber did not need his creative imagination to invent unusual events. It was sufficient, in most cases, to give his own interpretation of the materials in the Hasidic sources. Both Jaacob Yitzchak the son of Matel, the stranger who studied in the Seer's court until he was driven out, and also Jaacob Yitzchak of Pshysha (the Holy Yehudi) represent counterparts of the Seer of Lublin. The Seer views each double as a mirror of a different path stored up within himself, at the root of his soul. In his action against them he wants, in fact, to uproot a hidden aspect of his own soul. His doubles represent the true person within him.

There is a great affinity between the forms given to the problematic nature of the double in *For the Sake of Heaven* and that in Edgar Allen Poe's "William Wilson,"[72] an outstanding work based on the topos of the double.[73] Poe's image of the double develops and extends the fundamental outlines that, much later, informed Buber's view of character. Poe's double embodies the inner truth of man, the "anger of the conscience" whispering to him, or pricking him, or restraining him. The motto of the story is a quotation from Chamberlain, "What say of it? What say of conscience grim, that spectre my path?" When Poe's hero is stabbed to death by his reflection, "the world, heaven, and hope" die for him.

The archetype of every image of the double in western culture, and not merely in modern times, is probably the biblical verse: "And the man wrestled with him until the dawn rose" (Gen. 32:25).

When Buber came to present the double, he had before his eyes— we must imagine—both the manifestations of that motif in German romanticism, in which he was well versed,[74] and in nineteenth-century Russian literature. It seems quite likely that Buber was deeply affected by the literary expressions of the alter ego that embodies the "conscience grim," a kind of inner essence before which the conscious ego is judged. The conscience grim, or the feeling of guilt, was a factor in the conversion of which he testifies.[75]

A similar expression of a hidden inner center can be found in Rilke's "Saul unter den Propheten" (Saul among the Prophets). Buber and Rilke both created within the spiritual atmosphere of German culture. Scholars noted the affinity of influence between them at the time Buber published his philosophical-poetical work, *Daniel* (1913).[76]

The view of a person's double as a "conscience grim" can be helpful in understanding the inner connective strands between what Buber

terms "the counterpart" and the issue of his "conversion" in his intellectual biography. The connection between these two motifs bore further fruit in his intellectual work. Without it one cannot understand
his late study in philosophical anthropology, "Guilt and Guilt Feelings" (1957).[77]

A person's alter ego is that "second soul, . . . a primordial essence
different from his 'reality of life'."[78] It is "the deeper self of the person," different from "the trivial ego of the egotistical individual."[79]
Buber holds that in the depths of the human being there is a guiding
"center." That is the "dynamic center, which submerges all a person's
manifestations, acts, and customs." Buber devotes a number of sentences in a later composition to this idea,[80] but he does not go back to
develop and summarize it in his philosophical anthropology. Even in
"Guilt and Guilt Feelings" Buber does not refer to this root conception, though its presence has been evident in various fields of his work
over the decades.

4
EXISTENTIAL TENSIONS AND
EARLY STRUGGLES

Buber was born in Vienna. He spent most of his childhood in Poland, within a traditional Jewish setting. His mother abandoned her family when he was three, and he was sent to be cared for in his father's parents' home in Lvov.[1] There he was educated until he reached the age of fourteen, when he went to live with his father, who had meanwhile established a new family.[2]

He states that "the earliest of his memories" is related to echoes of the traumatic experience of separation from his mother, approximately a year after she disappeared from the horizon of his life (an event that was never discussed in his grandparents' home). This memory concerns a conversation with a neighbor's daughter, several years older than he, who was responsible for watching over him.

> We both leaned on the railing. I cannot remember that I spoke of my mother to my older comrade. But I hear still how the big girl said to me: "No, she will never come back." I know that I remained silent, but also that I cherished no doubt of the truth of the spoken words. It remained fixed in me; from year to year it cleaved ever more to my heart, but after more than ten years I had begun to perceive it as something that concerned not only me, but all men. Later I once made up the word *"Vergegnung"*—"mismeeting," or "misencounter"—to designate the failure of a real meeting between men.[3]

Buber's mother, an actress, absconded from the house to Russia with a lover, and there she married him. She refrained from any contact with her son for many years. In a letter to his wife Paula dated 25 October 1901, Buber relates, "Now I know: all the time I constantly searched for my mother."[4] He was not to see her again for thirty years. They held a conversation, which was not followed by any others, when she came to visit him in the company of her children. Buber tells of that meeting only the lesson it taught him regarding his dialogical worldview. According to his testimony, he could not look in her eyes without hearing from somewhere the word "mismeeting," as though directed at him. Echoes of this single encounter with his mother are connected with "his earliest memory" mentioned above. He finishes the story of his testimony with the insight: "I suspect that all that I have learned about genuine meeting in the course of my life had its first origin in that hour on the balcony."[5]

The passage from Vienna to Lvov was not only geographic and familial. The situations and history of Buber's childhood and youth penetrated him with awareness of the transformations that characterized Jewish existence in the late nineteenth century. The Jewish home of his grandfather in which he grew up and was formed was not closed to the new spirit. The orthodox way of life no longer bore a character of innocent faith. Rifts and gaps of the crisis in meaning were also to be noted within it.

Rabbi Shlomo Buber, Martin Buber's grandfather, was a scholar and the scion of a rabbinical family. He was "a genuine philologist who is to be thanked for the first, and today still the authoritative[,] critical edition of . . . the Midrashim." In addition to his scholarship, he was a grain merchant and owned an estate and mines. He left the management of his business to his wife, and he himself devoted most of his time to the study of Torah.[6] Buber's description of his grandfather does not provide a comprehensive picture of his personality, and it should be supplemented. He applied himself more than anything else to the Torah and to research in Torah, but he was a man of property, a businessman, and also "the president of the orthodox Jewish community of Lvov for many years, a commercial consultant, and the manager of two banks." He was thus a man of large-scale activities. In his method of study and research he combined the depth and precision of a Western European scholar with erudition in the Eastern European style. In his conduct he provided his grandson with the model of deeply rooted Eastern European Jewry and also of the western spirit of enlightenment.[7]

Through his grandfather the young Mordecai Martin Buber had an affinity with the ancient treasures of Judaism, whereas his grandmother endowed him with openness to "alien" culture. He relates that she had grown up in a small Galician town, where the study of "alien" books by Jews was proscribed. As early as age fifteen, she had "set up in the storehouse a hiding place" where she concealed German periodicals and reference books, "which she read secretly and thoroughly."[8] These two spiritual currents came together within Buber's spiritual world. Yet they comprised but one of the loci of opposing tensions with which he struggled.

The upbringing and education of young Mordecai Martin were not like those of a "normal" child. He did not play with other children in the "street," nor did he indulge in childish pranks. He was given personal guidance by private tutors. Thus, for example, he not only had an individual riding teacher but also his own horse.[9] Until the age of ten he studied only with private tutors.[10] Afterward he began to study in a Polish school of Christian character (the day began with Christian prayers and one of the subjects studied was religion).[11] From his first years there he experienced a plurality of languages that corresponded to a variety of cultures. For example, in the seventh grade his studies included the Latin, Greek, and German languages, along with Polish. Before reaching the age of thirteen, his world was already divided between orthodox Jewish patterns of education and western humanism and Christian religious ceremony. Interestingly, the language in which he gave his bar-mitzvah speech was German, while the biblical quotations in it were given in the original Hebrew.[12]

For a short while after his bar mitzvah

> the young Buber tried to keep the commandments with enthusiastic earnestness. In the large and somewhat modern synagogue of Lvov he attracted unwanted attention when, on the first Yom Kippur after his Bar-Mitzvah, he prostrated himself on the floor during the "Temple Service" section of the Musaf (Additional) prayers, instead of being satisfied with a polite bowing of the head as befit a properly educated, bourgeois young man (according to a letter from Buber to Franz Rosenzweig, September 28, 1922, in *Almanach Schocken*, [Berlin, 1937], p. 149). But he soon reached the opposite extreme and by his fourteenth year he had ceased laying tefillin."[13]

At the age of fourteen he moved into the home of his father, who had remarried and settled in Lvov, and he began to study in a Polish gymnasium (secondary school). Polish literature and Slavic culture did not satisfy his thirst, and in his father's home he could find no echo of his spiritual uncertainties.[14] At the age of fourteen and a half (on 5 November 1892), the young man gave a sermon in Polish, based on Bible passages together with verses from "Ode to Youth" by Adam Mickiewicz. The Bible verses were written in Hebrew in the Polish manuscript of his sermon. Soon afterward he grew quite distant from his Jewish origins and lived, as he relates, until the age of twenty "without Judaism, without humanity, and without the presence of the divine."[15]

In the beginning of this period, when he was given over to the "'Olam-ha-Tohu,' the 'World of Confusion,' the mythical dwelling of lost souls,"[16] Buber experienced a deep inner shock. Occasionally his spirit was so storm-tossed in his metaphysical search that he felt himself on the verge of insanity. He speaks of this adding, "[A]t times [I was] so closely threatened with the danger of madness that I seriously thought of avoiding it by suicide." He found an escape from this dilemma in reading Kant's *Prolegomena to any Future Metaphysics*, which distinguishes between infinity and eternity. "At that time," says Buber of himself, "I began to gain an inkling of the existence of eternity as something quite different from the infinite. Nevertheless there was a possible connection between me, a person, and the eternal."[17] This indicates not only extreme inner tension in his spiritual existence at such a young age, but also doubts concerning faith, manifestations of which were to accompany his spiritual biography until advanced old age.[18] At the time presently under discussion, he was attracted by powerful manifestations of European culture; he was enthralled by Nietzsche, and while Kant's *Prolegomena* was redemptive for him, Nietzsche's *Also sprach Zarathustra* "confused" him, made him "rebel," and even "led him astray into the kingdom of delicate inebriation," from which he did not escape for some time.[19]

Buber began to gain a grasp on his spiritual life when, after finishing his secondary studies, he moved from Lvov to Vienna. In 1896 he began studying philosophy at the university of that city. Later he studied at the universities of Leipzig, Zurich, and Berlin. In addition to philosophy he studied art, literature, psychiatry, German culture, and classics.[20] Among his other interests during his first years of study were Christian mystical doctrines from the time of the Renaissance. A prime expression of this can be found in his doctoral dissertation, presented in 1904 at the University of Vienna.[21]

In the first years of this century, while still in his early twenties, Buber was already beginning to be well known. In an article in honor of Buber's seventieth birthday, J. L Magnes addresses Buber directly, as though in a letter, saying: "I saw you for the first time in the semester of 1900–1901, when I was registered among the auditors of Professor Simmel's lectures at the University of Berlin. The audience was so large that it was necessary to transfer the lectures to one of the largest halls in the university. Although the auditorium was packed, you entered through a side door at the head of a group of young people, especially young women, and you took seats in the first row, which were apparently reserved for you. Your black beard, your slow and serious steps, your walking at the head of the group like a kind of zaddik with his Hasidim, led me to ask the student at my side, a blond Aryan, who you were, and he replied that that Jew was founding a new religious sect."[22]

Zionism provided Buber with a renewed tie to the culture of his people and helped him to form a living bond with a movement offering a common vision. He was attracted to it, under the influence of Herzl, during his studies in Leipzig (1898). In a poem, "Prayer," published in the Zionist annual *Die Welt*, of which he became the editor, he expresses ardent identification with the dream of returning to Zion at that time.[23]

On 31 January 1900, his grandfather's birthday, Buber wrote him a letter that is of interest, showing both his awareness of his roots and also his divided being: "Your vibrant kindness, . . . so often has brought me comfort and joy and firmness. . . . The unflagging and undivided quality of your creative work has often guided me back to myself from the bad path of incoherence."[24]

While engaged in Zionist activity, Buber began to identify his own personal crisis with that of German Jewry and strove to guide its course.[25] Zionism also served as the basis for the renewed interest which he began to show in Jewish sources. He relearned Hebrew, which he had neglected during his years of searching and wandering, and he once again turned to the Midrashim that his grandfather had edited (Gershom Scholem mentions that a copy of his grandfather's edition of some Midrashim stood at the back of Buber's desk until the end of his life).[26] This study prepared the ground for his interest in Hasidic literature, which was aroused when a copy of the booklet *Tzevaat Ha-RIBASH* (The Testament of Rabbi Israel, the Baal Shem Tov) came his way.[27]

Buber's mystical yearnings, mentioned above, and his activity in the Zionist movement drew him toward incompatible worlds. His discovery of Hasidism permitted him to create contact between these worlds. Therein the two directions in which he had hitherto sought his way in life suddenly met: Jewish mysticism and the Zionist renaissance.

During his studies in Zurich, in the summer of 1899, Buber met Paula Winkler, a young German woman who had maintained, since her childhood, a warm relationship with Jews, and now he joined with her in a life union. Herzl published her article "Philo-Zionist Reflections," in which she describes the manner in which she was impelled to understand the status of the Jews in Christian society and her adherence to Zionism.[28] Buber returned to his national origin and acquired Zionist identity, and at the same time he found expression of his yearning "in that young woman, who combined within her, like many people from southern Germany, a romance sensitivity to beauty with northern erudition. . . . He also saw in her a symbol of free humanity, beautiful and sure of itself. Indeed, from the beginning of the Haskalah period, many of the best Jewish youth found self-fulfillment particularly with non-Jewish women."[29] Buber's Zionism enchanted Paula Winkler, and he found within her the pole of inner unity and also the embodiment of spiritual tendencies that had drawn him to Germanic sources of sustenance.[30] Their eldest son Raphael was born in 1900. A year later their daughter Hava (Eva) was born.

Buber's intense involvement with the German cultural realm, which had begun at the start of his university studies, was not a revolutionary turning point for him, for he had already absorbed its spirit in his grandfather's home and had been acquainted with important creative artists in the German tongue during his youth, as we saw above. But this is not to say that Buber was free of spiritual remorse or tempests of the soul. He placed a double challenge before himself: to become involved with European culture and also to remain faithful to his Jewish identity; he wanted to dwell simultaneously at the poles of "Judaism" and of "humanity," of the "East" and of the "West," and to give himself over to the impulses of mystical aestheticism at the same time as he was involved with the issues of the Zionist movement. His spirit was subject to tensions between divided elements and distant worlds. He strove to reconcile them within his soul—to raise up from the opposites, which he sought to relate to each other, the unity of his spiritual life.

5
A CONVERSION

The concept of conversion (in German, *eine Bekehrung;* in Hebrew, *hafikhat lev*, an overturning of the heart) indicates a profound change in the structures of one's personality. At times this occurs all at once, like a flash of illumination that bursts through deep strata and brings out a new image of the personality. At other times it develops slowly, like a gradual maturing in which a person comes into being again in the course of a spiritual self-evaluation.

THE "MYSTICAL STAGE" AND DEPARTURE FROM IT

During the first fifteen years of the century, mystical tendencies, unconnected with religious tradition or authority, were prominent in Buber's views. At times during that period he isolated himself in a kind of aesthetic ivory tower, drawn by his spiritual yearnings to realms beyond earthly life. At this first, early stage in his path, Buber turned to lived experience *(Erlebnis)*. He believed that when a person concentrated on his mystical experience he would achieve "unification of the self with the all-self."[1] On the one hand, his writings show a conspicuous tendency to glorify creative individuality, and, on the other hand, a yearning to immerse that individuality within the "overall being." The inner unity to which he was drawn included the metahuman within it. And "there was a danger that the divine and the human would run

into one another" in that worldview, to cite the cautious phrase of
Hugo Bergmann.[2]

Buber himself used the term "mystical phase" as a possible definition of that early stage in his spiritual biography.[3]

A number of tendencies stand out at that stage in his work, among
them:

> 1. drawing upon Christian German mysticism, which was
> taken out of the context of German culture. (as he wrote of
> himself several decades afterwards: "Since 1900 I had first been
> under the influence of German mysticism from Meister Eckhart
> to Angelus Silesius, according to which the primal ground of
> being, the nameless, impersonal, godhead, comes to 'birth' in
> the human soul");[4]
> 2. the collecting and adaptation of mystical sources from
> Far Eastern cultures;
> 3. the literary "translation" of traditions and stories from
> the world of the Hasidism of the Baal Shem Tov;
> 4. articles on Zionism and "Lectures on Judaism";
> 5. the consolidation of a philosophical-mystical view,
> mainly presented in *Daniel* (1913).

It would seem that these areas of concern offer spiritual worlds
that are inconsistent with each other. However, one must recall that
Buber did not approach them as a scholar or scientist but rather from
a personal, existential point of departure, as we see in other chapters
of this study.[5] Moreover, this mystical phase is also expressed in spiritual inclinations and in the character of Buber's work and thought.
Actual mystical experience occupied an integral part of this period of
his life. Later, from a temporal and mental distance, Buber apparently
felt the need to tell and bear witness about these "sins of his youth."
"Now from my own unforgettable experience I know well that there
is a state in which the bonds of the personal nature of life seem to have
fallen away from us and we experience an undivided unity."[6]

The present chapter is mainly concerned with the essence of Buber's
"conversion," which represents the shift away from his early, mystical
stage and is also an indication of the beginning of growth in the direction of dialogue in Buber's thought. After it, he no longer expressed
yearning for the unity of fusion in which the individual self dissolves.

And when the conversion reached maturity, following that dialogical, philosophical turning point, it became consolidated as something existential, the realm of which was reality as it is lived and not the depths of the soul. The dialogical encounter is based on the duality of substances. Here we have no mystical unity. Buber even describes mysticism from the dialogical point of view after the appearance of his *I and Thou:*

> Here the mystic knows of a close personal intercourse with God. . . . But in erotic intercourse between being and being as in the intercourse between man and God it is still just the duality of these beings which is the elementary presupposition of what passes between them. . . . It is the duality of I and thou.[7]

Briefly, this is the background for Buber's explicit and implicit remarks in "A Conversion" (which he attributes to himself).

PERSONAL TESTIMONY

Buber testifies that he underwent a conversion at the time of the First World War, and to that conversion he attributes the shift in his spiritual biography from mysticism to dialogue. One gains the impression from various contexts in his writing that the term "conversion" refers to a long process in the course of which a decisive shift occurred in his worldview, but he also occasionally speaks of it as a single event or as the focus of a process. Most of his references to this change appear in his articles and in conversations meant for publication. In this respect the autobiographical piece "A Conversion" is of particular interest.[8] This personal testimony begins with a description of the time in which he was addicted to mystical experiences:

> There were hours that were taken out of the course of things. From somewhere or other the firm crust of everyday [reality] was pierced. . . . The "religious" lifted you out. Over there now lay the accustomed existence with its affairs, but here illumination and ecstasy and rapture held, without time or sequence. Thus your own being encompassed a life here and a life beyond, and there was no bond but the actual moment of the transition.[9]

Then, he says, the change occurred, following a meeting with a young visitor whom he received "without being there in spirit":

I did not treat him any more remissly than all his contemporaries who were in the habit of seeking me out about this time of day as an oracle that is ready to listen to reason. I conversed attentively and openly with him—only I failed to guess the questions which he did not put. Later, not long after, I learned from one of his friends—he himself was no longer alive—the essential content of these questions; I learned that he had come to me not casually, but borne by destiny, not for a chat but for a decision. He had come to me, he had come in this hour.[10]

This description gives its reader the impression that the "young visitor" took his own life, an impression probably shared by readers of many sorts. In a conversation held in his home in the early 1960s, I asked Buber, "Did the young man of whom you spoke in 'A Conversion' commit suicide?" He answered me in an angry tone, as though responding to a question well known for its marked misunderstanding: "That isn't so. He found his death in the [First World] War."[11] Nevertheless, the continuation of the cited passage and the way it is woven into the context of the discussion as a whole help give the feeling that the "young visitor" did indeed commit suicide a short time after his meeting with Buber:

What do we expect when we are in despair and yet go to a man? Surely a presence by means of which we are told that nevertheless there is meaning.[12]

This autobiographical passage may be divided into three parts:

1. the characterization of the mystical stage of Buber's life;
2. A description of the meeting with the young man, as typical of many other meetings between Buber and those who turned to him in need but different from them because of its latent connection with the young man's tragic fate;
3. an embodiment of the features of the dialogical conception.

A description of the conversion was apparently supposed to have been given between the second and third parts but instead it was merely implied, being indicated by the title of the chapter. After describing the fateful situation in the young guest's life, fateful for the host as well, the main point is presented wordlessly. Buber apparently means to engage his readers in a kind of mute dialogue, as though he is expecting us to feel the shock waves that struck him. The silence between the second and third part of this autobiographical passage, "A Conversion," is like "the silence in the heart between beat and beat," in the words of the Hebrew poet Nathan Alterman. Buber expects us to absorb the kernel of meaning that cannot be expressed in words. Here we must read, as taught by Rabbi Levi Yitzhak of Berdiczew, not only the printed words but also the space between letter and letter, word and word.[13]

The third and concluding part of "A Conversion" begins with the transition to the silence of the conversion that took place in the depths of the being of the one who presents it, and it is dedicated to its outgrowth:

> Since then I have given up the "religious," which is nothing but the exception, extraction, exaltation, ecstasy; or it has given me up. I possess nothing but the everyday out of which I am never taken. The mystery is no longer disclosed, it has escaped or it has made its dwelling here where everything happens as it happens. I know no other fulness but each mortal hour's fulness of claim and responsibility. Though far from being equal to it, yet I recognize that in the claim I am claimed and may respond in responsibility, and know who speaks and demands a response.
>
> I do not know much more. . . . You are not swallowed up in a fulness without obligation, you are willed for the life of communion.[14]

Extensive discussions have been devoted to analysis of the nature of "conversion" approached from the viewpoint of the academic study of varieties of religious experience. One approach argues that the basic meaning of this term, in its application to religions, is an absolute change—which sometimes occurs suddenly—in the individual's main beliefs, attitudes, loyalties, and aspirations. Starting with the assumption that this concept cannot be precisely defined, because each case of a conversion is largely individual, the *Encyclopedia of Religion* mentions ten types of conversion.[15] The seventh of these is "ethical conversion,"[16] a category that includes the kind of conversion discussed by Buber. I shall elaborate upon this below.

William James devotes two chapters of his famous work to conversion.[17] Included among the various approaches to this issue which he surveys are those of Professor Leuba, who emphasizes the moral aspect of religious life and dismisses the theological aspect.[18] James quotes Leuba as giving the word "religion" the sense of the totality of desires and feelings that flow from the feeling of sin, and redemption from it.[19]

The moral dimension of religion is embodied, according to Professor Leuba, in the feeling of sin, from which one must be redeemed. It would seem that he identifies personal redemption of this kind with conversion. There is a similarity between this approach and that of Buber, who, in his anthropological writings, develops his own approach to the essence of what he calls "existential guilt." He holds that the way to be redeemed from it is consistent with his dialogical conception, i.e., a "reconciling relationship to the world."

A proper understanding of Buber's approach to guilt and conscience must take "A Conversion" into account. Quite possibly the change that took place within him was implicit in the oppressive burden of "existential guilt" from which he sought to free himself by means of opening himself to the world of humanity (from which he had been alienated).[20] One must assume that this feeling of guilt stemmed not only from an examination of his relation to that young man, an independent examination that was, as it were, ordained. The meeting with the young visitor symbolized what had been typical of Buber's personal contacts at that time, as he himself relates. The conversion was meant to atone not only for the "feeling of sin" toward that young visitor, but also to change (to the degree that this was indeed possible) his relation to the world of men and to the living reality—as he testifies in the third part of "A Conversion."

A "feeling of guilt" is not a "modern" concept. The Talmud is familiar with it, illustrating it in its full poignancy in a legend involving Nahum Ish Gamzu:

> Rabbi Nahum Ish Gamzu was blind in both eyes. He had lost both hands and both feet and his entire body was covered with boils. ... "Rabbi," [his students] asked, "since you are a man holy enough to cause a miracle, why has God punished you so?" Rabbi Nahum Ish Gamzu answered, "Dear Children, I alone am to blame for all my afflictions. Once I was on my way to call on my father-in-law. I brought with me three asses. One was laden with food, another with drink and the third with sweet fruits. On the way a poor man stopped me. 'Give me something to eat, Rabbi!' he pleaded. I was in no hurry and asked him to wait until I had unpacked. But before I had time to do so, the poor man fell dead at my feet. When I saw

this I was filled with grief. I cast myself beside his body and cried out: 'My eyes that had no pity on your pleading eyes—may they become blind! My hands that had no compassion for your withered hands, and my feet that were not moved by the sight of your weary feet—may they be severed from my body!'

"And after that I could find no peace until I had said: 'Let my entire body be covered with boils so that I may forever more feel your torment!'"

When his students heard this they raised a great outcry. "Woe to us that see such afflictions visited upon you!"

"Woe to me it would have been indeed, my sons, if you did not see me in such wretchedness!" replied Rabbi Nahum Ish Gamzu.[21]

This is a story of a harsh decision deriving from a feeling of guilt and the desire for atonement. Nevertheless Buber would not under any condition accept atonement by means of self-punishment. He holds that one must atone before those against whom one has sinned.[22]

It would appear that one cannot distinguish between the way conversion is studied by scholars of religion and the approach taken in psychological and psychotherapeutical contexts, which also offer a background for clarifying Buber's experience.[23]

In Buber's writings we find both clear references to the change that he calls a "conversion" and less direct indications of it. However, I have found no reference to any single event (such as the one he recounts in "A Conversion"). In his references, both explicit and implied, it is generally viewed as a process that took four or five years, but which came to a peak.

The first of these references to the "conversion" seems to be woven into the preface to the collection of his eight lectures on Judaism that was published in 1923. There he recounts that he had come a long way, at the end of which, in 1918, he attained "clarity."[24] He tends there to interpret the change that took place within him not as a conversion but rather as a process of clarification and enlightenment:

> I can describe what has happened to me merely as a process of clarification; . . . for inherent in the process of clarification was the fact that my words became clear to myself, that I now understood what it was that I had then felt compelled to say.[25]

Just nine years afterwards his "Dialogue" was published, in which he included the autobiographical chapter in which he speaks directly of the conversion.

In various contexts within his works Buber speaks indirectly of the "conversion" without defining it as such (as he had in the chapter called "A Conversion"). Common to these contexts, to which I shall refer in detail below, is treatment of his dialogical worldview as a product of a deep personal change. This is not described as a unique illumination but rather as a process that took place within him during the First World War. Occasionally it is presented as a path of efforts and reflections that began in 1914 and ended in 1919:

> the grace of a relationship with the world that I did not attain except after long and complex wanderings, by means of decisive personal experiences. These experiences, which began in the first year of the war and ended a year after it, brought me from a hidden sphere of time and language to the sphere of the hour, between one chime of the clock and another. Everything is suspended and directed so that you can hear what is said to you, precisely at this very moment, in one of the innumerable living languages, and that you respond to it properly in one of them. I also found this belief from within language, whereupon every spoken language becomes the language of faith, in Rosenzweig's work, and within it was the kernel of our later work together: the translation from one language of speech to another . . . of that book, which is unique among all books, in that it transmits the history of man as a kind of conversation.[26]

These boundaries in time also emerge from another source, where Buber describes his experiences in one phase of the path that he calls, pejoratively, "mystical." In condemning that phase he proclaims his faith in the dialogical path of life: "Being true to the being in which and before which I am placed is the one thing that is needful." In the course of his remarks there we find that he noted the importance of dialogue and everything that it entails in 1914, but "it took another five years for this recognition to ripen to expression."[27] That is to say, this source corroborates the dates indicated by the other one, quoted above.

In one reference to the process under discussion he coins an expression for the area of faith[28] in his dialogical conception of life as it matured within him:

> Since my own thoughts over the last things reached, in the first world war, a decisive turning-point, I have occasionally described my standpoint to my friends as the "narrow ridge." I wanted by this to express that I did not rest on the broad upland of a system that includes a series of sure statements about the absolute, but on a nar-

row rocky ridge between the gulfs where there is no sureness of
expressible knowledge but the certainty of meeting what remains,
undisclosed.[29]

In that very context he also calls the narrow range of the existence of
dialogue with God a "narrow ridge of meeting."[30] In order to emphasize the decidedly autobiographical element of his account he points
out that he refers here to a "personal recollection," a "decisive [per-
sonal] experience."

Buber presented this process of change again as a decisive personal experience late in his life, in the beginning of a comprehensive
survey of his thought.[31] He writes:

> What happened to me was that all the experiences of being that I
> had during the years 1912–1919 became present to me in growing
> measure as *one* great experience of faith, . . . an experience that
> transports a person in all his component parts, his capacity for
> thought certainly included, so that, with all the doors springing open,
> the storm blows through all the chambers.[32]

This image seems to contain the echo of an experience that was not
dulled over the years. While elsewhere in his writings, referred to above,
the beginning of this process is attributed to the year when World War
I broke out, here it is dated two years earlier. Later in this work of his
old age there is a reference to what might be called the focus of this
prolonged process. Speaking of the cultural attitudes that influenced
him at an early stage in his path, Buber writes:

> My view was connected at that time not merely with *Lebensphilo–
> sophie* but also with aesthetic inclinations. The latter were already
> expelled from me by 1915; three years later, on self-examination. . . .
> I also found almost nothing more of the *Lebensphilosophie* in exist-
> ence.[33]

In one of his implicit references to the conversion he attributes the
problematic background of its occurrence to general historical and
social processes and not necessarily to its personal origin (as he generally did):

> During the First World War it became clear to me that a process was
> progressively taking place, one which I had not noticed earlier ex-
> cept hypothetically; a process of increased difficulty in true dialogue

between man and his fellow man; and there was an especially great difficulty in dialogue between people who are different from each other in nature and opinion. Face to face dialogue, without fences and barriers, becomes hard and rare, and the gaps between man and man widen with increasing cruelty, making the danger graver that it will no longer be possible to build a bridge between them. Then, thirty-five years ago, my eyes were opened to see that here was the main issue in the destiny of mankind.[34]

Another one of his references, the most important for our purposes, was made in Buber's old age during a conversation with Carl Rogers at the University of Michigan on 18 April 1957.[35] In answer to his interlocutor's question, "How have you lived so deeply in interpersonal relationships?" Buber reveals the focus of "conversion" (though there too he did not define it as such):

It was just a certain inclination to meet people. And as far as possible, to change something in the *other*, but also to let *me* be changed by *him*. At any event, I had no resistance—put no resistance to it. I began as a young man. I felt I have not the right to want to change another if I am not open to be changed by him as far as it is legitimate. Something is to be changed and his touch, his concept[,] is able to change it more or less. I *cannot* be, so to say, above him, and say, "No! I'm out of the play. *You* are mad." There were two phases of it. The first phase went until the year 1918, meaning until I was about forty. And then I, in 1918, I felt something rather strange. I felt that I had been strongly influenced by something that came to an end just then, meaning the First World War. In the course of the war, I did not feel very much about this influence. But at the end I felt, "Oh, I have been terribly influenced," because I could not resist what went on, and I was compelled to, may I say, to live it. Things that went on just at this moment. You may call this *imagining the real*. Imagining what was going on. This imagining, for four years, influenced me terribly. Just when it was finished, it finished by a certain episode in May 1919 when a friend of mine, a great friend, a great man, was killed by the antirevolutionary soldiers in a very barbaric way,[36] and now again once more—and this was the last time—I was compelled to imagine just this killing, but not in an optical way alone, but may I say so, just with my *body*. And this was the decisive moment, after which, after some days and nights in this state, I felt, "Oh, something has been done to me." And from then on, these meetings with people, particularly with young people were—became—in a somewhat different form. I had a decisive experience, experience of four years, many concrete experiences, and

from now on, I had to give something more than just my inclination
to exchange thoughts and feelings, and so on. I had to give the fruit
of an experience.[37]

There does not appear to be any connection between the event to which
he refers in the chapter discussed above, "A Conversion," where the
cause and motivation of the turning point was an unknown young
visitor whom he received "without being there in spirit" and the alter-
ation that took place in every fiber of his being after the murder of his
friend Gustav Landauer. But by means of these two stories he illustrates the profound change in his existence from experiencing life as
an individual concentrating on his own inner being (or on his spiritual
ivory tower) to that of dialogical responsibility based upon concrete,
earthly being.

It would seem that the change in Buber's spiritual biography was not
the result of the event described in "A Conversion." As indicated by
most of the sources cited above, this process mainly took place during
the First World War. It was connected to a letter which Landauer wrote
to him on 12 May 1916. Before discussing its contents and significance we must familiarize ourselves with the background: Buber's conceptions and positions from the start of the First World War until the
summer of 1916.

From the beginning of his path Buber was involved with German
culture, and of particular prominence was his firm base in the ideology of the German *Volk*.[38] It expressed itself in the patriotic identification with the land where he was living at the outbreak of the war.
Many European intellectuals at the time were virtually eager for war,
from which they expected a reawakening of the feeling of "unity" and
spiritual revival. Buber's mystical yearnings and neoromantic urges
also found expression in the bond of the fighting nation. He praised
the war with unquestioning, ardent pathos. Writing as a German pa-
triot on 16 October 1914, he said:

We here in Germany are astonished and horrified with a thousand
horrors, our hearts have expanded to discover that indeed we have
entered . . . an era in which the human soul no longer is congealed

and frozen; . . . in which human deeds are no longer crushed beneath many small goals, but achieves its liberty and fulfillment in
self-sacrifice for an absolute value. . . . Not in [people's] declarations
but in their devotion is the divine revealed. They throw off the trusted,
the certain, and the moderate and hurl themselves into the abyss of
the absolute. . . . Hence we must be glad in the midst of the horrors
and the bitter pains of this war, . . . a dreadful grace is this; the grace
of a new birth.[39]

Here Buber speaks simultaneously as a nationalist and a mystic, presenting a secular mysticism that is not connected to any religious authority but that views a projection of the inner human being as its
divinity.[40] Just as that approach was not exceptional in the European
intellectual community, it was also not out of the ordinary among the
Jews of Germany and Austria. On the contrary, when the war began
in the autumn of 1914, patriotic fervor enveloped most German Jews.
From the start, nationalist identification with the war was expressed
actively by the masses of Jews who volunteered for military service.
This was encouraged by the proclamations of large Jewish organiza-
tions at both ends of the spectrum, from the Central Union of German
Citizens of the Mosaic Faith (the largest Reform Jewish community)
to the German Zionist Union.[41] On 30 September 1914 Buber wrote
to Hans Kohn:

> The concept of "nation" never had such a concrete meaning as in
> those weeks. Among the Jews as well, almost everywhere, a serious
> and great sentiment prevails. Among the millions of volunteers were
> Karl Wolfskehl and Friedrich Gundolf. The latter was also accepted.
> I myself have, to my regret, no chance of being accepted for service.
> But I am trying to make my contribution in my own way. . . . If I am
> unable to be at the front, I still wish to be active near it.[42]

This active identification with the war was expressed by Zionists
throughout Germany. Among the members of the Bar Kochba Circle
in Prague who fought in the Austrian army was Sh. H. Bergmann. On
11 May 1915, before leaving the front with a wound, he wrote to
Buber:

> And now, after we have fought for German culture, more than ever
> we feel what its meaning is for us, and that we are subject to it with
> all our being. I cannot imagine that the ties of our generation with
> Biblical Jewry and with Hasidism, etc., which were formed, when

all is said and done, only in an artificial way, will ever be so natural as the ties of Fichte with those members of European culture who taught us the ways of human existence. Only because we had Fichte could we find the parallel streams in Jewish culture. We learned how to understand Judaism. . . . It is only as Germans that we can enter the life of Jewish culture.[43]

It is interesting that these words are written in the first person plural, and that they were written a number of years after Bergmann published a comprehensive article about Buber's early lectures on Judaism. Among other things, the following sentence appears in that article: "Messianism demands of us that we turn our eyes from our private, relative lives and direct them to the absolute life of our people."[44] There is a good deal of similarity between the polar tension with which Buber wrestled and that which is presented in Bergmann's words.

Buber's fervent German patriotism was expressed repeatedly in articles and speeches as well as in letters written from the outbreak of the war until the spring of 1916. Later he tended to gloss over this period of his personal and public life. Apparently that period was also forgotten or repressed, or relegated to a marginal position by his associates and other people from his circle.

Buber's views during the early years of the First World War are brought out in two scholarly projects: (1) the publication of the first volume of his correspondence, from the years 1897–1918, edited by Grete Schaeder, with an introductory essay that includes a section entitled "Friendship with Gustav Landauer and the First Years of World War I";[45] and (2) the appearance of Paul Mendes-Flohr's dissertation in book form, as well as the separate publication of a chapter of it as an article, which touches upon the topic of our present discussion;[46] his arguments are of primary importance for an understanding of the sharp opposition between Buber's and Landauer's approach during that time.

Buber's personal ties with Landauer were very significant for him. Landauer was perhaps his only intimate friend, and, as would become clear in the future, the thinker who exerted decisive influence on his social utopianism as it was consolidated from 1918 onwards.[47]

Landauer was uncompromisingly opposed to the war. It was hard for him to understand Buber's approach to it, nor did he wish to accept it.[48] Their relations underwent a crisis, the height of which is embodied in a very vehement letter from Landauer to Buber written on 12 May 1916. This long letter was written in anger and with a distant tone not typical of their personal relationship. In reference to "Die Losung" (The slogan), Buber's opening article in the first issue of his new publication, Der Jude, published in March 1916, and to a passage in "The Spirit of the East and Judaism" (1912), which indeed was omitted when the article was reprinted in 1916, Landauer wrote:

> These are very painful to me, they are very repulsive to me, and I can barely grasp them. . . . I call that entire genre aestheticism and formalism, and I tell you that you have no right—regarding yourself—to speak out in public on the political events of the present which are called a world war and to include these shameful things in your lovely and wise generalizations: the result is very deficient and very upsetting.

He dissects Buber's assumptions and theories in "Die Losung" with a sharp scalpel, saying of one of them that it is "simplistic and almost childish." He calls Buber's attitude to the world a "vacuous system." Landauer tells his friend:

> You deny what is essential especially to yourself: you regard the quotidian and take it for a miracle, but you don't regard it with a glance that gives it shape but rather with a regard that accepts it . . . and behind that lies the desire to see great things here; but this desire is insufficient to transform blunt baseness into greatness. "Virility, the spirit of sacrifice, devotion"—true, all that is found here, but not in the leadership, not in the content, and not in the significance of this foul deed.

As opposed to the mystification of war, with which Buber became involved, Landauer presents a Jewish-humanistic approach at the conclusion of his letter: "Alas for the waste of Jewish blood; alas for every drop of blood spilled in this war. How wasteful it all is, you shall see in time from the results, which are still hidden from sight."[49]

Buber's answer to this letter has not been found. Mrs. Margot Cohn, Buber's secretary during the last eight years of his life and the director of the Buber Archives in the National and University Library in Jerusalem, states that she was informed that Buber traveled to Berlin to resolve this conflict with Landauer in a face-to-face meeting.[50] Paul Mendes-Flohr brought out the repercussions of the influence of this letter, showing that, among other things, Buber expurgated it from the collections of Landauer's letters that he edited and published in

1929.[51] Mendes-Flohr also notes the absence of any reference either to the quarrel between Buber and Landauer or to Buber's attitudes to the First World War in the biography of Buber written by Hans Kohn, "under the close supervision of the hero."[52] Apparently Buber wished to suppress Landauer's sharp letter of response just as he wanted to divert attention from the positions he took during the first years of that war. Sh. H. Bergmann, who maintained close ties with Buber from early in the second decade of this century and was known for his excellent memory, did not know about the aforementioned quarrel.[53] Nor is there any reference to it in most of the studies by A. E. Simon devoted to Buber's spiritual world and path.[54] In contrast, in the article by Simon devoted to the living tradition of Buber on the hundredth anniversary of his birth, there is a discussion of the change with which we are dealing in this chapter, and I shall refer to it below. It is interesting that encyclopedia articles about Buber also contain no hint of the aforementioned positions, to his quarrel with Landauer, or to its background.[55]

Mendes-Flohr's study of what Buber wrote after receiving the letter from Landauer led him to the conclusion that this letter was the main factor in Buber's shift from mysticism to the direction that gave rise to his dialogical conception of the world.[56] He brings out three elements of this change:

1. explicit opposition to the war and to nationalism;
2. reevaluation of the significance of inner experience *(Erlebnis)* that had, until then, occupied a central place in presentations of his mystical worldview;[57]
3. reevaluation of the significance of community *(Gemeinschaft)*.[58]

In a later article A. E. Simon also attributes primary importance to Landauer's letter of 12 May 1916. "It was Landauer," he states, "who first turned Buber away from the exalted concepts back to reality, which is always less exalted, but which is sometimes more dependable." In his opinion, there was a "real turning" here, which took place as a process of "slow and hesitant awakening from the ecstatic pathos" that had previously characterized Buber's writings.[59]

Both Mendes-Flohr, in his scholarly discussions based on documentary evidence, and Simon note the developmental process in the change in Buber's worldview and do not view it as a one-time conversion. Interestingly, in their discussion of this change, neither of them refers to the autobiographical piece discussed above, which Buber called "A Conversion."

It seems that some significance must be accorded to a passing comment of Buber's in which he states, among other things, that the spring of 1916 was the time of "the beginning" (meaning the first planning or writing) of *I and Thou*. Only about fifty years later, after he had made this comment on the margins of the first edition of this work,[60] and with the appearance of the German original of Buber's correspondence edited by Grete Schaeder, did the aforementioned letter from Landauer, which also dates from the spring of 1916, come to light.

Mendes-Flohr's research, which thoroughly investigated the changes in Buber's thought during the period following the spring of 1916, shows that at that time it did not have even the germs of the dialogical philosophy that Buber was later to develop. We find these only in his articles beginning with 1918,[61] the year when he noted for himself a sketch of the plan of a new intellectual conception that came to full maturity with the appearance of *I and Thou*.[62] In 1919, when Landauer was killed, Buber had already entered the new period in his biography. The shock of the tragedy merely hastened the consolidation of ideas that had already been embodied in his articles of 1918. Hence it is difficult to accept Buber's testimony, given in his conversation with Rogers, that an "episode in May 1919," Landauer's murder, was the focus of the process of change or the point when it matured. In some of Buber's autobiographical hints discussed above he mentions 1919 as the date when the change was complete. But only in his conversation with Rogers did he explain why that year was so significant for him.

"A CONVERSION" AND ITS PLACE IN BUBER'S BIOGRAPHY

In most of his references, explicit or implicit, to the change which took place in his worldview, Buber himself refrained from calling it a conversion. Significantly, this process of change was not the only crisis event, whether short or prolonged, in his spiritual biography. Both before and after the First World War he experienced tragic events and "moments" of crisis that gave rise to changes or clarifications in his spiritual world.[63] "A Conversion" should be compared with a letter from Buber, dated 4 February 1926, to Max Brod, in which he responded to Kafka's *The Trial*.[64]

This letter was not intended to be made public. Hence it lacks the linguistic veils that generally characterize Buber's intimate revelations when they are included in his letters. Here he switches to the first-person plural by saying "all the pollution" in these hearts, which he identifies with himself. Similarly, "A Conversion" treats a situation in the first-person plural by stating: "When we are in despair." "Pollution" and "despair" are mutually conjoined. They lead to dissatisfaction with oneself, to doubt, and to the feeling of "whirlpool," and/or "chaos," in Buber's inner self. At the same time they have a vitalizing force like "redemption from the fall," or like creative despair similar to that of which he speaks (not in reference to an individual but to the whole nation) in a biblical essay:

> From the moment when the national disaster appears inevitable, and especially after it has become a reality, it can, like every great torment, become a productive force from the religious point of view: it begins to suggest new questions and to stress old ones. Dogmatized conceptions are pondered afresh in the light of the events, and the faith relationship that has to stand the test of an utterly changed situation is renewed in a modified form. But the new acting force is nothing less than the force of extreme despair, a despair so elemental that it can have but one or two results: the sapping of the last will of life, or a renewal of the soul.[65]

This discomfort with himself is also implied in Buber's extremely personal interpretations of "thou shalt love thy neighbor as thyself," for which the point of departure is that "man does not love himself."[66] The root of this inner discomfort was, one assumes, sunk deep in the feelings of guilt mentioned above.

The conclusions of "A Conversion" are implied, it seems to me, by means of the concept of return *(Umkehr)*, which had a place in most fields of Buber's work,[67] and also in concepts or terms that were useful to Buber in his calls for rebirth or renewal (in his social-Zionist writing). Thus, for example, we find it in his discussion of the "crucial overturning of the soul and the relation with the world."[68] The term "overturning" *(Umwandlung)* has related terms in his articles, such as "a drastic change" *(Umschwung)* and "the decisive movement" *(die entscheidende Bewegung)*.[69]

The feeling of guilt is central to a poem which Buber wrote late in life (1964):

THE FIDDLER
for Grete Schaeder

Oddly here, at the edge of the world
I have now settled.
Behind me, in an infinite round,
There is silence in the universe, only that fiddler fiddles.
Dark one, already I have forged a covenant with you,
Willing to learn from your sounds
Of what I was guilty unbeknownst to me.
Let me feel it, reveal
To this uninjured soul every wound
That I wickedly inflicted and which remained illuminated.
Sacred minstrel, do not stop before then![70]

It would appear that one may also find a clear reference to "A Conversion" in a confessional sentence of Buber's embedded in his article, "Spinoza, Sabbatai Zvi, and the Baal-Shem" (1927): "I early had a premonition, indeed, no matter how I resisted it, that I was inescapably destined to love the world."[71]

IMPRINTS OF "A CONVERSION" IN VARIOUS WORKS BY BUBER

Several of Buber's ideas that are of primary importance for understanding his worldview may be properly understood when seen against the background of the event in his life that he calls "a conversion":

1. *I and Thou,* which presents the systematic statement of Buber's dialogical thought, contains a short discussion, unique in all his writings, of the concept that he calls "self-contradiction." This discussion was devoted to the final outcome of a life of monologue, man for himself. According to this passage, a life entirely of monologue leads to the "edge of life."[72]

During the first ten or fifteen years of the century, Buber's spiritual tendencies apparently lay hidden in the darkness of the background of his repugnance for "self-contradiction." He presented these tendencies critically in the autobiographical passage, "A Conversion." His descriptions of his propensities and the traits of his spiritual world in his "mystical phase" could be an illustration of the process, or at least of the start of the process of "self-contradiction."

2. A clear resonance of Buber's two paths—the one he leaned toward during the mystical phase of his creative life and the one toward which he began striving after the change had taken place in the depths of his being—reaches us in the chapter "Of Death and Life" of his *For the Sake of Heaven*.[73] There too, as in "A Conversion," we have a charismatic spiritual personality facing the test of responding to a person in extreme existential distress. How can one offer guidance to someone else, within whom seethes the question of "To be or not to be?" The approach of the Seer of Lublin, on the one hand, and the response and personality of the Holy Yehudi, on the other, represent two diametrically opposed answers. These two answers, two opposing conceptions of life, are parallel to the duality of Buber as a mystic, the power of whose personality is hypnotic, and that of the other Buber, who accepts the responsibility of dialogue. "Of Death and Life" tells the story of the Holy Yehudi, that Hasidic sage who was directed towards the service of God with his whole attentive being in this vale of tears. The Yehudi happens to encounter a sick Jew who is filled with consciousness of his approaching death. "I am about to die. . . . I know I shall die soon," he tells the Yehudi, who speaks to him "as though he had long known him."

The Yehudi identifies with the man's plight and tries to understand why he has lost all hope of living. It turns out that the sick man is a disciple of the Seer, who met the sick man when he visited Kosnitz, his hometown: "When the Rabbi had visited Kosnitz the last time, this man had been there, too. The Rabbi had greeted him and looked at him long and intently. Then he had said: 'You must get your soul in readiness to die within the year.'"

The Seer, trusting his mystical vision, virtually imposes the loss of hope to live upon the man. Immediately afterwards the man went to Lublin with his son "and brought his shroud with him." In this plight he held "his soul in readiness to die within the year" in passive expectation until he met the "Yehudi."

Out of his deep faith that human life emerges from a willed determination and from a person's struggle for his truths, the Yehudi rebelled against the decree of the Seer. He struggled with the man, at his bedside, until dawn and, very gradually, he repaired the damage done by the Seer, and the man's hope for life was restored. Afterwards, when the Seer asked him, "You seem to have saved a man who was destined to die. How did you go about it?" the Yehudi answered, "I persuaded him not to let death get the better of him."[74]

Buber believed that human freedom of choice was consistent with a dialogical responsiveness to people. This way emerges from the denial of the deterministic tendency that, in its religious contexts, depends on mystical visions. The mystic, who is directed beyond the crooked byways of existence in this world, is viewed by Buber as a person of monologue, shutting himself up within the four walls of his own spiritual urges against the duties of responsibility within the human vale of tears. In this respect there is an affinity between the ways of the Seer of Lublin and Buber as he presents himself in the first part of "A Conversion." There are also parallels between the quality of the responsiveness of the Seer to his disciples, as portrayed in "Of Death and Life," and the character of Buber's response to the appeal of the young man who was "in despair and yet [went] to a person" (as described in "A Conversion"). The subject of these two chapters is the responsibility of the educator, who might be entrusted with "life and death."

While it would appear that "Of Death and Life" was a product of Buber's imagination, expressing a reflection of his profound experience (that of the conversion), surprisingly, we find that it has a parallel source within the Hasidic tradition:

> The holy Rabbi Mordecai David of Dombrowy, the father-in-law of the holy Rabbi Beer Moshe, and the holy Rabbi of Moglanitsa, were two of the greatest disciples of the Rabbi of Lublin. And the Rabbi told him that this year Rabbi Mordecai David would pass away. Therefore he should come to Lublin for that time. After Passover he went there with his son. . . . His late wife was amazed at that, and he did not tell her or anyone what was the matter with him. Every evening he went to the Rabbi, and the Rabbi blessed him. Of course he did not eat or drink, only [devoting himself to] prayer and service and study until he should possess the truth. The Holy Yehudi was in Lublin and came to visit him and heal him. Soon he understood there was something to the matter and he ordered everybody to leave him and go outside. Then [the man] told him what the Rabbi had said to him. Then the Holy Yehudi said to him: I do not see anything in you. Take my advice, and drink some brandy with me. And with blessed God's help you will live. And that is what hap-

pened. That night at two hours past midnight, the time when the Rabbi had told him that he was to pass away, it was heard in the house where the Rabbi dwelled that Reb Mottl [a nickname for Mordecai] Shenker, who lived there, suddenly became ill. And when they mentioned his name, Mordecai David ben Mishka, to the Rabbi, then the Rabbi said that what he had seen was about that man, since their names and the names of their mother were the same. The holy Rabbi, Rabbi Mordecai David, came to him at that time, and [the Seer] saw that his vitality was still upon him and he started to doubt. And people said that the Holy Yehudi had done it, reversing things, i.e., this one will live and this one will die.[75]

The contrast between the Seer and the Yehudi as it emerges from this story is the contrast between a way of life based on choice and a deterministic way of life. This contrast greatly concerned Buber, and he came back to it in various contexts in his thought and work. A very concentrated and comprehensive expression of it is included in his scholarly study "Prophecy, Apocalyptic, and Historical Hour." There Buber asks:

Do I dare the definitely impossible or do I adapt myself to the unavoidable? Do I dare to become other than I am, trusting that in reality I am indeed other and can so put it to the test, or do I take cognizance of a barrier in my present existence as something that will eternally be a barrier? Transposing the question from biography to history: does the historical hour ever experience its real limits otherwise than through undertaking to overstep those limits it is familiar with? Does the future establish itself ever anew, or is it inescapably destined?[76]

Do these questions not receive living significance, not merely theoretical and abstract meaning, when we view them against Buber's self-revelations in "A Conversion" and "Of Death and Life"?

3. Buber apparently finds an equivalence between closing oneself off to "demands and responsibility" that are in "the abundance of every passing hour"—which characterized him during his mystical phase (as he states in "A Conversion")—and "flight out of selfhood and environment" by means of drugs.[77] One must suppose that he recalled his mystical experiments when, years after they ceased, he condemned Aldous Huxley's praise of mescaline.[78] Buber states that "The 'chemical holidays' of which Huxley speaks are holidays not only from the petty self, enmeshed in the machinery of its aims, but

also from the person participating in the community of logos and cosmos."[79] The "petty self" referred to here is the one that is subject to "'lower' periods," as he said in *Pointing the Way*.[80] Buber calls the "vacation" from the personality and the environment, achieved in a short time by means of drugs, "situationlessness."[81] In the same context he defines the "dream state" and "schizophrenia" and "situationless, because they are in their essence uncommunal."[82]

In the continuation of his rebuttal to Huxley's paean to the marvelous intoxication of mescaline, Buber states that in that intoxication "one experiences to some degree what the mystics experience." It seems evident to us that he links Huxley's descriptions with mystical experiences of another kind, those which he himself had undergone. It is clear from his criticism that not only does he disagree with the lessons which the English thinker seeks to draw from his experience, but he also is combating Huxley's tendency to immerse himself in "a strictly private special sphere."[83] He describes the experiences derived from mescaline intoxication with almost the same language that he used in describing his own immersion in mysticism in "A Conversion."

In this context we must note a trait common to all loss of individual identity, whether achieved by wonder drugs, by mystical experimentation, or by immersion in a "collective." The "collective," in the dictionary of Buber's concepts, represents "the organized atrophy of personal experience," and it is the polar opposite of his concept of "community," the "increase and confirmation" of the element of dialogue.[84] Redemptive movements and political theologies that supply absolute answers free man from times of the eclipse of God or from hopelessness, and from prolonged struggles for significance.

"The self is a focus of torments. Redemption is the denial of the self. Absolute self-obliteration in the masses," writes one of Amos Oz's protagonists.[85] And just as there is a horizontal flight from independence, there is also a vertical flight—in self-immersion that could lead to "self-contradiction" as well as to an ecstasy that grants one "otherness which does not fit into the context of life" (as Buber wrote in "A Conversion").

6
DUALITY AND ITS STRUCTURES

The individual's consciousness is consolidated on the basis of the spiritual possessions and behavior patterns of his society. A person is born into the reality of the group or society's life, and as he grows up he internalizes its concepts and values, making them the inner components of his personality. In other words, his existential reality as well as his consciousness come into being within the context of his social environment; the world is flat to the eyes of a child of the South Sea islands and round to the eyes of a product of western culture.[1] Society determines the boundaries of the spiritual reality of its members and also creates them, according to Peter Berger, who points out that personal identity is consolidated in concepts and idioms, and these are implemented and brought to life in the course of mutual social intercourse.[2] To become human means to become an individual, and this is possible, according to Clifford Geertz, only if we are directed by social patterns: "We become individual under the guidance of cultural patterns, historically created systems of meaning in terms of which we give form, order, point and direction to our lives."[3]

These very same cultural patterns, which are discerned within systems of belief and behavior, serve as social consolidators for the group.

101

They are both the means by which the present creators link their ac-
complishments with those of previous generations as well as the basis
for communal cultural identity and cohesiveness.[4]

A concept is a linguistic sign by means of which images are linked
and phenomena are combined within the individual's consciousness,
turning his or her attention away from the private and the sensory and
directing it toward the essential and general. It is an idiom indicating
abstraction and generalization. The meaning of a generalization is the
capturing of many impressions in a single image, whereas abstraction
means to turn consciously away from the multifarious to the unitary,
and from the phenomenon to the essence.[5] General, abstract concepts,
which belong to the area that Buber calls "the sphere of pure
conceptuality,"[6] should be distinguished from the type of concepts that
represent a society's spiritual possessions, concepts that embody the
ideas shared by a society, or, in other words, value concepts.[7] According to C. Geertz, these concepts constitute the matrix of the social
fabric by being "organized systems of significant symbols," or, as he
explains, they are "conceptual structures molding formless talents."[8]

The totality of a given society's value concepts is identified with its
cultural design, constituting a means of transmitting its tradition. Every culture-society struggles with reality by means of the idioms that
embody its values. Its structure of value concepts indicates its characteristics. In any changing historical situation, a generation is likely to
shape various dimensions of the concepts of their culture, and to endow them with new meanings. Personal and collective attitudes are
interpreted in the contexts of the cultural tradition.

It is difficult to elicit value concepts from the language of a society
in an era of change and turmoil. It is difficult for the individual during
a time of transition, when historical traditions lose their authority, to
find a spiritual handhold and existential security in life.

Buber came to maturity at the fin de siècle, a period marked by the
weakening of social and traditional ties.[9] Hugo von Hofmannsthal, a
poet with whom Buber expresses spiritual identification,[10] portrayed
the crisis of that time as embodied in the disintegration of concepts.
The main protagonist of his story "The Letter of Lord Chandos" says
of himself: "I have lost completely the ability to speak or to think of
anything coherently."[11] This statement is interpreted later as the loss
of "abstract words." "They disintegrate in my mouth," he says, "like
rotten mushrooms."[12] The spiritual situation at that time is summed

up in words that Hofmannsthal places in his hero's mouth, to the effect that everything is falling into fragments and fragments of fragments, and nothing can be encompassed with a concept. Individual words incessantly swirl about him in maelstroms, leading to the void.[13] The concepts of the past have lost their coherence and also their ability to maintain their meaning. This is true of European culture and also of the worldview of the Jews who were involved in it.

The structure of concepts underlying European culture, as well as Jewish society within it, had lost its power and the sources of its authority even before the fin de siècle, but the processes of spiritual and social change that had been at work from the time of the Enlightenment were strengthened. Many of the changes that took place at that time could be interpreted as the results of confrontations between traditions whose authority had been weakened and the processes of the modern world.[14]

The processes of social change may stimulate the growth of a new personal identity. Individuals possessing spiritual power are capable of erecting a spiritual world for themselves from within the maelstrom of the streams of thought current in the new era of change. They continually try to bind the tattered concepts of the past to new life values. In their spirits they confront the various extremes of their time while seeking to consolidate a worldview out of the tension between opposites.

In speaking about the identity or uniqueness of a nation, Buber pointed out two central components: (1) "the innermost stratum of man's disposition, which yields the basic structure of his personality"[15] and (2) "community of blood, land, language, way of life."[16]

He called this duality both "experience" and "existence." Experience is "the physical being" of the people, and existence is their shared "spiritual being." And thus they become a "nation."[17]

The critical encounter with manifestations of modernity was a stimulating challenge for Buber. His exposure to "the hidden questions" made them an impetus for his own cultural creativity, which in turn served to forge a new self-identity. In Buber's idiom of the first decade of the century there are many expressions of the zeal for "innovation," "revolution," and "rebirth." There is also a conspicuous call for a Renaissance type of cultural design, which would emphasize the individual creator. In the first of his early Speeches on Judaism he gave this very picturesque expression:

Let us get hold of ourselves: let us draw our life into our hands, as a pail out of a well; let us gather it into our hands as one gathers scattered corn. We must come to a decision, must establish a balance of power within us.[18]

This passage expresses more than the urge for cultural renewal, and I shall return to it in the following sections.

Looking back with the perspective afforded by the passage of about two decades upon this desire to create a culture, Buber says of himself and of his comrades:

Later we saw that culture was not subject to will; that it did not come to the world as the outcome of premeditated intention, but rather always . . . as something secondary to the course of life. Like a personality, so culture grows absentmindedly.[19]

CONCEPTS AND STRUCTURES: THE BACKGROUND
OF THEIR REFERENCE

The dangers of the "World of Chaos"
and the aspiration for unity

The mystical-experiential subjectivity that marked the early stage in Buber's progress and his aspiration for personal creativity that breaks through the accepted cultural patterns[20] was inconsistent with a systematic attitude toward the multiplicity of the phenomena of reality. In the introduction to an article written in his youth, which advocates the new life values signaled by Nietzsche, Buber argued that the spheres of life are "large and undefined like life itself," making it impossible to confine them "in a *single* little room."[21] In his early work "Speeches," this argument is advanced by way of rejecting "conceptualization," "schematization," or "forms," and as an appeal to the motive power of personal "yearnings" and to "forces."[22]

These formulations and others like them expressed his anarchical-mystical tendencies in those years—his opposition to general opinions, to principles, and to methods of thought. These tendencies seem to have distanced him from any methodical scholarly approach. He began to develop these patterns of thought as early as his articles of 1901.

In early 1901 an article of his named "Lesser Uri"[23] was published. In striving for new life values, Buber presented Lesser Uri as an
artist "who is among those who seek a new language, expressing everything, because the old language is not sufficient for them."[24]

In the "hues" of Uri's work Buber found "the characters and movements of the human soul."[25] This artist's landscapes seemed to him
"so void of content, so full of fanciful vision, that it is almost impossible to explain them, rather one must only see them and feel them."
He felt in them "a moment, in which a thousand eddies of life mix
together. The sun shines down and the prominence of the sun makes
things brilliant beyond their essence. . . . The sun slants down, and
everything reverts to itself, and then each thing restores its fire to its
essence."[26] It seems that he identified with the ecstatic quality of Uri's
colorfulness, seeing it as representing a restless movement[27] of "whirling," to which he had been subject in his youth, but not only to it.
Until the end of the First World War he continued to experience the
spirit of straying as well as the birth pangs of new life values.

Buber's tempestuous existence sought to get a grip on life and to
find an answer in realms that were distant from each other and even
diametrically opposed.[28] His mystical yearnings were bound up with
breaking through the bounds of regulatory and organizational ratio-
nalism, and at the same time he was aware of the dangers of the "world
of chaos" from which he was extricated. An "aspiration for unity"
stirred within him, by means of which he hoped to overcome the oppositions in his existence. For him "unity" was a longing and not a
real human possibility.[29] In the absence of unity what he needed was at
least the solidity of conceptual patterns and organizing guidelines for
his thought.

*The dual-level principle and its early
conceptual expressions*

Buber's aspiration, which achieved formulation and presentation only
after the "Speeches," was "to gather the [directionless] forces of life
and to bring them 'to equilibrium.'"[30] However, his articles from as
early as the beginning of the century testify to the growth of a way of
thinking that would help attain it, and this was along a double course:
(1) the consolidation of value concepts[31] with the aim of placing them

within dual structures; (2) the clarification of the relationships between these dual structures, which constitute the theoretical level and the primary, basic level of experiential reality, which was to him the main focus of interest. Buber's recognition of the need for a theoretical level is implied in his grappling with concepts and structures, even though he himself never explicitly declared this to be so.

In the article "Lesser Uri" there is a multifaceted effort to grapple with the first tendency, as well as an attempt to conceptualize the interrelationship of the theoretical and primary levels. The second tendency received a much clearer and more direct expression in his article "Jewish Science," which was also published in 1901.

The range of ideas and conceptual idioms exemplified in the article "Lesser Uri," is surprising. This article is laced with the embryonic forms of the very same concepts from which Buber later developed the most central structures of his dialogical thought. Some of these concepts may already be seen here, at the time of their first presentation, as parts of dual structures:

1. A structure whose two parts are "color" and "form" was presented in it. From this pattern were developed the structures of I-Thou and I-It, which are the focus of Buber's dialogical thought. Their stages of development will be pointed out below.

2. A structure by means of which the relation between the concepts of "time" and "eternity" was formed.[32]

3. A conjunctive duality between the individual's inner life and the social and historical world into which he is born. This duality, which Buber could have found in the writings of his teacher Dilthey, gained further consolidation in one of his early "speeches" on Judaism, and upon its foundation he developed the structures: "distance – relation" and "vortex – direction."[33]

This dual relation to the world, which should, I submit, be applied to all areas of Buber's thought[34] is evident and palpable as early as "Lesser Uri." It is evident that all the structural patterns above are dual.

In the article "Lesser Uri" one may also locate germs of ideas that were later developed and formulated in Buber's thought. I shall mention only two of them.

1. "The Future." This idea is hinted at in reference to a figure that appears in Uri's work entitled *Jerusalem*. Less than ten years later, Buber presented "the Future" as a consolidated concept embodying the aspiration for redemption and also combining within it the concepts of Unity and Deed. These three concepts in combination are viewed in the early "Speeches" as the basic ideas of Judaism.[35]

2. Self-destruction inherent in human solitude is described at length in an interpretation of one of the paintings in Uri's triptych *Man*. In time Buber was to give this concept a special place in *I and Thou*, where he calls it "self-contradiction."[36]

The article "Lesser Uri" could only have been written by someone who viewed Uri's work as a reflection of his own world. It contains a reflection of Buber's torments and an expression of his yearnings. He did not treat the artist's creativity from a contemplative distance, nor was he content with an experiential identification with it. Rather he combined it with theoretical assumptions, which were intentionally hidden, as it were, in the mystical poet's language. In my interpretations of this article, two levels are located: both an experiential-empathic level and also a level of abstract concepts.

An approach based on the principle of dual levels like that which is demonstrated in "Lesser Uri" was already formulated in the article "Jewish science,"[37] published near the end of 1901. In this early article, the double-faceted approach is presented within the expression of Buber's attitude toward "Jewish Science." It is clear that there is a distinction between an entirely subjective level and a theoretical level built upon it. This attitude is indicated in the very title of the article. In his articles about Judaism published after the beginning of the century and, more pronouncedly, in his earlier "Speeches" on Judaism, Buber understood *Jewishness* as subjective and anti-intellectual. Thus, he viewed a *scientific* approach to it as positive only if based upon a personal, experiential approach.

In the beginning of the article Buber points out that the science of Judaism can take three directions: it can be (1) the science of Judaism; (2) the science of the Jewish question; or (3) the science of Zionism. He denied the validity of objectivity in the first two directions, and afterward he stated: "[O]bjectivity in the science of Zionism will be even more difficult. It will derive not from a question, but rather from an answer; from an answer which in most cases is not scientific, but rather intuitive, and in any event it is discovered in subjective fashion, and now it must be justified."[38] Thus, the *scientific approach* is valid only on the basis of a personal approach. It must explain and ground what was achieved by *intuition*. This combined duality is expressed in two spiritual acts: love and cognizance. The second act is based on the first: "to know what we love."[39] From the context of the discussion there may be inferred, among other things, criticism of the blurring of the boundaries between "love" and "cognizance" in the science of Zionism. Buber states later in that article that indeed, "one must examine what is given so as to determine what is needed for our nation and what it can expect, its needs and its possibilities." But this is "in order to formulate the program of Jewish politics [on the basis of the needs and possibilities] in a maximally scientific style, that is, to reach the state which we call 'the Science of the Jewish Question.'"[40]

The duality of intuition and science, or of love and cognizance, is parallel to the duality of color and form presented in "Lesser Uri." Buber identified with Uri's "color values," in which he found, as we have already seen, "the characters and movements of the human soul." But at the same time he knew that it was impossible to dwell solely in the world of "color." For, "reality has placed obstacles of form and boundary in the path [of color]."[41] Love, like color, embodied the inner experience *(Erlebnis)* that was its main source.[42] But Buber knew that in reality there was no place for love without cognizance, for intuition without analysis and scientific synthesis.

The stages of consolidating the dual-level principle as a two-faceted approach to existence

In the two articles just discussed, dating from the beginning of the century, the structure whose members are "love" and "cognizance" was not yet developed. Later it began to be consolidated so that it could be applied in various areas of thought. It served as the matrix for yet another approach in the article called "Buddha," which was written in 1907, though not published at that time. It was later included twice in collections of Buber's articles.[43] This article, too, is founded upon an approach that presents two realities. The first of these is grasped as possessing great, inner actuality. It is stamped within our creation and by means of it we contact mythic and archaic sources—which are symbolized in "the great primordial words." The second reality is presented as something external, thin, and limited by natural law and abstract concepts. Unlike the articles of 1901, which were discussed above, in "Buddha" the approach is entirely mystical. It does not contain even limited, obligatory endorsement of the reality that is subject to scientific thought. It expresses yearning for mystical penetration beyond mundane existence. Buber writes there:

> The inexhaustible consolation of human life these days, is that the great, primordial words remain open for our entry.[44] The reality which they express cannot be reconciled with the image of reality presented by Western culture. These two contradict each other. . . . If this is our way of living things, that is, by determining an "aesthetic" or "philosophical" or "religious" attitude toward them, then we shall remain outside. . . . If we accept the primordial words, the unification of which I call Buddha, as a theory—we have lost them. What remains with us will be "Buddhism," an existence among existences, with a beginning and an embodiment in history, with a thesis and its justification according to logic. By means of these things we shall only become poorer, and we shall accept as our fate an area of existence such as was not ours by the nature of our creation. We sell our eternity to Satan for a sack of wishes full of interesting combinations of concepts.[45]

On the one hand, Buber created concepts and strove to unite them in dual structures; on the other hand, he harbored yearnings for mystical elevation, for a state of "illumination, ecstasy, rapture,"[46] in which "the instant" and "eternity"[47] were combined in an existence beyond place and time. An examination of the worldview in the article "Buddha" against the background of the concepts in the other articles that we have mentioned in this discussion reveals the contrary tendencies that strove with each other within Buber's world and the spiritual struggles in which he was embroiled.

Despite his mystical tendencies, Buber apparently did not permit himself to express once again the yearning or the call for "consolation" in absolute transcendence of this world. The characteristics of the duality that is presented in "Buddha" later helped him to develop and deepen his two-faceted approach to existence. But this was not just another duality of which one component was acquired by the negation of the other.

In his mystical-philosophical work, *Daniel* (1913), this duality attained conceptual consolidation, presented in the terms Realization and Orientation. It is also presented there as a polar duality, and its character is described at length.[48]

Buber's two-faceted conception of reality underlies his article "With a Monist" (1914), which in many respects comprises an expansion of the dual tendencies expressed in the aforementioned articles of 1901. There is an especially close connection between the ideas exhibited in "Jewish Science" and those of "With a Monist," though the defined subjects of the two articles are different.[49]

The duality that was merely intimated in the articles from the beginning of the century received an extensive and consolidated discussion in "With a Monist": "Each thing and being has a twofold nature: the passive, absorbable, usable, dissectible, comparable, combinable, rationializable. And the other, the active, non-absorbable, unusable, undissectible, incomparable, uncombinable, nonrationalizable."[50] The first reality is "an ordinary reality, sufficient so that things may be equalized and organized."[51] This is an existence that depends on patterns of "doctrine" with tenets and general rules, subject to the laws of logic—is this not the external reality that was condemned in his article "Buddha"? In "With a Monist" it is not condemned, but it is made subject to another reality, which he calls "the great reality." It is identified with "the intensity of our experiencing."[52]

"The great reality" is irrational. It is the reality that embodies the meaning and essence of human life. Its being brought to life depends upon the conjoining of all the human faculties and powers:

> And how can I give this reality to my world except by seeing the seen with all the strength of my life, hearing the heard with all the strength of my life, tasting the tasted with all the strength of my life? Except by bending over the experienced thing with fervour and power and by melting the shell of passivity with the fire of my being until the confronting, the shaping, the bestowing side of things springs up to meet me and embraces me so that I know the world in it? The actual world is the manifest, the known world. And the world cannot be known through response to the things by the active sense-spirit of the loving man.[53]

We find that this reality has an aspect that is entirely experiential, and it also has a second level, by means of which the surrounding world is perceived, and it is colored with its colors. And the two cannot be separated. Revitalizing experiential intensity by concentrating all the powers of the personality is what enables it to know the world "through response to the things by active sense-spirit of the loving man." Buber apparently intended the term "active sense-spirit" to mean intuition, a concept to which he had already attributed fundamental importance in his article "Jewish Science." In the article of 1901 "intuition" and "love" were placed on the same footing, and both were set in opposition to "cognizance" and "science"; the same is true of "With a Monist." Only in later years, in the dialogical stage and through it, Buber once again presents *his* concept of intuition, clearly an extension of the meaning embodied in his expression the "active sense-spirit of the loving man":

> If we want to do today's work and prepare tomorrow's with clear sight, then we must develop in ourselves and in the next generation a gift which lives in man's inwardness as a Cinderella, one day to be a princess. Some call it intuition, but that is not a wholly unambiguous concept. I prefer the name "imagining the real," for in its essential being this gift is not a looking at the other, but a bold swinging—demanding the most intensive stirring of one's being—into the life of the other. This is the nature of all genuine imagining, only that here the realm of my action is not the all-possible, but the particular real person who confronts me, whom I can attempt to make present to myself in just this way, and not otherwise, in his wholeness, unity, and uniqueness.[54]

The dual structure "love – cognizance" resonates in another important article from the year of 1914: the introductory essay to the German translation of the Finnish epic *Kalevala*.[55]

The two concrete ways by means of which Buber grasps the world are not mutually exclusive. In his early mystical stage of thought, primacy is awarded to the way of Realization (a concept discussed extensively in *Daniel*) of "the great reality" (a term found in "With a Monist"). However, this reality is not unique: human existence on earth is not possible without "ordinary reality" (as he says in "With a Monist"), which is based on the way of "Orientation" (in the conceptual language of *Daniel*). In Buber's view, one ought to ascend to or penetrate the "great reality," which is experiential and intuitive, and by means of which one "realizes" oneself. But at the same time it is impossible for a person to exist without the reality that is controlled by his intelligence and organized by means of scientific method.

Later, in Buber's language of dialogical philosophy, both the I-Thou relationship[56] and the I-It relationship[57] supersede the ways of Realization and Orientation and may be seen as developmental extensions of them. Buber himself was not accustomed to revealing the stages of the formation of the basic concepts underlying his thought. In his article "The History of the Dialogical Principle," he often conceals more than he reveals. Thus we can only learn from him that the paired concepts of Realization and Orientation, which were presented in *Daniel*,[58] are the roots of the duality that is central to *I and Thou*. This combined duality of love and scientific cognizance, which emerged in his thought as early as 1901, continues to underlie his approach in works besides *I and Thou*. It also appears in the later dialogical works, such as "The Foundations of the Interpersonal": intuition does not cancel the intellectual approach, but rather it is primary and more essential.

Certain basic differences between the duality in *Daniel* and in *I and Thou* should be pointed out:

1. The duality in the first work refers to the individual himself, both in terms of Realization and of Orientation; however in the second duality, presented in *I and Thou*, a person's worthy and essential existence is no longer grasped as embodied in the realization of the person himself, but in the realization of the *Thou* which is stamped upon him, and orientation is not conceived as a relationship.

2. The concept of Realization is used to express the striving to achieve unification of the soul and to melt with the universe. The I-Thou relationship, by contrast, is impossible between a person and himself. In the world of dialogical encounter there are no longer any connotations of blending, as in *Daniel*.

Major milestones in the consolidation of concepts in the "mystical stage"

Some of the tendencies that characterized the premystical stage of Buber's thought are represented in the concept of Realization, to which he accorded a place in his work even before it was included in the structure "Realization-Orientation." This concept embodies the individual's desire for self-expression, for actualization of the creative powers within him. This desire resonates in his early writings before it was consolidated conceptually. Various idioms represented this aspiration in the original German of his writings. Most of them continue to serve him in the dialogical stage as they had served him in the mystical stage.

A few years afterward a new role was accorded to the concepts of Realization and Determination in consolidating assumptions that were expressed in his articles "The Spirit of the Orient and Judaism" (1912)[59] and "Jewish Religiosity" (1913).[60] The call for Realization in these articles on Judaism was consistent with renewed desires and aspirations for personal creativity that were formulated in *Daniel*, a philosophical-mystical work that lacks any indication of its author's Jewishness.

A place was also set aside for Jewish historical concepts in these articles on Judaism. We find "exile" and "redemption" in "The Renewal of Judaism" (1910), "repentance" in "The Spirit of the Orient and Judaism" and in "Jewish Religiosity." But these terms were not interpreted in the spirit of Jewish homiletical traditions. To a great degree they were meant to express the spirit of realization, creativity, and spiritual renewal.

Both the concepts that derived from the historical literature of Judaism and the other concepts mentioned above possessed decided value meaning. Their function was not essentially intellectual. Each of them (except for the concept of exile) embodied a value that was to be expressed in life as it is lived. They replaced, as it were, tenets, principles, and commandments, which Buber rejected. At the same time no clear and distinct content was expressed in these concepts. They did not bear concrete personal obligation. They were meant to arouse and awaken one's emotions while not necessarily pointing to paths of positive action nor to ways of behavior that were to be shared by the community. Every single individual could interpret and implement them in accordance with his propensities and abilities.[61] However, as mentioned above, as early as his article "The Renewal of Judaism," Buber had spoken about the "deed." But he saw no need, during all of those years, to clarify *how* to realize the deed. It is therefore very difficult to reconcile the meanings of his concept of Realization with the demands of the positive commandments of faith, and also with a social vision that requires the responsibility of participation. This is shown both in his writings and in his personal correspondence.[62]

*The change in the character of his concepts and its embodiment
in a structure of ideas in the articles of 1918*

The inner change that took place in Buber's world during World War
I brought about a shift in the direction of his thought: on the one
hand, the emphasis on the subjectivism of his experience was blunted,
and, on the other hand, his conception began to assume a communal
character, which was subject to tension with the "political element."
The new image of the world was developed and formulated conceptually in four articles that Buber wrote in 1918: "Zion and Youth,"
"The Holy Way," "Herut," and "Community." Buber, the artist of
language, here shows himself to be an artist of composition as well.
Various threads are woven between the articles, tying them into a unified structure of ideas with three axes: communal, social, and religious. This subtle work of design enhances the meaning of the structure as a whole, while also highlighting new and different aspects of
each article taken separately. The article "Community" presents Buber's
new conception in terms encompassing all of humanity, whereas the
three other articles interpret it coterminously with the foundations of
Buber's Zionist vision. Only in "Community" and in "Zion and Youth"
are the three elements of his conception presented clearly, and in "Community" it also serves to form the triple structure of the article.[63]

The three Zionist articles of 1918 are centered upon the term Realization, which appears explicitly in two of the articles and is the implicit foundation of the third. Now, as opposed to its meaning in Buber's
articles about Judaism from the years around 1910, it means the creation of communities in which there arises "the immediate relationship between man and man, the carrier of the Divine."[64] Proper understanding of the concept of Realization here requires reference to the
concept of Community, and vice versa. In the aforementioned Zionist
articles, Realization expresses the focus of the new worldview, and in
the fourth article it is mainly revealed in the concept of Community.
"In the waste and confusion of a disintegrating society," he calls for
the endeavor "to take seriously at once God and the community, God
as being in the community."[65] He refers to the establishment of religious communities with a utopian vision, aspiring for total social renewal. "The community in its various forms" will come into being out

of the communes in an organic process.[66] This appeal combines the three components of his new conception, and it fully expresses the propositions, the various aspects of which are discussed in the four articles.

Within the totality of the aforementioned 1918 articles a change is indeed expressed in the tendencies that had characterized the mystical stage of Buber's thought, but they do not yet have a systematic consolidation that presents a different way of thinking. No intrinsic importance should be attributed to this change. It should be seen as the basis for the continued development of his dialogical philosophy.

Only one of these articles, "Zion and Youth," was published in the year when it was written. The other three were published a year later. Buber did not indicate the dimensions of sharing and affinity that bind these four articles, and he also refrained from joining together those with a Zionist subject. In 1920, upon collecting in a single volume his articles from the years 1916–20 on questions of Judaism and Zionism, he included "Zion and Youth" but refrained from including "The Holy Way" and "Herut."[67] In all four of these articles Buber plays, as it were, the same score, but on various musical instruments; and the individuality of their sounds does not mute the single melody which is heard in them.

*Central concepts in the dialogical thinking
and their structural integration*

About the time of "The Holy Way," "Zion and Youth," "Herut," and "Community," Buber wrote the outline of a short work on dialogue. This draft indicates "an effort to construct a system"[68] and bore fruit five years later in *I and Thou*, which is regarded as the systematic and comprehensive presentation of his dialogical thought. At the center of this work stands a structure built on "the double face" (the dual relationship): I-Thou, and I-It. I have already pointed out the ideas that may be seen as the roots of this structure. Their tendrils lead to Buber's articles from the beginning of the century. All the other structures that occupy a central place in his thought were also interpreted by him in accordance with his dialogical thought. I shall devote chapters to each of them.

In Buber dialogical thought is an attempt to transcend the restrictions of the narrow space of inner experience while moving toward interpersonal experience. Correspondingly, the concept of Realization came to mean realization within shared human existence. This is reflected in the series of articles from 1918. A new stage in the maturation of the dialogical worldview is represented in a series of lectures, "Religion as Presence," which Buber gave in January–March 1922 in the Frankfurt Lehrhaus. Rivka Horwitz, whose scholarship first illuminated what was implicit in this series, points out that the concept of Realization appears in these lectures together with other expressions of the Thou-world and as a synonym for the Thou-relationship. She points out that a short time afterward, in *I and Thou*, the tendency is evident to present dialogical concepts and expressions under the concept of Realization. Perhaps it was Rosenzweig who influenced the change in Buber's relation to this concept.[69]

Several concepts occupy a fundamental place in Buber's dialogical thought, having a status of their own and at the same time fitting in as members of a structure. We have become acquainted with a number of them in the discussion of the complex of articles formed in 1918. To these concepts must be added first of all the concept of responsibility, which had not received a significant role in Buber's writings in the first and second decades of the century. Hence this concept is different from all the other concepts and also from those into which new meanings were cast later on, or whose emphases were changed.[70]

In *I and Thou* the concept of responsibility was given only a marginal place. It was first presented as having meaning beyond the individual and his individuality, as a bearer of dialogical value. In that work Buber alludes to "the infinite responsibility" (which is responsibility before God), stating that it is realized when a person acquires "the power of loving responsibility."[71] And for him "love does not cling to an I, . . . it is between I and You."[72]

When Buber speaks from the distance of many years of the conversion that took place within him, he mentions its results as expressing "claim and responsibility" embodied in "each mortal hour's fullness."[73] Implied here is the conception of two realities, one being the substantiality that comes into being with every passing hour, and the other, built upon the first, is the actuality of the world of the spirit. The metahistorical level comprises an authority above the life of the present and is based on "distinguishing between what is conditioned by the times and what is timeless."[74] The claims of the spirit are embodied in value concepts (one of them being Responsibility), which are supposed to give a direction beyond the life of the present to historical reality.

Perhaps because the concept of responsibility did not have a place of its own at the beginning of the dialogical stage, Buber saw the need to base special discussions upon it, mainly during the 1930s: the section entitled "Responsibility" is included in one of the three "topics" of which the essay "Dialogue" is composed.[75] One of the six chapters of the work *The Question of the Single One* (1936) bears the title, "The Single One in Responsibility."[76] Similarly, discussion is devoted to this topic in one of his articles on the subject of education.[77] It seems that the concept of responsibility began to occupy a place of its own in Buber's dialogical thought in early 1929, in an article dedicated to its value.[78] This article was reworked and expanded to become the basis for the section "Responsibility" in the first version of the work "Dialogue," which was published in that year.[79]

Personal responsibility, i.e., a person's responsibility for his life, has two aspects in Buber's thought. One aspect is Decision, which is situated in the depths of a person's essence, and in its context Buber frequently uses the term Conscience.[80] The second aspect is Response to the other, the "other" implying both the human other and the divine: "Responsibility presupposes one who addresses me primarily, that is, from the realm independent of myself, and to whom I am answerable."[81]

From the time when Buber began to develop this concept in the 1930s until the end of his life, he repeatedly emphasizes that Responsibility has only a concrete and obligatory meaning, which is embodied in "real responding."[82] The realization of Responsibility in a life of dialogue anchors itself in the reality of life—where Buber wants the principles of his teachings to take root. Responsibility to the other and responsibility to reality are the same: "We respond to the moment, but at the same time we respond on its behalf, we answer for it."[83]

In Buber's conception, Responsibility is bound not only to Decision but also, on the other hand, to Realization. This triangle of concepts—Decision, Responsibility, and Realization—resonates especially in his articles about Jewish existence and the paths of Zionism. It seems that only in his article "Education and Weltanschauung" (1935) do all three of the concepts appear in combination in a direct presentation. After treating each of the three independently, Buber combines them and concludes that education that responds to the needs of the hour must elevate man "to the test and to withstanding it, to Responsibility, to Decision, to Realization."[84]

Between lived reality and the guiding principles beyond it

In his dialogical writing Buber upholds the unique vitality of every situation, proclaiming: "It is the sense of the situation that is to be lived in all its antinomies—only lived—and lived ever again, ever anew, unpredictably."[85] In the dialogical stage of his career it often seems that his declarations sanctify lived reality and that they contain reminders of the mystical stage.

The sanctification of lived reality appears together with the rejection of "the world continuum in space and time." Thus Buber alludes, as it were, to the duality of aspect he presents in *I and Thou*: "The It-world hangs together in space and time. / The You-world does not hang together in space and time."[86]

During the mystical stage Buber did not particularly strive for self-realization within the context of shared human experience. In the dialogical stage, by contrast, he proclaims the existential reality embedded in the realm of dialogue. The reality of "this world" is embodied in his dialogical writings in terms such as "concrete reality," "present realization," and "what confronts me."

His dialogical worldview is not supposed to be at all "subjective." It does not arise from emotions or feelings within the individual, which are then projected onto the reality of things, but rather it is the meaning that the individual discerns within reality. It grows out of dialogue with reality:

> For the most part we understand only gradually the decisive experiences we have in our relation with the world. First we accept what they seem to offer us, we express it, we weave it into a "view," and then think we are aware of our world. But we come to see that what we look on in this view is only an appearance. Not that our experiences have deceived us. But we had turned them to our use, without penetrating to their heart. What is it that teaches us to penetrate to their heart? Deeper experience.[87]

Conclusion

Even in the midst of the mystical stage of his spiritual biography, Buber was not satisfied with addressing experiential reality and basing himself upon personal experience. Such a view was presented in his article "Buddha" (1907) but was not typical of his thinking even when he was in the throes of mystical yearnings.[88] He wanted to dwell in a "great" internal reality, but not at the cost of negating external reality, and he wished to be given over to a Realization together with acknowledgment of an Orientation. The central embodiments of his worldview during the mystical stage figure in his article, "With a Monist" and in the book, *Daniel*, both of whose central concepts have been discussed above. The distinction between Realization and Orientation allowed him, among other things, to indicate the need for a dimension of theoretical, abstract, or scientific thought. And the acknowledgment of this dimension gave him a basis, or served as a means of (self-)justification, for the very use of these concepts and of conceptual structures in general.

The many contexts of discussion in which Buber glorifies lived reality, whether it possesses decidedly mystical traits or whether it is embedded in the realm of dialogue, cannot fully express his worldview.

He fears "man's fleeing before the taxing infinity of the moment into a uniform system of Is and Ought."[89] He states that "the ordered world is not the [proper] order of the world," and at the same time he recognizes the importance of systematic thinking in the sciences and in a state's legal system. However, he demands of the orders in the spiritual world what he demands of the orders of the state: recognition "of culture as the expression of those inner forces which also bear it, the state."[90] The spirit of these words is consistent with a short article that he published in honor of Gershom Scholem's sixtieth birthday in late 1957; in the article he writes:

> Gershom Scholem founded a new field of philological-historical knowledge. He has given us a historical approach to the Kabbalah and to those messianic movements which emerged from it, an approach based upon authoritative knowledge of the texts. Thus Scholem succeeded especially in showing us the countenance of Sabbatian reality, for the first time revealing it to us as it was. Now we may discuss what happened there, and speak words which are concerned with cognizance.[91]

Implied by these remarks is a distinction between the philological-historical approach and personal interpretative understanding. This distinction is very similar to the duality presented in the introduction to his Hebrew book, *Be-Fardes Ha-Hasidut* (In the orchard of Hasidism), which is based on the distinction between, on the one hand, "combinations of thought" and "knowledge of ideas" (both of which are dealt with in the context of abstract discussion in general, as well as in the specific area of the scientific study of Hasidism), and, on the other hand, "the knowledge of Hasidic truth, as an embodiment of truth deriving from life, as a unique way of living human life."[92] Buber's own interest is concentrated on his personal approach to the living reality of historical phenomena, in the search for the "message"[93] in them, yet he does not refrain from referring to the discoveries of scientific research. This, fundamentally, is the hermeneutic of a creative thinker who discovers principles consistent with his worldview in the sources and in historical phenomena. Buber's approach is founded upon assumptions that were presented as early as his article on Jewish science in 1901.

THE QUALITY OF HIS UTILIZATION
OF "PURIFIED CONCEPTUALISM"

Buber's negative attitude to systematic and methodical thinking is not to be placed on the same footing as his complex relationship to concepts. The references to conceptualism in his writing are generally principled and do not appear in the context of his use of concepts in the processes of molding and constructing his thought. The point of departure for his relation to them is implicit in a letter of 17 March 1917, in which he responds to the invitation of the International Institute for Philosophy in Amsterdam to establish an "Academy for the Creation of a Uniform Conceptual Language." The task envisioned was to create "words of spiritual value for the speech of Western peoples," which would be freed of ambiguity. In rejecting this plan, he states: "The generation, the creation of words, is . . . one of the most mysterious processes of the life of the spirit. . . . The coming into being of words is a mystery that is consummated in the enkindled, open soul of the world creating, world discovering man." Therefore, he continues, a public body "can and may assume only the goal of purification of the word. One must combat the misuse of the great ancient words but not teach the use of new words."[94]

This basic attitude resonates in the lecture that he gave ten years later in Jerusalem, where he points out the need to clarify and purify the concepts of the humanities while learning them. According to him these fields "are encumbered by unclear concepts. . . . Study must begin with criticism of the concepts. A 'customs house' for concepts must be established, which would not permit any concept to pass without examining its true content."[95] The clarification of concepts, he says elsewhere, "begins with the dominion of the Socratic system, which intends to enhance human existence by improving consciousness." Clarifications will lead to reform. In this context he quotes Confucius: "In a place where concepts are not correct, words are not fitting, and when words are not fitting, actions are not done."[96]

The admission of the necessity of concepts in the area of the humanities, which is implied in the foregoing remarks, is accompanied not only by an indication of the need for their frequent and constant examination but also, and perhaps prior to that, by the determination that there is an existence liberated from the uncondemnable necessity of conceptual thinking. In an article of 1918 he argues against concepts that are liable to petrify religiosity: "Religious truth is not a conceptual abstraction but has existential relevance."[97] These words are consistent with the spirit of his distinction, found in the same article, between living and creative faith (religiosity) and the principles of faith bound into a system of obligations and commandments (religion).

Buber's attitude toward concepts is clarified in his responses to questions posed to him and also in remarks made during public debates. Thus, for example, in response to a question he distinguished between the "realm of concepts" and "the realm of meeting."[98] It is also noteworthy that he stated: "Concepts step between myself and the Thou, the other person. Sometimes I may have to use concepts, but we should avoid them as much as possible."[99]

Buber's view entails reserved admission of the importance of concepts, after relegating them to the world of the It, to the area of the I-It relation.

The essence of his relation to conceptualism is found, I believe, in the statement that "Concepts are formed from our highest experience of a certain kind, which we recognize as being repeated."[100]

THE CHARACTER OF HIS CONCEPTS

So far we have been discussing Buber's attitude toward general, abstract concepts. However, in the following chapters we will be discussing other concepts that are not identical in any way to those which have already been considered. The concepts referred to below are those which occupy a place in more than one area of his work, and belong to more than a single period of time. We have seen above that concepts began to take a focal position in his writings from the first decade of the century and that, with one exception—the concept of Responsibility—they are found, with changes in linguistic dress and metamorphoses in meaning, both during the early mystical stage of his thinking and also in its dialogical stage.[101] In the following chapters of this work, we shall become acquainted with additional concepts that in their entirety comprise the basis of his later thought. Buber does not refer his readers to his concepts, he does not explicitly state their fundamental place in his writing (which is what I deal with in most of the chapters of this study), nor does he refer directly to their general identifying traits. It is my intention to elicit, locate, and reconstruct these basic traits.

Buber's concepts were consolidated against the background of tension between his experiential subjectivism and the theoretical and abstract tendency that attended it.[102] There is an indissoluble connection between his spiritual personality and the subjects of his thinking; as he said, "I know that my interpretation, like any interpretation, is conditioned by my existence."[103] He defines this conditioned connection as a relation between the "Matter" and the "Personality."[104] This duality is reflected in the ambivalence that characterizes his attitude toward Max Weber (1864–1920). He expresses deep respect for Weber's personality and makes use of his objective-scientific concepts, with which he agrees, although he is in confrontation with Weber's approach. He writes:

> I shall never forget—it was about 1910—after a lecture on Jewish piety which I had delivered before Heidelberg students, Max Weber, requested by the young people to open the discussion, stepped up to me and asked me whether it were agreeable to me if he spoke now; he could, to be sure, offer "only science about religion and not religion." Also my book here is not intended to express faith, but a

knowledge about it; it asserts admittedly that one can possess a knowledge about faith legitimately only when the eye remains directed upon the cosmic margin, never given as object, as which faith is given a habitation.[105]

In this context Buber points out that his "view [is] essentially different" from that of Weber,[106] whom he calls an "eminent man," saying of himself that he "made use of Weber's concepts and ideas."[107]

In the year when the aforementioned preface to *The Kingship of God* was written, Buber devoted an essay to sharpening and emphasizing his conception by means of the distinction between two kinds of consciousness: (1) theoretical and abstract consciousness that dwells "in the untouchable province of pure ideation," that is, "reality framed by thought";[108] and (2) consciousness that is not awareness bounded by itself but rather constitutes an expression of all of a person's powers and behaviors. This latter consciousness is directed at the reality of life and its questions derive from "the basis of human existence, situation and present."[109]

This distinction also clarifies the connection between distinctively Buberian concepts and concepts that are entirely theoretical; the latter "lack valuation" because they are not necessarily directed at the reality of life.

It seems to me that the matrix of concepts at the foundation of the edifice of Buber's thought is meant to express the "spirit" in its relations with historical and social reality. All references to its substance can be found in the writings of the second stage of his thought, that of Dialogue. He does not comprehend the spirit as part of social reality, but rather as a kind of partner and interlocutor. It dwells above the life of the present as the source of its authority.[110] It is not an abstract idea, but rather an experience that bears a mission toward life.

The relation between spirit and reality, however, is not unidirectional. Buber refers to the action of life upon the spirit no less than the action of the spirit upon life. The spirit "does not plunge into life and remain there, but it returns to its own sphere and renews itself there by itself, by the influence from below," as he wrote in a Hebrew article from the time of World War II.[111] This is also the goal of his value concepts. Their nature emerges, among other things, from the negation of what he calls "the sphere of precise conceptualization,"[112] in which concepts in their abstractness are severed from the relationship of responsibility to the depths of earthly human existence. Philosophical thought grounds itself upon an "objective thought-continuum ... with a static system of concepts." According to Buber, it has completely "abandoned the relationship with reality of life."[113] The value concepts that indicate the system of his thought are entirely different. They are not static, nor are they subject to systematic lawfulness.

It can be said of almost every one of Buber's value concepts (I shall point out the exceptions in the following section) that it is "a living force, a formative force, growing and active, a force that adapts the materials which are absorbed by it and shapes them both into the figure of personal life and into the figure of social life."[114] We have seen that there is a mutual relation between his concepts, as embodiments of the powers of the spirit, and historical and social reality. To the same degree there is also a mutual relationship between them and the individual who is embedded in his society and culture.

The purified concepts lacking value—which Buber condemns— could be called "inert ideas," to use an expression of A. N. Whitehead, who defines such values as those which one absorbs in one's mind without actually using or examining them, and without putting them into new combinations.[115]

The importance of Buber's concepts may be seen in the assumption that "permission is given" to man's creative and formative power. Thus the value concepts constitute a yardstick, and every individual who uses them imprints them with the image of his personality and path. Buber's distinctive concepts are meant to serve as signposts in the processes of self-examination of both the individual and the community in their determination of the direction they will take and in their realization thereof. Their purpose is to provide shared ideas, which are meant to be used as guidelines for ways of life. They also have an abstract and formal function, the introduction of a unifying and organizing dimension in his antisystematic approach.[116]

THE ESSENCE OF HIS STRUCTURES

Most of the focal concepts in Buber's system of ideas are not grasped by him singly and by themselves, but rather as erecting dual structures—both latent and manifest—with all sorts of relations existing between their members. This even holds true of the first manifestations of his thought at the start of the twentieth century.[117]

The role that he destined for the value concepts discussed above is the same as that of his dual structures. Like the structures that he formulated, the concepts upon which he stamped the impress of his conception have no static or unequivocal essence; rather, everyone who uses them adapts them to his own character, as it were (one person's Realization is not similar to someone else's, nor is anyone's inner vortex like that of another person's, etc.).[118] . Everyone interprets the value concepts of his society in his own way. And, according to Buber, this also applies to the way people join them together and weave them into structures.

These are the structures that have a place beyond a certain area of thought and a given time period in Buber's view:

- Distance *(Urdistanz)* – Relation *(Beziehung)*
- Vortex *(Wirbel)* – Direction *(Richtung)*
- Moment *(Augenblick)* – Eternity *(Ewigkeit)*
- I-Thou *(Ich-Du)* – I-It *(Ich-Es)*

Each of these pairs has an early form or at least the roots of crystallization in Buber's early thought, and they were developed fully only after the start of the dialogical stage in his spiritual biography. Each of these structures is represented in various guises, and I shall try to provide a full portrayal of three of them in separate chapters. There we follow the processes of weaving together and clarification of the value tendencies embodied within them. No separate chapter is devoted to the well-known and central structure of I-Thou – I-It, since most Buber scholars treat the I-Thou – I-It duality very fully, and there is little reason to rehearse again their conclusions.

Not until the 1950s—that is, at the sunset of Buber's life—do his writings seem to show indications of his dual conceptual schemes in the guise of structures. These indications are brief and made in passing. In a work dedicated to the duality of I-Thou – I-It, it is presented as "the double structure of human existence itself. . . . The two basic modes of our existence within being, they are the two basic modes of our existence in general."[119] In another work he argues that it is impossible to relate to "the dynamic of lived life" that takes place between the spheres of I-Thou and I-It from a systematic point of view,[120] and this statement serves as the background for his statement that "no system was suitable for what I had to say. Structure was suitable for it, a compact structure but not one that joined everything together."[121] In another source from the same era, he points to only one of the members of the aforementioned duality as a structure.[122]

Although the central structures listed above underlie the presentations of Buber's ideas in all the fields and genres of his idiom, it is essentially only in his philosophical and anthropological-philosophical writings (and in his view philosophizing had to be anthropological) that he refers to them as such. And most of his few references to his structures are not explicit, nor are they clearly indicated; frequently it is up to the reader-researcher to locate and identify the structures implicit in the fabric of a discussion.

Occasionally Buber points out the basic duality of his structures, and while so doing he presents it as having general application. Thus, for example, he states, in presenting the "I-Thou – I-It" duality: "The world is twofold for man in accordance with his twofold attitude. The attitude of man is twofold in accordance with the two basic words he can speak. The basic words are not single words but word pairs."[123] Twenty years later this general applicability becomes clearer in the formula presenting the world of relationship and the world of Its as "the two basic modes of our existence." In the context of the dual structure of "Distance – Relation," Buber speaks of a "twofold movement" in human existence in general, saying that "the principle of human life is not simple but twofold."[124]

He is far from intending that his structures should be based on a system or structure with static principles. Not once did he try to place them within a single arrangement and to bind them together as having functions with a dimension of correlation or of complementarity.

An existential approach to a transitory situation is formed in every one of the structures mentioned above, at the same time as a gaze beyond it; in each of them there is emphasis on processes occuring within the lived moment, accompanied by a perspective vision of the living movement:

• Someone who concentrates on his individuality, on Distance, which is the area of individualization, must, in Buber's view, realize that the formation of personality is not an end in itself but rather a stage prior to a life of Relationship, to dialogical existence (see the chapter "Distance – Relation").
• Someone subject to the Vortex of his innerness should

see Direction on the hidden horizon, toward which he should strive (see the chapter "Vortex — Direction").

• Someone living in the Moment must be guided by orientation toward Eternity (see the chapter "Moment – Eternity").

• Someone dwelling in a dialogical existence should know that human life is impossible without the existence of the world of Its, which is the I-It relationship.

Each of Buber's structural schemes with which we are concerned includes at least one member (= concept) embodying a longed-for destination. This does not refer to an ideal existence but rather to an attainable reality. Deep in this longed-for destination is a beckoning and impelling power. According to Max Kadushin, every value concept of any given society contains a drive for realization, and its image is the image of the individual and the society that adopt it and strive to attain it. Hence it will be understood that each of these structures is based on breaking through the narrow limits of the individual in himself.

Each of these structures provides a viewpoint and a relationship toward human life and social existence. In each of the structures is a dimension of inclusiveness, not of exclusion.

Each of the structures is made to grow according to a tendency imprinted on it by its creator. Each determines the character of its members and the nature of the relations between them. They present and express dynamic life processes, with their polysemous complexity. Hence each of Buber's structures has its own typology, which is susceptible to elucidation by means of locating the relations between its members. I shall attempt to indicate them:

1. Correlation between two members, in which the first is the background and preparation for the second, exists in the structure "Distance – Relation." Buber calls it a "twofold movement which is of such a kind that the one movement is the presupposition of the other."[125]

2. A dichotomy, in which the two members cannot coexist at the same time as two dimensions of reality, exists between the members of the structure "Vortex – Direction." The first member serves as a background and preparation for the decision, by means of which a person transcends the realm of inner chaos (the Vortex).

3. There is the possibility of a dialogical relationship between the members of the structure "Moment – Eternity." This dialogical relationship does not contradict the conception of Eternity as being a yardstick for the Moment, as being the object of ideal, superhuman direction.

4. The dimension of complementarity between the members exists within the "I-Thou – I-It" structure. It is impossible to remain, for better or worse, in an existence that is stamped uniquely with the imprint of either of these members.

There are partial overlaps between the members of some of the structures, and I shall mention them:

• The concept that is meant to embody dialogue constitutes a member of three of the structures. Its meaning changes according to the character of the structure, one of whose components it embodies. Dialogue is embodied, respectively, as "I-Thou," "Direction," and "Relation." There is also a considerable presence of the member "Moment." The assumption implicit in many contexts of discussion in which the term "Moment" appears is that it is an existential situation that properly expresses the realization of a life of Relation.

• There is some overlap between the structure "Distance – Relation" and that of "Vortex – Direction." The point of departure in both of them is the inner world of the individual: in one it is "distance" or the "originator instinct," and in the second it is "vortex" or "chaos." In both of these structures the first stage constitutes the ground for the growth and becoming of the second. The first member of "Vortex – Direction" expresses negative value, or what is liable to be negative if one does not transcend it. Both Relation and Direction represent proper human experience, the realization of a person in "die dialogische Existenz" (the dialogical existence).[126]

The structures of "Distance – Relationship" and "Vortex – Direction" are bounded in the human world, in inner personal and interpersonal processes. The other two, "Instant – Eternity" and "I-Thou – I-It," have a dialogical dimension with "the eternal You" or "eternity." These typological gropings will be fleshed out in their respective chapters.

The concepts and their structural bonds give Buber's worldview clear "directions,"[127] which can be interpreted in every area of his thought. It seems that in his untiring effort to reject systems and principles of thought, he constructed a kind of antisystematic system. Fundamentally one may say that neither current concerns nor existential situations of unique character are what aroused a unique and personal response in him; the lived situation that he glorifies is not, essentially, closed within itself. It is interwoven with a "structure of situations" and stands within it, equipped with the assumptions of a consolidated worldview; on the basis of the conceptual and structural formulations of his worldview, Buber responds to personal existential situations as well as to matters of historical moment. In the chapters devoted below to his central structures, I shall trace the continuity of this tendency of his spiritual world.

Buber's concepts are very often implicit in his writings, not manifest in a linguistic symbol. Their value content underlies both the contexts of discussion and the consolidations of ideas, without the concept itself being present in them (or represented in them by a term). This is also true of his structures. Frequently a direct and manifest representation of them is absent from his writing, and they are neither indicated nor alluded to, but they provide the underpinnings of his discussions.

7
DISTANCE – RELATION

CREATIVE VITALISM

From the time of its earliest expressions at the beginning of the century, Buber's worldview had been based on elements that were imbued with his personal experiences. He aspired to develop them and to implement them. In a letter to his friend Paula Winkler (the woman he was to marry within less than two years), dated 15 August 1899, he used language characteristic of the mood guiding him:

> Why must I say that the time has not yet come? . . . Perhaps the flash of lightning will yet come which will bring out my essence.[1]

From the outset, abstract principles as well as general concepts were alien to him. He was inclined toward personal creativity, denying systems and principles while emphasizing emotion and intuition. He rejected scientific analysis, advocating vitalism and rebellion against the logos.[2]

The spiritual environment in which Buber came of age was marked by a polar tension between the individual's "inner law" and "external and borrowed patterns of thought."[3] Human action was viewed as "deriving from people's spiritual condition and from their mutual relationships." This thought, which is found in a letter to Gustav Landauer dated 9 April 1907,[4] resonates in the first of Buber's early *Lectures on Judaism*, where he states: "The forces that carve man's life are his inwardness and his environment."[5] He called the interconnected elements of this duality "experience" and "existence."[6]

The experiential subjectivism in which Buber anchored himself was a refuge from a worldview that no longer offered "existential security,"[7] and it was meant to provide a point of departure for a revival from fin-de-siècle decadence. In his essays and articles, the creative individual is the object of yearnings and is destined to provide the foundation for a new conception of reality, in which the drive for personal renewal is the basis for a "renewal of Judaism."

The duality which we have noted—human inwardness and the world surrounding it—is not coincidental in Buber's world. Its conceptual posture was not created, as we have already had occasion to note, ex nihilo. Buber's knowledge and concern were concentrated on "experience," whereas he did not view "existence" as being an entity in its own right; for him the surrounding world was, essentially, a platform for individual creativity, and it was not apprehended as embodying obligations or as the object of responsibility.

As early as 1900, in a lecture that he delivered to a circle in Berlin that year,[8] Buber, who was then twenty-two, advocated free creativity. This was an expression of the inner affective experience *(Erlebnis)* of a personality seeking the joy of giving *"in the greatest freedom,"*[9] beyond the patterns of life, laws, and religious dogma. In that lecture he contrasted the "old and new community." The object of his yearnings was the latter, in which the goal of life was creative, as opposed to the goal in the old society, which was utilitarian. His ideal was "the growth and free creativity of the personality."[10] At the base of the dream picture that he presents to his listeners is a "pure community," in which the power of creativity raises life to the level of a work of art, harmonious and enchanted.[11]

A short time after delivering this lecture, with its decidedly anarchistic character, Buber gave this fundamental approach Jewish and historical consolidation. In an article dedicated to the work of the Jewish artist Lesser Uri, he expressed the inclusive duality of the "inner" and the "exterior" by anchoring it in the "Jewish historical idea: the image of the destruction of Jerusalem in the artist's heart."[12] This outline was also spelled out in the duality of "soul" (or "inwardness") and "cosmos," which was represented by

> an aged man, covering his face with his hand. A man whose soul— erect, mourns quietly, knowing how to gather the power of resis-

tance and also to live it in his inwardness. . . . Perhaps he is one of
the long chain of those Jews . . . who leave the ghetto and direct
their steps directly towards the cosmos, without any transition.[13]

Buber used this duality to present the fate of the individual and that of
his nation as interconnected; he pointed out that Lesser Uri "experienced the fate of his people, within his soul," and he expressed it in his
work.[14] Even then, early in the century, this duality was crystallized in
a clear structure based on two axes, of which one pole embodied the
inner essence, while the second embodied its realization in the exterior
world.

The yearning for the actualization of inner strength by means of
creativity was also contained in Buber's Zionist articles. He lauded
and exalted creativity, even attributing sanctity to it: "To create! The
Zionist, who feels the full sanctity of that word and experiences it,
stands before my eyes upon the highest degree."[15] The historical and
the individual mingled together in this dramatic appeal (which was
removed from the dimension of a true personal obligation by mystical
obscurity). He then continues:

> To create new values, new enterprises—which were bound for such
> a long period to the fetters of non-productivity—this is the ideal of
> the Jewish people, and this comes from the depths of its primordial
> individuality, from the particular and incomparable force of its blood!
> To erect monuments of its essence! To let its nature resonate in a
> new vision of its life. To raise up a new form against infinity and to
> give a new shape to latent possibilities! To allow new beauty to
> blaze up, to let a new star rise in the enchanted sky of eternities![16]

Buber did not merely accord a central place to "creativity" in his lectures and articles. In 1903 he wrote a small book, which was never
published, entitled *Creativity as Redemption or Development and Revolution*.[17]

A direct line leads from the aforementioned Zionist article dating
from the beginning of the century to his early lectures on Judaism,
which date from the end of its first decade. They too bring out the
image of the individual as a "great creator" and a "hero":

> Once the great doer expected to alter the face of the world with his
> deed, and to inform all becoming with his own will. He did not feel
> that he was subject to the conditions of the world, for he was

grounded in the unconditionality *(Unbedingtheit)* of God, whose word he sensed in the decisions he made as clearly as he felt the blood in his veins. This confidence in the suprahuman has been undermined; man's consciousness of God and deed had already been stifled in his cradle; all one could hope for was to become the exponent of some small "progress." And whoever can no longer desire the impossible will be able to achieve nothing more than the all-too-possible. Thus, the power of the spirit was replaced by busyness, and the might of sacrifice by bargaining skill. And even the longing for a new heroic life was corrupted by this tendency of the time. The most tragic example of this corruption is probably the man who, though he longed for such a life more intensely than any other man, could not free himself from the dogma of evolution: Friedrich Nietzsche.[18]

In the spirit of this approach, Buber called for a "renewal of Judaism" through a spiritual revolution.

Buber's view of Judaism and his identity as a Zionist touched upon each other only lightly and without creating a sense of obligation. In this regard, his article "He and We" is interesting. In this article Buber presents a confrontation between the path embodied in the personality of Herzl and that of diaspora Jews (with whom Buber identified himself). Speaking of the diaspora Jew, he said, "For the man of problems, existence is given in a form full of contradictions, which demand correction by him and which may be corrected only in what is above nature and not in experiential reality."[19] Hence, the spiritualization of the diaspora can be reformed only through Zionist earthliness. However, the writer of these sentences had inner affective experience *(Erlebnis)* in mind rather than the concrete reality of life on earth. The "problematic situation" that concerned him was primarily that of "blocking the creative power." He said explicitly: "The soil of the Land of Israel will not renew us, if we do not renew ourselves from within. It can only strengthen, fix, complete. *However, there can be renewal through will.* All creative Jews have known this."[20] He perceived the liberation of the "creative power" as a channel for self-realization, which obligated one to be faithful to oneself and not to deviate (from oneself) in order to share in a common vision. Everything, both ultimately and from the start, revolved around the individual and his objects of longing. Along with "creativity" went "greatness," "longings," "expectation," "happiness," and "unity."[21]

Even the "Jewish religiosity" that Buber advocated was identified by him with "the creative foundation" in the personality, which permits every generation to renew, and be renewed in, its quest for its own God. This is in contrast with "religion," which is founded and based upon a system of obligations that passes from generation to generation. "Religiosity is man's sense of wonder and adoration, an ever anew becoming. . . . [It] starts anew with every young person, shaken to his very core by the mystery." In contrast, "religion" leans on a static system that "wants to force him into a system stabilized for all time."[22]

Fertile spontaneity was henceforth the basis of Buber's religiosity. He depended upon the foregoing distinction even in his dialogical writings and in his later articles about Judaism. One noteworthy example was included in a lecture he delivered at the Free Jewish House of Learning in Frankfurt in 1934, where he said:

> In a living tradition it is not possible to draw a line between preserving and producing. The work of concretization takes place spontaneously, and that person is honest and faithful who utters words he had never heard as though they had come to him.[23]

During the first years of the century Buber regarded the laying bare of the creative foundation of the Jewish people as the central ambition of his generation. In an article he devoted to a portrait of Berthold Feiwel he describes the time of "their common youth" in the Zionist movement as "the heroic period in the history of Zionism. . . . The time we were given to live we felt truly to be a heroic time. This was not only a time of great hope, but also a time of great initiative, truly a time of commencement."[24]

This account does not lack overtones of romanticism. It describes his friend and partner as a "romantic of the present" and his friends as children of a "new spring" who were prepared for an "active sacrifice" in a dreamlike reality, that which preceded another reality, the reality of realization, into which they later entered. "We wished," he said, "to reveal to the Jews and to the whole world the creative power which dwells within our people." The people's creative power is none other than the combination or concentration that comes into being in their creative enterprise together; this was then embodied above all in the revelation of the individual in spiritual and artistic activity.

Sh. H. Bergmann calls the ideal that aroused Feiwel and his comrades, among whom Buber was the most prominent, "the aesthetic ideal of Zionism." However, he made it clear that, although this artistic-aesthetic expression occupied an important place within their Zionism, their ideal was mainly that of "the people's coming into being, the encounter of eastern European Jews who create out of their rootedness in the nation and the tradition, and western European Jews, who draw upon European culture—moving towards a modern Jewish national ideal."[25]

In a letter to Jakob Wassermann (dated 12 December 1912), Buber seized upon one of Wassermann's assumptions regarding the Oriental man in order to present him as "a man who creates himself." He even compared him to "God," for, similarly, "he distinguishes between light and darkness and makes a firmament above the water."[26]

Buber also continued expressing this view prominently in his writings that were devoid of Jewish connotations. In his philosophical work *Daniel*, creation and implementation were raised to the same level. The "creative man" was praised as one who bears "the power to create and to implement."[27] Very frequently inner essence was not only a point of departure for the expression of Buber's creativity but also its goal. However, this tendency and the tendency to view creativity as a passageway to outer existence subsisted together within his world.

Even the assumptions of his Zionist worldview were formulated upon a matrix of vitalism and of yearnings for self-realization. Did Buber's view also include a message regarding the concrete content of self-realization implying personal responsibility? This question should be addressed in connection with interpretations of Buber's conception of creativity during the years when his dialogical thought was coming into being. His expressions of this conception were directed towards the substance of concrete life and the responsibility connected with it. I shall deal with this topic in the following section.

THE EMERGENCE OF THE DUAL STRUCTURE: "PERSONAL
CREATIVITY — COMMUNITY" IN THE ARTICLES OF 1918–21

Personal creativity was also accorded a primary place in Buber's conception at the same time that his dialogical thought was beginning to blossom. From that time on, the interpersonal and social element begins to occupy a place alongside it (though this may not yet be identified with the element of dialogue). In early 1918 he published the article

"The Conquest of the Land of Israel,"[28] around the time when he composed a first draft of *I and Thou*, the work that was to mature over the following five years.[29] This article shows Buber's Zionist viewpoint as identical with that of the Labor Zionists and pioneering settlers. The "young pioneers" are, in his eyes, "the sincere, the straightforward, the brave," who conquer the Land of Israel "by labor throughout life and with the investment of their entire personality." Observing from afar, he praises the values of personal self-realization, which are reflected in his concept of "creativity." The object of his longings is a "dictatorship of the creative spirit."[30] If in his articles from the early part of the century creativity expressed the individual's self-realization within his individuality, now it is identified with the "labor" of the pioneers. Both in the body of the article and in its conclusion labor is presented as the embodiment of the "creative spirit." The concluding sentences emphasize the transformations of the concept of creativity, while at the same time they are linked with personal-pioneering self-realization: "And to create that essence, which we are capable of creating. The creative spirit, creative labor, the sacrifice of the creator— this is what is demanded."[31]

At that time Buber leaned towards giving the creative axis a Zionist connotation. This inclination is reflected in his presentation of it as the polar opposite of the axis of diaspora life, which is embodied, for him, in "the spirit of commerce." "In our soul," he states, "two creatures are struggling, two nations: . . . the essence of creativity and the essence of commerce." He calls for the "extirpation of the spirit of commerce by the spirit of creation."[32]

In "The Conquest of the Land of Israel" he also makes one mention of the concept "community," meaning social cooperation accompanied by "labor." However the combination of the element of labor (i.e., creativity) and that of social cooperation is as yet external, not organic. It is not yet a duality in which there is a relationship between its components.

During the year in which the foregoing article was written Buber wrote three of his better-known articles about Judaism: "Zion and Youth," "The Holy Way," and Herut." In that year he also wrote an article called "Community," which is universalist in tone (without any Jewish or Zionist resonance), though it is linked to the other three articles, forming a single unit.[33] Two of these articles, "The Holy Way" and "Zion and Youth," were first delivered as speeches in May 1918.

The first contains repeated instances of phrases that emphasize creativity and social cooperation, without, however presenting these two elements as playing a shared role. The last part of the article lists the elements that are "stamped in the inner history" of Judaism. Among them are "labor" and "congregation" (meaning the basic cell of society that is based on the coming into being of *direct* relationships among people").[34] However, these too were not given a prominent place, nor was any particular connection between them indicated.

In "Zion and Youth," by contrast, one notes a tendency to combine the values of labor and congregation, even though they are not discussed together directly nor at the same time. The inner foundation for the realization of these two elements is embodied in the duality of the values of personal creativity and communal bonds, but this duality had not yet crystallized into a conceptual structure.[35] The values of (personal) creativity and communion (among human beings and in the congregation) together provide the fertile source for the ideas that are set forth in this article.

The third of these well-known articles about Judaism which Buber wrote in 1918 is "Herut: An Essay on Youth and Religion." The discussion there is based on the concepts of "creativity" and "communion" in their application to the question of faith. The basic assumption is the need for "awakening youth's own latent religion."[36] The creative power of the Jews and the renewal of their faith are presented together; personal creativity is seen as implementing the "primal forces" of the people that are embodied in their inner being.[37] The faith that creates the individual and the faith that creates the people are the same faith; and thus creativity and social bonding are present in organic unity. However, in the 1918 article the communal dimension is still not equal in value to the dimension of creativity. Very gradually these two dimensions are given a common role and become reciprocally connected with each other. Thus, for example, in Buber's speech at the congress of Ha-Po'el ha-Tza'ir - Tze'irei Tzion in Prague (1920), he stated: "There is no creative life in the pure ego, all creativity necessarily requires a 'Thou.'"[38] A year later, in more concrete fashion, in his speech to the Twelfth Zionist Congress in Karlsbad (in the framework of the first of his two speeches there, on 2 September 1921), he said: "Our settlement, which is meant only to save our people and to renew it, . . . is intended to be creative work of free people upon communal land."[39] He stated that a "congregation of young people" was to be the standard bearer of the idea of the conquest of the Land of Israel by means of "organic and non-doctrinaire socialism,"[40] and this statement has the connotation of the concept of "community." The social character of Zionism is significant, in his opinion, not only inwardly but also outwardly. Upon this foundation a "renewed humanity" will arise in organic fashion, and it will give shape to the new Hebrew nationality in the Land of Israel. Buber saw the socialist character of "our national aspiration" as the "guarantee [that] solidarity will be created between us and the laboring Arab people based on true interests which will do away with the oppositions deriving from momentary misunderstanding. Out of recognition of this bond, feelings of caution and mutual regard will be formed in the hearts of members of both nations. Only then will the great encounter between the two nations arise once again."[41] Here a segment of Buber's faith regarding the development of community is translated into political language: the growth of a "commonwealth in the manner of the bonding of cells," and from it, in widening organic circles, into "mankind as an association."[42] This takes place "by means of the formation and subsistence of relations between one person and another, between one group and another, and also between one nation and another."[43]

The link between work or creativity and interpersonal relations (making community grow) that shaped Buber's Zionist views toward the end of the second decade of the century is similar to the link between the element of realization and the social element. We see this, for example, in his statement that "the Jew's drive for realization . . . makes him the authorized assistant in promoting great social change."[44] Within a few years the linking of the values of "creativity" and "community" was to assume the guise of a conceptual structure in his thinking.

At this point it is appropriate to inquire whether these articles from the years immediately following the end of the First World War indeed embody a new relationship to concrete reality and shared human experience, one that is different from his view during the first fifteen years of the century. In other words: are the connotations of the concept of creativity in these articles close to those which characterize that concept in *labor Zionism*, and especially those in the views of members of the Second Aliyah?

Signs of Buber's affinity to the world of labor Zionism (i.e., to the approach of the Workers' Movement of the Land of Israel), had been emerging since 1916. He published writing by A. D. Gordon in *Der*

Jude (the first issue of which was published in April 1916 and contained an article by Gordon called "Arbeit"). Gordon's "Four Letters to the Diaspora" were also first published in Buber's journal in 1917, and they were translated into Hebrew from that source in that very year.[45] Zalman Rubashov-Shazar was working with Buber at that time both as his permanent assistant at the newspaper and also in a clandestine Zionist organization Zion ba-Mishpat Tafdeh (Redeem Zion with Judgment), which Buber led. Later Buber joined the Ha-Po'el Ha-Za'ir party.[46] He identified with the projects of the pioneers and admired A. D. Gordon, who embodied for him the combination of a vision and its fulfillment, of spirit and reality, for which he yearned for many years. However, Buber himself reached the Land of Israel and settled there only a very short time before the outbreak of the Second World War.

During the Second Aliyah (1904–14) utopian visions were formed out of the difficulties of daily life. The "better world" for which the pioneers of that period pined, was woven out of the given time and place, "here, on the earth," as if it were a *utopia in creation*.[47] Their understanding arose out of action without any hiatus between word and deed. In its first year, the leaders of the Second Aliyah, the immigrants of 1904–5, "took upon themselves systems of behavior which were the opposite of the existing ones, and hence there began the dawn of a new reality"[48] that was characterized by "the unity between physical and 'metaphysical' life.[49]

The yearnings of the members of the Second Aliyah for *tikkun olam* (reformation of the world) were combined with their *creative* impulses. Their daily labor demanded all their powers of body and soul, and it was like a holy labor for them, directed beyond itself—to building up the country. At the same time, it was also directed to reconstructing the nation and to making a new man, the main steps on the path toward reformation of the world in general. H. N. Bialik used the biblical phrase "the day of small things" (Zech. 4:10)—meaning persistence in small, colorless actions, day by day, hour by hour—to signify the Jewish-Zionist path that they developed.[50] Every action, every creative act, whether material or spiritual, is imbued with its own intrinsic value and serves a goal that is both distant and invisible. Those who blazed this path, which guided the fulfillment of Zionism from the time of the Second Aliyah until the 1960s, were not merely setting the course of a single stream or one main road for Zionism. Rather their actions should be viewed not only with regard to the history of Zionism but also from the general Jewish-historical view-point. This was Buber's conception, which grew out of his identification with the path of labor Zionism (and with the members of the Second Aliyah): he viewed this path not only as a "direction" guiding toward the future of Zionism but also as an expression of the spirit of Judaism and a way of reforming the world, toward the completion of creation for the sake of all mankind.[51]

The active members of the Second and Third Aliyah were Buber's contemporaries, and some of them belonged to his generation. They were privileged to be at the center of a historical change because *they themselves made a decision and fulfilled* their vision. The identity forged between themselves and their enterprise corresponded to what Buber called the unity between "person" and "cause."[52]

Still, the creative significance of labor is not exhausted in physical work or in productive tendencies alone. Creative work is grasped as an expression of personal fulfillment, a path of visionary life. In A. D. Gordon's view (which is a direct expression of the creative existence, just as, conversely, it influenced that existence), the creative significance of labor is formulated in theoretical fashion as well. "A creative act," Gordon states, "is the secret of life—because every great or small action reflects the world of emanations, of the spirit, of thought, of knowledge, just as the heavenly host is reflected in a drop of water. This is the soul of the life of action. Without that soul there is no living action, and this is the difference between a creative act and a mechanical one."[53] In A. D. Gordon's worldview labor expresses not only the creativity of the individual but also the "creative power of the nation." The significance of this is inconsistent with a differentiation between manual and intellectual labor. Gordon's credo was: "In labor we seek life, both matter and spirit, and we must not sunder what is joined together—material labor in the name of socialism and spiritual labor in the name of nationalism—if we desire to live."[54] The enterprise of Zionist rebirth is viewed as a "living creation" that cannot be cut in two, "just as we do not divide life in two, saying, 'This is matter and this is spirit.'" Creativity takes in all spheres of the nation's life and also that of the individual who is involved with his nation, and all of this finds expression in the project of renewal:

> Our entire spirit living within us, all the powers of our body and spirit, must be repaired. They must find expression in our entire life,

in the creation of our life from start to finish, in every labor and
every kind of work and in every deed, just as in everything within
our hearts.[55]

In his entire way of life and behavior Gordon embodied this view of
creativity no less than he expressed it in his writings. This effort stresses
the vision of labor Zionist creativity from its origins in the Second
Aliyah.

Buber, by contrast, presents a conception of creativity in which
the aspiration of the private ego is not only the origin but also the
ultimate purpose. One might have assumed that in the writings of the
"dialogue stage" of his career he might have given the significance of
clear personal obligation to the emphasis on common human reality.
In an autobiographical chapter he proclaims abandonment of the confinement of the individual within the four ells of his world and opening
oneself to "each mortal hour's fullness of claim and responsibility."
However, in these words he implicitly refrains from insisting on what
is embodied in "claim" and "responsibility," except to indicate that
they are found in the sphere of dialogue.[56] It seems that he has not yet
gone beyond the dimension of the individual's proclivities and yearnings to find "his path." He does not indicate that contents or essences
of objective or nonpersonal creativity have autonomous status in reality. This attitude of his stands out especially in his writings on Judaism
and Zionism. "With admirable consistency Buber has always refused
to pin himself down on any content of such action, on the *what*."[57]

In Buber's thought one does not find an emphasis upon contents
or principles with objective existence. Personal creativity becomes a
norm for him that need not be conquered by a visionary command,
nor need it be pressed into the service of a "cause." He maintains that
"You cannot tell a person what way to take."[58] The "way," the "destiny," the "direction" are all one in his view, and their only meaning is
decidedly personal.[59]

It should be added that in Buber's world, as in the manner in which
labor Zionism grasps creativity and realization, emphasis is placed on
the situation being lived here and now. But in neither view is that
reality self-contained. It has a resonance beyond place and time: it
strives toward time beyond time—toward an era of future redemption.
Yet the strong similarities of these two worldviews do not obscure the
difference between them: the national ideas and Zionist visions that
Buber advocates ultimately serve as an expression of personal identity,

and they are not discussed beyond its contexts. However, in the world of the pioneers the vision is actually lived in the form of a day-by-day, personal exigency.

CONSOLIDATIONS OF THE STRUCTURE OF "CREATIVITY – COMMUNION" (BUBER'S "DOCTRINE OF POSITIVE IMPULSES")

A short time after the appearance of the "dialogue stage" in Buber's thought, a new structure begins to make way for itself in his writings, the components of which are identifiable with the values of creativity and communion. Its basic development is first found in a work entitled "Education" (1925).[60] The primary axis of this structure was one of the prominent features of his thought from the start, as I have shown above, and the second axis is parallel to his dialogical thought.[61] He calls them "the instinct of origination"[62] and "the instinct of communion."[63] This approach is presented at the same time as Buber rejects the psychoanalytical approach to human instinct.

He points out that "modern psychologists are inclined to derive the multiform human soul from a single primal element—the 'libido,' the aggressive urge, etc. . . . In opposition to these conceptions, we must continually point out that human inwardness is in origin a polyphony in which no voice can be 'reduced' to another, and in which the unity . . . [is] only heard in the present harmony."[64] These voices of human inwardness are "the creative powers."[65] Buber means "the power to produce things," "the natural activity of the self," which every person possesses.[66] I propose calling Buber's approach to human instinct and the anthropology that he bases on it the "Doctrine of Positive Instincts." The meaning of this term is clarified below.

Attentiveness to oneself and to the stirrings of these natural traits permits man to locate among them "one of the leading voices" that can be a path for development and growth for him.[67] The stage of the consolidation and growth of that urge takes place within a person, in solitude: "as an originator, man is solitary."[68] In the lecture under discussion ("Education") Buber had not yet developed a clear and comprehensive conception of the essence of this "instinct of creativity." However, it does show a clear turn toward the connotations that had already characterized his conception of creativity during the years preceding World War I. During the mystical stage in his progress he occasionally stated explicitly that a person can create himself;[69] but from the outset of the dialogue stage, the identification of "creativity" with "creation" in his writings no longer means creation ex nihilo. It seems that his formulation during the 1950s regarding the quality of creation that is within human ability is also valid regarding the expression of his view in "Education." During the 1950s Buber stated, in a controversy with J. G. Hamann: "Creation means . . . a bringing forth, certainly not out of nothing but rather out of the inner self of the creator; it is independent of all otherness."[70]

In his discussion of the "instinct of origination" Buber presents a distinction between "instinct" and "greed." In his view, "instinct" is fundamentally positive—embodying a fruitful value; human instinct "does not snatch the world to itself." By means of it the individual can also go beyond the confines of his own little world. This is not true of "greed," which is characterized by "lust" (which is in turn different from "passion"—by which Buber characterizes "instinct").[71] He seems to identify "greed" with "urges . . . of hunger, sex, and the will to power," which are called "elemental urges" in his writings.[72] The last greed, "the will to power," is treated extensively in "Education."[73]

Fundamentally, the liberation of "the powers of creation" (as one concentrates one's efforts within the "instinct of origination") can only be a contribution to a person's self-realization. "The decisive influence is to be ascribed not to the release of an instinct but to the forces which meet the released instinct."[74] These forces are dialogical forces (which are embodied in the "instinct of communion"). In his writing, Buber created a dual structure by combining the expressions that presented the "instinct of origination" with the dialogical "instinct of communion." This dual structure became the foundation of his anthropology. Its clear crystallization is presented for the first time in "Education." Prior to that, expressions of the "instinct of communion" are notable in his dialogical writings, as I shall show below; however, their relation to the "instinct of origination," in the sense that we have noted above, is merely apparent. Buber posits that infants have an "instinct for contact" and "an instinct to become an originator" that is expressed later (in the child's world). However, he explains that his meaning regarding this second instinct is "the drive to produce things synthetically or, where that is not possible, analytically."[75]

Whereas a crystallized expression of what Buber calls the "instinct of origination" is not found in his writings prior to "Education," manifestations of a dialogical relationship as a positive instinct are already presented in *I and Thou*. There he speaks of "the drive to turn every-thing into a You."[76] Buber coined other terms for this drive, such as "the craving for the You"[77] and "the You-sense."[78] These terms indi-cate the rooting of dialogue in instincts or inner drives, in "the innate You . . . realized in the You we encounter."[79] Later on, in his article, "Education," the "instinct of origination" is also grounded on this foundation.

Buber's attitude to the traditional Jewish concept of "the evil im-pulse" (or to the aforementioned "elemental urges") is connected to this basic approach. On the one hand, he is a realist who recognizes the limitation of "the human soul's freedom of choice" and acknowl-edges that freedom of choice is limited by the powers of destiny and nature.[80] On the other hand, he believes in the possibility of uprooting evil. In interpreting the "will to profit" and the "will to power" in the first systematic presentation of his dialogical thought, he states: "[T]here is no evil drive until the drive detaches itself from our being. The drive that is wedded to and determined by our being is the pleasure of com-munal life, while the detached drive spells its disintegration."[81]

An additional development of his "Doctrine of Positive Impulses" is presented in Buber's essay "What is Man?" The background for this development is a confrontation with the ideas of Max Scheeler (1874–1928), in which Buber finds expression of "the constitution of the modern soul" against which one must struggle, as well as an expres-sion of the sources of influence with which he was in conflict. Buber views the duality of "spirit" and "instincts" in Scheeler's doctrine as a version of the gnostic conception of the two primal gods: an inferior and material god, who created the world, and an exalted, spiritual god who redeems it.[82] Scheeler maintains that a blind, aimless, "pri-mal power" is embodied in the "instinct" or "drive," whereas the spirit itself is helpless. Therefore, "it can influence the world-process only by holding ideas and meaning before the primal powers, the life impulses, and guiding and sublimating them till in ever higher ascent spirit and impulse penetrate one another, impulse being given spirit and spirit being given life."[83] Buber finds the clear stamp of psycho-analysis in this conception of the relation between the sphere of the spirit and that of the instincts, separating them in a kind of gnostic dualism.[84] Just as he rejects "the central significance of Freud's concepts

of repression and sublimation," so, too, he rejects Scheeler's use of the
Freudian conceptual vocabulary.[85] The problematic nature of modern
man, says Buber, is similar to the problematic conclusions implied by
Scheeler's views: the barrenness of the spirit that is separate from life,
on the one hand, and the aimless power of the instincts, on the other
hand. He proposes a way of his own to deal with this dualistic crisis,
by presenting an anthropology founded upon the organic unity of spirit
and instincts: "The instincts listen to the spirit, so as not to lose connection with the ideas, and the spirit listens to the instincts, so as not
to lose connection with the primal powers."[86] One finds that the instincts have a value of their own, and it is an error to identify the
demonic with the instinctual: the essence of the instincts is spiritual.[87]
"Spirit," in Buber's view, is something that takes place, something
unexpected, but that happens suddenly, and it can express "the concentrated manifestation of the wholeness of man."[88] The unity of spirit
and instinct underlies "spiritual impulses," which are the foundations
of Buber's concept of man. Both the "instinct of origination" and the
"instinct of communion" are presented in the work with which we are
dealing as urges that are inherent within man. In the discussion devoted to this subject, he makes combined use of two other dual structures of his: "vortex – direction" and the one that is based on the
spiritual instincts mentioned above. First he depicts the birth of the
spirit on the basis of the duality which combines chaos (vortex) and
cosmos (direction): "Only with the passion to bind the experienced
chaos to the cosmos does the spirit arise as a separate being. The picture emerges distinctly from the wild flickering light, the sound from
the wild tumult of the earth, the idea from the wild confusion. Direction
comes out of the chaos of all things: in this way the spirit arises as spirit."[89]

This spiritual instinct to create (the "instinct of origination") can
subsist only when united with "the spiritual instinct to the word" (the
"instinct of communion").[90] The unity of spirit and instincts arouses
and fosters man's self-realization in a life of relationship. "What is
Man?," the work we are presently discussing, does not emphasize this
dimension to the degree to which it is emphasized in the anthropological works that we shall discuss below. Nevertheless, it is expressed
here in various contexts, as when Buber says "the instinct to the word"
is "the impulse to be present with others in the world of streaming communication,"[91] and when he points out that "the divorce between spirit and

instincts is here . . . the consequence of the divorce between man and man."[92]

The manifestations of the "instinct of communion" or "the spiritual instinct to the word" are central to Buber's dialogical thought, and it does not appear to be necessary to make further reference to them in this discussion. However, it is necessary to pursue the manifestations of the "instinct of origination" or the "creative instinct" in his anthropological writings. In a work written during the 1940s, Buber speaks of "Man's most powerful desire," saying, "It is necessary that the power of even this feeling . . . be diverted."[93] It is not difficult to identify these remarks with the "instinct of origination" mentioned in "Education."

In his essay "Essence of Culture" Buber states that there are two main principles of a cultural happening: "growth in form and growth in consciousness." Both of these, form and consciousness, permeate human existence with their potential for power. From his remarks on the transition of form from potentiality into actuality one may understand that he portrays it in his mind's eye as the "instinct of origination." He states that its coming into being is the product of self-fruition: "The form grows, as it were, by itself. Once I saw a clay cup, made by an ancient Japanese potter; . . . it gave the impression that the creative power of nature had passed through that man's hand, and he used it for his project. Thus, from the womb of our spirit, are born . . . artistic, conceptual, and social forms."[94] Whereas Buber generally describes the "instinct of origination" as preceding the "instinct for communion," and, in any event, he distinguishes between these two instincts, in the source quoted here the creative urge also applies directly to social forms. Thus we see that Buber is not imprisoned by the structures he consolidated; he makes creative use of his structures in his thinking, without becoming subservient to them.

"Creativity" and "communion" are two basic channels for human self-realization, as Buber grasps it. Even though each term seems to play an independent role in his writings, it is never absolutely alone, but rather always one of two components of a dual structure in which it is combined with the other. There is also no unequivocal division between the components: creativity also has a dialogical function, just as "social spontaneity is creative."[95] These two spiritual instincts are interdependent and express themselves best in unison.

CONSOLIDATION OF THE "DISTANCE – RELATION" STRUCTURE

It seems that the preceding discussion has already clarified the relationship between the dual structure "Creativity – Communion" and the dual pattern "Existence – Experience" (or: "man's inwardness and the world surrounding him"), which occupied a place in Buber's early thought.[96] From 1918 on, significant new values are alluded to by means of this structure.[97] One finds a clear reference to this dual pattern "where . . . individual beings open themselves to one another, help one another; where immediacy is established between one human being and another."[98] This is an entirely individual stage (in which the individual is by himself), and it is prior to an interpersonal relationship, in which the dialogical connotations have not yet been expressed.

In *I and Thou* only a very marginal place is given to the importance of individualization as an anticipation of a life of communion.[99] It seems that, at that time, Buber needed to blunt the strong emphasis he had placed on the potential for creativity that characterized the mystical stage in his thinking. In *I and Thou* the outer world is no longer grasped as an anvil upon which the individual's drive for self-realization is hammered out. A short time afterward, Buber found a way of presenting inwardness (the source of creativity) in combination with dialogue, which had leaped to the fore in his thought, by means of a structure whose components are the "instinct of origination" and the "instinct of communion." Henceforth, interwoven in his writings is an aspect *that was not to take a prominent place in them for years*, and that was based on the assumption that a life of communion requires an earlier stage that takes place within the domain of the individual in his individuality. Thus, for example, he presents the dialogical domain of faith as "communion with God in the world," which is anticipated by "ever renewed preparation and hallowing."[100] The duality that joins inwardness (the personal-creative) and dialogical reality appears again after a few years in the following terms: "Certainly in order to be able to get to the other, you must have the starting place, . . . you must be with yourself."[101] This formulation is clear and explicit; however, the dual-axis structure that is embedded in it is not discussed in the comprehensive work in which it is included.

Not until the late 1930s, after Buber had arrived in Palestine and had begun to develop his anthropology,[102] does the relation between the "starting place" and dialogical self-realization (which he viewed as central and essential) become anchored in his thought. From the appearance of *I and Thou,* until 1938 no actual importance is given to individuation in his dialogical thought. In "What is Man?" he states for the first time that, "besides man's threefold living relations,"[103] "there is one other, that to one's own self."[104] He emphasizes that "*a great* relationship exists only between real persons.*" Although the centrality of dialogue in his worldview is blunted, he now says, "only the man who has become a Single One, a Self, a real person, is able to have a complete relation in his life to the other self."[105] This basic approach can also be found underlying another work published at the same time, where he defines the area of individuation of the personality and its consolidation in its singularity as "the sphere of the relation of the individual to his own self." Again he states clearly that, in order to create a relationship (in the same context he speaks of forming a relationship with the "absolute"), "it is first necessary to be a person."[106] In this article, the joint duality, the manifestations and concretizations of which I have been following, comprise the latent structure for the establishment of "the link between what this individual is and the sequence of his actions and attitudes, which, in Buber's thought, signify personality."[107]

In "Dialogue," an essay dating from the early 1930s, the significance and extent of a man's being with himself are reduced ("a person must be with himself for once, to be himself"), and this is only considered to be the "starting off point." This is not true in either of the essays, "What is Man?" or "The Education of the Character," which date from the end of that decade. That which is accomplished in these two works becomes the basis for the broader and more fundamental development of the same structure, which will continue to be latent in presentations of his ideas for many years. For example, he presents it by means of Hasidic sources in his work, *The Way of Man According to the Teachings of Hasidism.* The first three chapters in this work deal with man's relation to himself, with the process of becoming a "true personality" (to use the phrase from "What is Man?"). Their titles indicate their orientation: "Heart-Searching," "The Particular Way," and "Resolution."[108] The fourth chapter focuses on the combination of the personality's coming into being, with its realization in the life of dialogue. Its intention is indicated by its title: "Beginning with Oneself,"[109] and it implies that individuation does not have full intrinsic value, but rather it is meant mainly to serve what is beyond it. The fifth chapter is dedicated to man's self-transcendence toward his mission in a life of dialogue. Its subject is presented in its title: "Not to be Preoccupied with Oneself."[110] The sixth chapter, called "Here Where One Stands,"[111] is meant to emphasize the "how" of dialogical self-realization.

Chapter 5 of this anthropological-dialogical work summarizes the relation between the path of dialogue and its anticipations in processes of individuation that are not exhausted within themselves:

> One need only ask one question: "What for?" What am I to choose my particular way for? What am I to unify my being for? The reply is: Not for my own sake. This is why the previous injunction was: to *begin* with oneself, but not to end with oneself; to start from oneself, but not to end with oneself; to start from oneself, but not to aim at oneself; to comprehend oneself, but not to be preoccupied with oneself.[112]

The personal path, which is described in plastic form here, has two foci: the first is personal and internal and prepares the way for the second one, the basis of whose expression is the experienced concreteness of the world as it is delivered to man so that he can live a life of encounter (dialogue).

These two axes are conceptualized as two parts of a structure only in Buber's essay "Distance and Relation," written in the early 1950s. There the part that embodies the individual's singularity is called "distance," and the life of dialogue is called "relation."[113] Buber regarded this work as an important element of his anthropology in its own right, and it should be examined in order to see whether new horizons in his thought are indeed opened.

The starting point in the discussion, as it is presented there, is the statement that man is superior in the living world. Buber declares that mankind exists in a "world" that he apprehends as being beyond the "boundary" of his elementary physical needs. The animal, in contrast, lives within the "boundary" allotted to it. This condition of mankind as an independent being in its own right and distinct from the world is what determines the difference between him and the world of nature. However, this distinctiveness is not yet sufficient to embody his human essence; for that is expressed properly only when man creates relationships with the world around him. Hence we have two stages:

distance, "which provides the human situation," and *relation*, which provides man's becoming in that situation."[114] These two stages are not separate from each other. Consequently we have here a "double principle" of human existence being built up "in a twofold movement which is of such a kind that one movement is the presupposition of the other."[115] We find that "distance" serves to indicate man's distinction from the subhuman world just as it is a presupposition for "relation." However, aside from these statements, Buber does not discuss any further the nature of "distance and relation," and, therefore, on the basis of this work one cannot learn the full meaning of "distance" in Buber's conception of man. The stress in this discussion is ontological. Processes of self-analysis and self-improvement are not mentioned or discussed in the context of pointing out the quality of "distance." That is the difference between this work and *The Way of Man According to the Teachings of Hasidism*, in which the emphasis is placed on self-awareness and on refining the personality to serve its goal in the world.[116]

The distinction between the world of man and the world of nature that Buber presents in the introduction to his essay "Distance and Relation" is not new in his work; this distinction was also evoked several years earlier in an article entitled "On the Great Crisis":

> Two actions or attitudes precede everything, and by means of them the inwardness of man emerged, as it were, from nature, and, despite his weakness, he withstood it and even subdued it. One of these actions is that man prepared objects, each with a specific function, which are called tools, and he used them whenever needed for his purposes; and the second was that he joined together with members of his kind for protection, hunting, and labor, and this union was formed in such a way, to some extent from the start and afterwards increasingly, so that he viewed the other people before him as independent creatures, and he saw himself as an independent creature facing them, and in that aspect he entered into conversation with them. These two actions or attitudes of man's, the creation of a "technical" world using objects which were formed especially for that purpose, and the formation of a "social" bond with people who are both dependent upon each other and independent at the same time, are different in kind from all similar actions of animals.[117]

In the continuation of this discussion, the stage of "the creation of a 'technical' world using objects which were formed especially for that purpose" is identified with the "feeling of *enterprise*, that is to say, . . . the inner relation with what he does and accomplishes."[118] This phrase, the "feeling of enterprise," is a version of the "instinct of origination" or the "creative instinct." Here we seem to have a link, clarifying the close affinity or congruence between the "relation – distance" structure and the "creation – communion" structure.

Buber's "fundamental double stance" of distance and relation has extended existential significance. It should be recalled that the "working together" of these two elements is not a one-time process; rather, "Unlike all other living beings, man stands over against a world from which he has been set at a distance, and, unlike all other living beings, he can again and again enter into relationship with it."[119]

From this point of departure found in his essay "Distance – Relation" (the distinction between man and the living world), Buber expands upon his exploration of "distance" in another anthropological work, where he lists "four powers . . . with which man transcends the natural." He refers to four potential forces that spring up from the innermost recesses of man. The boundary of "distance" is viewed as a corridor, from which "open the doors of the four potencies in the inner rooms of knowledge, love, art, and faith."[120] Buber discusses each of these potencies and describes them as embodiments of relations of various kinds, by means of which man transcends himself and fulfills a life of relation.[121]

In Buber's anthropology, the structure with which we are dealing is applied, among other things, to the area of psychiatry. It comprises a structure with two axes for his essay "Guilt and Guilt Feelings," the central concern of which is "existential guilt." Buber contrasts "existential guilt" to the "guilt" that is discussed by theologians and to the "guilt feeling" that psychiatrists attempt to lay bare. Buber maintains that "existential guilt" is "a reality in the relations between the human person and the world entrusted to him in his life."[122] He calls the two main stages in the process of curing it "self-illumination" and "reconciliation." In the first stage, man attempts "to illuminate the depths of the guilt," and this can only be done "in the abyss of the I-with-me."[123] The stage of illumination makes possible the next stage, which takes place beyond the individual in his singularity. This stage is reconciliation and means renewing communion with the world, or, in Buber's words, "that I approach the man toward whom I am guilty in the light of my self-illumination."[124] The illumination takes place in the domain of "distance," and reconciliation takes place in the world of relations in life.

Certain manifestations of Buber's conception of the world overlap with the two-part structure with which we are presently dealing, and they occupy places of their own in his thought. One topic, "soul peace" and "world peace," merits separate treatment.

SOUL PEACE AND WORLD PEACE

The division between personal, inner experience, and the outer world, which is evident in Buber's thought from its early expressions,[125] was the source of his yearnings for unity.[126] The foundation of these yearnings is a striving for "unification of the soul";[127] and he testified that the individual (Jew) first experiences the fate of the world within himself, "in his innermost self, as the duality of his I."[128] He assumed that the attainment of soul peace would lay the foundation for the striving for unity in the circles of the world beyond the individual. This is only possible for an individual as a member of his nation, rooted in his culture: "[E]very individual among us will feel that he is the people, for he will feel the people within himself."[129] This organic conception, whose foundation is the individual and whose horizons are set by the vision of universal redemption, is alluded to in an expression he used at the end of the first decade of the century. At that time he already indicated the stages of development that would lead toward "unity within individual man; . . . unity between sections of nations and between the nations; . . . unity between mankind and every living thing; . . . for unity between God and the world."[130] However, and this must be stressed, this allusion was marginal at the time; it belonged to an early stage of his thinking, with its emphasis on inner experience *(Erlebnis)* and yearnings for personal redemption, and these were not as yet combined with the ideas of social responsibility and social action to improve the world.

The assumption of an organic connection between the individual and his nation lay behind his pointing out that "just as in the life of the individual the decisive virtues are none other than passions which are elevated to spiritual levels, so the decisive ideas in the life of a nation are none other than the passions of the people which are elevated to the level of the spiritual and the creative."[131] The key to the realization of these virtues is a person's *determination* both within the confines of his own world and also those of the people. Buber continues to express this basic approach after freeing himself of the tendencies that had characterized the early stage in his progress. Just as there is a "personal" element in the individual's soul, which is involved in his nation, there is also a "group" element in it. Hence, among other things, public responsibility is identified with personal responsibility: there is no group responsibility for life different in essence from the responsibility of the individual, states Buber, and "anyone who is severe with himself as an individual and lenient as a group member will eventually vanish and be as naught, whether consciously or unconsciously, when he sets about fulfilling personal responsibility."[132]

Just as in deduction one proceeds from the general to the particular, so it is impossible to understand the fate of an individual except through the spiritual processes of his nation. One cannot separate reference to the nation from reference to its components, including their mutual relations, or from reference to relations beyond the nation— between nation and nation. Following the marked change that took place in Buber's work in the last year of World War I, it takes on new meanings; one of these is based on the identification of the renewal of Judaism with pioneering Zionism in the Land of Israel; from this renewal, he believes, will emerge and develop the renewal of the family of man in general.[133] The Zionist dimension and the universalist dimension in his thought are joined together. After the personal creative tendency in his thought was linked with the idea of community *(Gemeinschaft)*, its implementation in social reality becomes its true test.

From 1918 there is a correspondence between Buber's conception of Judaism and his social conception. Renewal *from within*, whose kernel and focus is "community," nourishes both these conceptions. And as Buber's view of a utopian society was consolidated, it also became consistent with his eschatological approach.[134]

Buber's socialism may also be interpreted on the basis of the parallel between the processes of inner renewal of individuals in their individuality and the processes of national renewal. He expresses it in the spirit of the socialist dream of his friend, Gustav Landauer:

> At this critical hour in the world rescue cannot come from anywhere except from within ourselves, from an innermost decision

and from innermost change. Redemption does not indicate anything external to us, other than from our new birth, the new birth of nations in the spirit of the congregation. Can such a thing be? We do not know, answers Landauer, we cannot know. "We do not know this, and therefore we know that we are obliged to try." "There is nothing before us, everything is only within us." Thus we must begin, we must found a true community, a community out of the congregation, a new covenant, a new nation. "Socialism is repentance and a new beginning." Wherever a true social cell is formed and lives, this is the beginning of new life.[135]

Buber's social utopia is not detached from political realism. He maintains that relations between two nations begin by coming to know the foreign in its difference; every culture can draw upon the abundance of other cultures and graft their spiritual growths upon its own. There must be mutual influence both between cultures and also between the polarized spiritual worlds on the globe. In his own personality Buber embodies the possibility of bridging the contrasts within Jewish culture: between Haskalah and Hasidism as well as between deeply rooted eastern European Jewry (Galicia) and the Jews of Vienna and Berlin, who were characterized by deracination and assimilation. He is familiar with the productive power of the stranger, who need not be threatening or repulsive. From the multiplicity of his roots he also strives for cultural fertility beyond the boundaries of the west. He seeks a reciprocal relationship between the West, with "its inner disorder and goallessness," and "the vision of the eternal truth" in the meditation of the Far East.[136]

We must distinguish in Buber's writings between the "East," meaning the cultures of the Far East, and the "East," meaning the Middle East. Occasionally he combines these two meanings. Thus, for example, in "Conversation with Tagore," in which he and Tagore mainly discussed the cultures of the Far East, he also mentions the need "to accomplish the work of settlement in Palestine in agreement with the peoples of the Orient, yes in union with them."[137] As early as 1913 he states:

We, who intend to serve as intermediaries between Europe and Asia in the Land of Israel, must not appear before the East, which is awakening from its dull slumber, as agents of a West which is doomed to destruction, lest justified suspicion fall upon us. We were called to herald an Occident in the process of regeneration. We must help our brothers in the Orient, on the basis of a covenant with that Occident, and on the basis of their own strength, to lay the foundations of a true social existence. Granted, until now the *effendis* of both East and West have succeeded in suppressing the very aspiration for such an existence. However, it is in our power, on the basis of our socialist principles, to build the bridge that the evil genius of Versailles will never succeed in erecting. By bringing the call for liberation to the suppressed classes of the peoples of Asia, we shall redeem them from the false rule of nationalism, aggression, and the thirst for power. Their exploiters, the talented pupils of the Europe of Versailles [namely, the effendis], endeavor to divert their awakening aspirations from their natural aims by means of nationalism.[138]

In the introduction to a collection of his articles on Judaism and Zionism that was published in 1920 (which also included the German original of the article just quoted) Buber relates his first awakening several years previously to an understanding of the importance of the Middle East and its problematic nature:

Among my notes I find, dated September 14, 1914, the sentence: "The horror which is taking place [meaning World War I] has three times double meaning for me: the liberation of the central European man, . . . the arousal of the Russian to constructive life, the success of Asia Minor, and Semitic rebirth." Later I became aware that each of these processes had to bring a new, difficult, and problematic situation, in accordance with the essence of our period and the atmospheric situation in which [the processes] are taking place. The growing clarity of the foregoing problems and the summons to overcome them are the essential contents of this volume.[139]

The Arab question disturbed and concerned Buber until the end of his life.[140] The question of the connection between western culture and the worlds of the Far East also resonated or was discussed more than once in his writings before being presented in the account of his conversation with Tagore. This issue deserves a separate discussion, which goes beyond present concerns.

It seems that a continuous line of development extends from these early expressions of Buber's attitude and reaches political issues, which are discussed in broad perspectives not limited in time and place, and in which the human dimension is central, culminating in important expositions in his later thought. Prominent among manifestations of the latter is the speech "Genuine Dialogue and the Possibilities of Peace"

(1953), which brings together basic tendencies that were interwoven in his writings from various times: the personal, inner root of the campaign against evil in international structures; the political dimension of dialogue; and global perspectives upon relations among nations, the high point of which would be "the Great Peace."[141] The point of departure there is the assumption that "the great inner struggle of all peoples [is] being fought out today, more or less consciously, more or less passionately, in the vital center of each people. The preparation for the final battle of *homo humanus* against *homo contrahumanus* has begun in the depths."[142] In this internal contrast, which is subject to struggle, there is an echo of the Hasidic-Kabbalistic conception of the *sitra achra* (the force of evil) that secretly lies in wait to ambush the divine element and subjugate it.

Later on in the essay "Genuine Dialogue and the Possibilities of Peace," Buber notes that "the front is split into as many individual fronts as there are peoples, and those who stand on one of the individual fronts know little or nothing of the other fronts. Darkness still covers the struggle, upon whose course and outcome depends whether, despite all, a true humanity can issue from the race of men."

Buber's utopia does not seek realization only in mutual relations between cultures and in political dialogue among nations. In his vision of the end of days he saw the redemption of the entire human race in "the common world of God":

> Each religion is a human truth. That means it represents the relationship of a particular human community as such to the Absolute. Each religion is a house of the human soul longing for God. . . . Each religion is an exile into which man is driven; . . . and not sooner than in the redemption of the world can we be liberated from exiles and brought into the common world of God.[143]

Buber believes in the possibility of overcoming the split among the various faiths but not in the disintegration of organic membership in a nation; he maintains that society is not composed essentially of individuals but rather of social units and of the combinations of those social units.[144] His belief in world peace leans upon individuals "as members of the people into which they are incorporated and from which they are undetachable. . . . This is, indeed, a universalism not of the individuals but of nations, through which it reaches out to the individuals."[145] As Buber puts it, the Jewish religion is founded upon "social humanity" and on "religious humanity," and they in turn are based upon a true relation between man and his fellow man as well as between man and God. The individual (as a member of his nation) must strive to better the world, "lovingly to take part in the still uncompleted work of creation. Creation is incomplete because discord still reigns within it, and peace can only emerge from the created. That is why, in Jewish tradition, he who brings about peace is called the companion of God in the work of creation."[146] Thus Buber's unified, organic view includes dimensions of the individual, society, and faith. And thus his emphases upon mankind are mingled with his connections with the apex of human history—the achievement of world peace.

The concrete reality of life in which Buber anchors his worldview is not exhausted in and of itself. Realization "here" and "now" is nourished and fertilized by drives towards redemption, the meaning of which are the "completion of God's creation to the Kingdom of God." He does not refer to the replacement of this world by another. This is, rather, "the faith in a new world *on this earth*."[147] To use an expression of Buber's, which appears in his writings on Hasidism, in general one could call his approach "Messianic realism . . . [which] means fulfillment."[148]

I have already noted that the emphasis on the individual in his individuality (as a stage in the formation of his personality and its devotion to a life of relationship) does not occupy an essential place in Buber's thought until after the late 1930s.[149]

After the early 1940s, a complete and comprehensive understanding of Buber's conception does not appear to be possible without taking the starting point into account, that is, the relation of the individual to his essence so that he may attain peace in his soul, or without his orientation toward the yearned-for future in which world peace will be achieved.

At this point, the structure with which we are dealing here overlaps that of "the moment – eternity" (which will be discussed in a separate chapter below). A Hasidic legend that Buber entitled "World Peace and Soul Peace," offers a full presentation of the attitude we are discussing:

> Rabbi Bunam taught: "Our Sages say, 'Seek peace in your own place.' You cannot find peace anywhere but in your own self. In the psalm we read: 'There is no peace in my bones because of my sin.'

When a man has made peace within himself, he will be able to make peace in the whole world.'"[150]

By making use of Hasidic sources in his own manner, Buber points out that "a man should himself realize that conflict-situations between himself and others are nothing but the effects of conflict-situations in his own soul." He also emphasizes the need for a person to repair himself (to achieve "reparation of the soul," as Rabbi Nachman said).[151] Man is a microcosm. His inner soul is a reduced reflection of the outer world, just as the outer world reflects the inner world on a larger scale.

8
VORTEX – DIRECTION

THE FORMATION OF THE STRUCTURE

Buber's worldview was formed within a spiritual climate where the subjective point of view determined the relation toward external reality.[1] Strongly conflicting inclinations agitated his spirit, with the potential danger of subjecting him to an all-encompassing vortex; he struggled with the tension between contradictory desires and strove to impose a guiding direction upon them.[2] This problem is reflected in his writings from the beginning of the century. One of the early expressions of it reverberates in his interpretation of the works of Lesser Uri, in whose landscapes Buber found "the moment in which a thousand whirlpools of life are mingled. The sun beats down and then its prominence inflames things beyond their essence, and at the same time . . . things inflame each other."[3] It seems that in struggling with the multiplicity of "the whirlpools of life," Buber formed a dual structure for himself whose first member represents spiritual and psychic "chaos" and whose second member is departure from it in "direction." In the article on Uri, he points on the one hand to a greatly extended sense of power that inflames the spirit, and on the other hand a kind of dam is erected to halt the sweeping eruption, by returning the whirling elements to their essence. In another of his articles from that period, it is also evident that Buber had already begun to work toward the process of spiritual clarification and *to the creativity that is beyond it*. He states

there that man "dissolves his soul into its urges in order to find the
most ancient and best one, out of which to build the creation that he
wants."[4] Creation is also an objective essence outside of and beyond
its creator.

    These lines contain the earliest expression of a duality that was to
be concretized within a few years in a structure occupying an important place in Buber's writings. The process of this concretization is
evident in his early "speeches" on Judaism, given in the years around
1910. The first of these "Speeches" presented variants of the duality
of "experience" and "existence" (of the "world of inner impressions"
and of the world surrounding a person).[5] Emphasis was placed on the
first member of this structure, namely, that which expressed the inner
turmoil, the psychic whirlpool. He stated, "We must come to a decision, must establish a balance of powers within us."[6] Decision
(Entscheidung) was viewed as the point of transcending the inner world,
which lacked "existence," to an environment ruled and guided by man.
A year later, in expanding discussion of the issue of "the aspiration for
unity," Buber presented it as the "experience of inner duality and redemption from it."[7] This expression presented the topic to which this
chapter is devoted as a dual structure, but still without the conceptual
terms that would characterize its members. His article of the same
year, "He and We," presents a clearer expression of the ideas latent in
"Judaism and Mankind," with linguistic sophistication and cloudi-
ness; the structure that concerns us here is presented there as an opposition between "the whirl of battle" and "the face of man."[8] In this
article, too, Buber's attention is mainly directed to the given inner world.
Regarding the lack of direction it also says: "Judaism is within us as a
problem; because our inner being is given to us as a problem; because
existence is given to us as a problem." This is an existence of which
the traits are degeneration (Entartung), guilt (Schuld), and inner con-
straint (innere Hemmung).[9] In an article from 1912 he has already
reached equilibrium in the presentation of vortex and direction, in
that he identifies the rift and directionless confusion with exile, and he
identifies directed existence with Zionist self-realization in the Land of
Israel.[10] For him the Land of Israel embodied reformation: "[T]here a
nation will live that actualizes its new religiosity in culture.[11]

    The ideas that echoed in the aforementioned articles from around
1910 were further developed and consolidated in his article, "The Spirit
of the Orient and Judaism," written in 1912. The focus of the aspira-

tion expressed there is striving for inner unity and locating obstacles on the path toward it within the person himself:

> The unified world—yet to be built—exists within man himself, intended and projected as the "will of God"; but also within man himself, it is opposed by a resistant, reluctant element. Man feels called to the former, but is held back by the latter; he perceives himself as a battleground of prodigious contradictions. A Jew who in this respect is representative, Paul, expressed this perception in movingly simple words: "For I do not that good which I will, but the evil which I hate that I do." When man is so beset, he is in a state of bondage of duality, of conditionality, of division, of "sin"; for sin means nothing more than a divided, unfree existence. He is the bearer of the world's division, he experiences within himself the fate of the world which has fallen from freedom into bondage, from unity into duality. But it is within his power to be as well the bearer of the world's unification. Just as the Indian brings the world to unity by his insight, so the Jew brings the world to unity by his decision. On the surface both actions seem to be a process taking place only within individual man; in actuality, the process takes place within the essence of the world.[12]

This passage embodies an anthropological conception whose prominent assumptions are:

1. A person's inner world is a microcosm.
2. The achievement of peace or unity of the soul is a necessary prerequisite for the struggle to perfect the world.
3. The unification of the soul is insufficient. This serves as a precondition for a "decision" that permits unification in the external world.[13] In those years, the concept of "decision" had already been accorded great importance in Buber's worldview.[14]

There is also found there a full development of the concepts of a duality whose structural consolidation I am attempting to trace. It is called "powerful impulses" and "direction," and it is identified with the duality of "evil" and "good."[15] To live in inner turmoil means to live "in the midst of 'sin,' that is in decisionlessness."[16] The "sinner" lacks direction. His words are a reflection of very powerful inner struggles; from a feeling of danger and a whirlpool, which is bound up with the multitude of authorities that he tried to establish simultaneously, he sought a "direction" that would have the character of "reality restricted and chosen as opposed to the overburdened chaos of potentiality."[17]

In most of Buber's discussions cited above, there is no symmetry between concern for the first member of the structure being consolidated ("powerful impulses") and reference to the second member ("direction"). During the year when he first elaborated the conceptual scheme of "powerful impulse – direction," he published the philosophical dialogue devoted to "direction"—the subject of the first of the five dialogues that were to compose his book *Daniel*.[18] Direction is described in that book as a channel for the actualization of the individual: "[D]irection, this is the basic tendency within the human soul, motivating a person from time to time to choose just one and none other from among infinite possibilities and to realize it."[19]

Central to *Daniel* stands the distinction between two types of relationships between the individual and his world: "orientation," which characterizes the passivity of a person overcome by inner turmoil; and "realization," which embodies the ability to give form to personal self-realization.[20]

It seems that in the process of Buber's treatment of the duality of "chaos – direction" in his writings of 1912–13, its structural solidarity began to take shape. Later the presence of this duality is clearly evident as a structure, manifest or latent, comprising the armature that bears the representations of his ideas in his writings. One should take note of its representation in the opening article of the periodical *Der Jude*, which began to appear, edited by Buber, in 1916; on its basis and by means of it he presents the Jews of the West there as "lacking direction," needing a national "objective."[21] It seems that this article of his is connected closely with a fundamental turning point that took place in his spiritual biography,[22] following which the second member of the structure was imbued with new value significance, the manifestations of which are examined here.

MANIFESTATIONS OF THE STRUCTURE AFTER THE END OF THE
FIRST WORLD WAR AND IN THE "DIALOGICAL STAGE"

In an autobiographical essay dating from the last part of the First World War, Buber describes the opposition between the various experiences of his youth and a tendency of which he had just begun to develop the first harbingers at that time. He speaks of "'Olam-ha-Tohu,' the 'World of Confusion,' the mythical dwelling place of the wandering souls," and about "the whirl of the age," to which he was then subject. To these he contrasts existence formed by "Judaism," "humanity," and "the presence of the divine."[23] The "vortex – direction" duality reverberates in this presentation, and from it we may infer the biographical background. He relates to experiences of childhood and youth, also in a general way, when he states:

> Youth is the eternal chance for human happiness. . . . Once again and repeatedly the generation of the twenty-year-old appears on the stage, ablaze with yearning for the absolute in his heart, with devotion to the ideal, he is ready and willing to break through the sealed gates of the Garden of Eden. . . . But during the time of preparation, the abundance of petty goals proposed by society takes over his young soul, vain selfish urges take control of him. . . . The pure power, which was about to achieve a life of truth on the earth, is subjected to the yoke of lies and the yoke of walking without in a rut, walking without spirit.[24]

In the representations of the structure that were surveyed above, misdirected potentiality represents the first member, and the second member is the tendency to give-form. Here the first member represents "pure power," the value aspect of the structure, while the other one expresses the lack of clear direction.

In our search for the earliest representations in Buber's writings of forces of the personality that are misguided or lack direction, it already has become clear to us that he did not relate to them in an all-inclusively negative manner, but rather he maintained that *from them* a channel must be found for actualizing the personality. Later, in the first systematic presentation of his dialogical thought, he even stated clearly: "There is no evil drive until the drive detaches itself from our being; the drive that is wedded to and determined by our being is the plasma of communal life, while the detached drive spells its disintegration."[25] In the same context, he points to urges that are positive, "natural and legitimate as long as they are tied to the will to human relations and carried by it." Henceforth Buber does not advocate the self-actualization of the individual in his individuality but rather the actualization of the inner goal of the personality in a life of dialogue. He begins there with the development of a conception of the positive instincts according to which the instinctual potentiality in itself is not bad. Man is capable of transforming it to a creative tendency by means of the decision, henceforth directed toward a dialogical life.[26] In contrast, passivity, which is contrary to freedom of will, draws man to inner chaos—which is identified with "evil." Good requires overcoming and choice, evil is a result of submission; henceforth Buber was to return repeatedly to these ideas, to develop and enrich them against the background of his dialogical worldview. And in *I and Thou* he refers to them again; they reverberate within his proposal of the unification of the soul as an inner human process. This event permitted the "decision" that opens a person's "vocation" before him.[27] The concept of "vocation" alludes to what is called in the passage quoted above, "the will to human relations," and it was later to occupy a representative place in the "Vortex – Direction" structure in Buber's anthropological writings of the 1950s, as we shall show below.

The same direction of thought is expressed by him in his reference to the concepts of the Hasidism of the Baal Shem Tov:

> Nothing, in fact, is unholy in itself, nothing is in itself evil. What we call evil is only the directionless plunging and storming of the sparks in need of redemption. It is "passion"—the very same power which, when it has been endowed with direction, the one direction, brings forth the good in truth, the true service, the hallowing. Thus there no longer exist side by side in the soul of man the worldly and the spiritual, qualitatively sundered, there is now only power and direction. He who divides his life between God and the world, through giving the world "what is its" to save for God "what is His," denies God the service He demands, the giving of direction to all power, the hallowing of the everyday in the world and the soul.[28]

The members of the structure with which we are dealing are called "power" and "direction" here. Below he describes the process represented by the concept "power" in more detail, as an event within the human interior: "The directionless storming and plunging of the sparks in need of redemption—temptation, turmoil, and undecided deed."[29]

These short contexts of discussion prepared the background for a more basic exposition of these ideas in his article "The Faith of Israel" (1928), which explains Buber's conception of good and evil as implied in the dual connotations discussed in this chapter. In contrast to the ancient Iranian concept according to which light and darkness (as well as good and evil) constitute two separate realms, Buber presents the unificatory concept of Judaism in which evil does not exist as an independent realm. There is no evil, he declares, except in the human soul—and it alone is capable of doing evil.[30] "There is no evil except the 'shell,' the envelope, the cortex surrounding good; the shell which is easy to break through in action."[31] In his repeated reference to this essence of evil, he presents it as "the power to act without a path," and "lust . . . gone astray with no path."[32] Lust cannot be repressed or conquered, Buber maintains. Only a positive direction can be given to its energy—to draw "all the ability of lust to the side of the path that one has chosen for oneself.[33] Here again it is implied that a path is personal, that an individual decision determines its quality.

The conception in its Jewish-historical context is embodied in the article "The Faith of Israel"; it was later presented in universal terms in a work of 1936. But this, too, was against the background of the ancient Iranian duality, with which it is not consistent.[34] That work also includes reference to the nature of the conscience,[35] to which Buber was to make similar reference in further discussions of his touching upon "vortex" and "direction," and he also developed them in his comprehensive anthropological work, "Images of Good and Evil," which will be discussed below.

Among other things, the structure with which we are dealing here provided Buber with an armature, often an implicit one, upon which he draped his ideas in various areas. I shall here present two examples from times far removed from each other.

Under the Nazi regime, in the beginning of the summer of 1933, he strove to present an "educational goal" to the Jews of Germany. As a background to this he discusses the state of German culture since romanticism; he notes the disintegration of the ideal figure of the "citizen of the world," a unifying, organic figure that had been crystallized in the writings of Lessing and Herder. Its place was later taken by the approach of "general education," in which "the objects and values of mankind are placed in a pile which appears to be classified systematically." It is easy to identify the structure implicit in this representation. It becomes manifest later in the article, when he asks regarding the Jews of Germany: "Do they have any goal of their own? Or have they, perhaps, been abandoned to a vortex with no goal and no direction?"[36]

The duality of "vortex" and "direction," the opposition between "evil" and "good," is also used to embody the duality of "lie" and "truth." As early as the end of the First World War he identifies "direction" or "destiny" with "truth" (in declaring that "from within the din of erring voices [youth] will hear the clarion call of truth").[37] His tendency to present the "correct response" as direction, in opposition to "tactical response,"[38] is especially notable in the articles from his first years in the Land of Israel; thus, for example, he states: "Truth is the straight path, and falsehood is an infinite vortex."[39] Truth is identified with "a man's path," with "direction," with his personal self-realization, which in Buber's conception was embodied in a life of dialogue. One of the core expressions of this is presented at the conclusion of the autobiographical chapter, "A Conversion." It speaks of transcending "fullness without obligation" and "vortex," toward "communion," for only in it and from within it can "direction" be found.[40]

IMAGES OF GOOD AND EVIL

The essence of the evil that people commit against their fellows does not come from their being so evil at bottom, but because they don't understand each other, because they don't understand their own souls to their full depth.
—A. D. Gordon, "The Authors and the Workers" (1921)

The various manifestations and guises of the structure "vortex – direction" converge in the work, "Images of Good and Evil" (1952), in which the ideas which Buber repeatedly developed are crystallized.[41] Buber indicates it as the formation of his ethical teaching,[42] which cannot be distinguished from his anthropology, his conception of man; he is not concerned with "ethical abstractions," in theory for its own sake, but rather in "existent states of human reality."[43] "We find the ethical in its purity," he says, "only there where the human person confronts himself with his own potentiality and distinguishes and decides in this confrontation."[44] He does not speak of "good and evil" except "in the factual context of the human person."[45]

Buber begins discussion of the source of evil with the individual and his inner world, arguing that evil must first be recognized in the conduct of the soul toward itself. In his opinion the source of evil in the world and in man can be found in the dynamics of the life of the soul:

A man only knows factually what "evil" is insofar as he knows about himself, everything else to which he gives this name is merely mirrored illusion; but self-perception and self-relationship are the peculiarly human, the eruption of a strange element into nature, the inner lot of man. Here also, then, the demoniac, whose desire is towards us, as a woman's is towards a man—to arouse this association in the reader, one of the phrases God addressed to Eve is incorporated in his speech to Cain—is first to be encountered directly; from this point too it first becomes accessible and demonstrable to us in the world.[46]

Within the person, in his soul, is where "the struggle against evil" must open, and all the rest is the outcome of that.[47]

Instinct, says Buber, is the product of imagination.[48] "The storm of adolescence of imagination," instinct, sweeps man off into infinite possibilities, and this is "the greatest danger and the greatest opportunity at once."[49] He states that imagination is not entirely evil. "It is evil and good, for in the midst of it and from out of it decision can arise, . . . master the vortex of possibility, and realize the human figure purposed in the creation."[50]

Buber claims that there is evil or negative imagination, just as there is fertile and positive imagination. He condemns "the fantasy" whose place is only within the confines of the soul, such as lust or "alien thoughts." By contrast, he values vision or a utopian dream rooted in the soul but raised beyond it—to the level of formation or actualization. He does not advocate the repression or conquest of imaginations, but rather "their elevation." He expresses this in the contexts of his Hasidic writings, saying,

We should not thrust away [the alien thought's] abundance that waylays our hearts, but receive it and fit it into real existence; only in the strength of such an act shall we attain to that unity that does not look away from the world but embraces it. But to do this we must accomplish what is hardest of all: the transformation. We must transform the element that wants to take possession of us into the substance of true life.[51]

However, a negative tendency is also possible as a result of succumbing to fantasies and idle dreams. The distinction between these two tendencies is described in one of his articles as the opposition between the paths of two leaders, Lenin and Mussolini. The former "gave shape to what he foresaw," whereas the latter "sets out from time to time to give shape to what he has evoked in his imagination from time to time."⁵² "Vision," so it seems, is based on deviation from man's inner being. By means of it "something which was hidden in nature is drawn and lifted out of it." Raised up within it is the direction "toward figuration."⁵³

Buber does not intend to combat human nature, but rather to bring forth the value implicit in it. Man, he believes, is fundamentally good. "That it is called the evil urge derives from man's having made it so. . . . Only through him, man, did it become evil."⁵⁴ His discussion is based on the rabbinical conception of man, according to which man is born with two drives, the evil impulse and the good impulse. In the spirit of this conception, Buber states that "man's task . . . is not to extirpate the evil urge, but to reunite it with the good."⁵⁵ The unification of the two urges means directing the evil impulse (which, in itself, has no direction) toward the self-realization of man; thus the evil impulse is made "capable of great love and of great service."⁵⁶ In these terms Buber alludes to the central positive urges on the basis of which he constructs his anthropology: "the instinct for communication," and "the instinct of origination." The path of elevation and actualization is thus based on the development and nurturing of the good while including evil within it. There can be no vacuum in human existence. If he does not turn toward the good, inevitably, even if unintentionally, he falls into the realm of evil: "Sin croucheth at the door" (Gen. 4:7).⁵⁷

We find that the evil impulse in isolation is identified with the inner "vortex," whereas when linked with the good impulse individuation takes shape.

The overcoming of evil requires an additional step, according to Buber. He refers to it in a very early stage of his thinking: breaking down the soul into its forces by locating "the most primordial and the best" of them.⁵⁸ This process is not alluded to in "Images of Good and Evil." Its sharpest expression in Buber's writings appears in connection with a Hasidic source: "Everyone has in him something precious that is in no one else. But this precious something in a man is revealed to him if he truly perceives his strongest feeling, his central wish, that in him which stirs his inmost being."⁵⁹ The location of this force must precede the unification of the soul and "decision" regarding the "direction" of the self-actualization of the "strongest feeling," of "the

central wish." This central inner desire is identified with what Buber
calls the "instinct of origination."[60]

What kind of "decision" is this? From our discussion in the first
section above, it could be inferred that the concept of "decision" had
an important place in the structure "vortex – direction" from the beginning of the second decade of the century. But it is difficult to find a
discussion of its essence in all of his references to it. From them it
emerges that this term refers to the inner decision of the individual
within himself, in the secrecy of his world; a person's decision, Buber
stated, "takes place in these elemental depths of the soul that are closed
to reflection and inaccessible to analysis."[61] The "lightning flash of
decision," he states, comes out of the "darkness of the soul."[62] Without it there can be no transcendence of the inner turmoil. A person
draws the quality, purpose, and direction of this decision from his
conscience.[63]

A fence-straddler lacks the ability to muster determination to de-
cide, but "Doubt is unchoice, indecision. Out of it arises evil." So
Buber identifies the inability to choose, the state of "indecision," with
the dimension of evil itself, and he even states unequivocally that "evil
action stems primarily from indecision."[64] Hence, too, flows the conclusion that decision can only be reached in a unified soul: "Good can
only be done with all the soul. . . . Evil is lack of direction, and what is
done in it and out of it is the grasping, seizing, devouring, compelling,
seducing, exploiting, humiliating, torturing and destroying of what
offers itself. Good is direction and what is done in it."[65]

Before the decision, unformed powers swarm in the soul. Its processes are characterized by contradictions and inner collisions. After
the decision, the soul stands at the gate of a single direction, on the
long path of self-actualization. In this course various decisions are
necessary, and these cannot be resolved by the basic decision. Decision
is founded upon self-control, the forgoing of tempting possibilities that
are not consistent with the single direction.

Hence Buber maintains that a person can express only good, and
not evil, with his whole being. This assumption has particular importance regarding the reinforcement of the ethical approach. Buber argues
that the decision "with a complete soul, a unified soul" necessarily
leads to a "path," to the "good," to the realization of one's personal
vocation. Since the decision has this character, it constitutes and serves

as the sign and symbol of nondependency upon the illusions of self-deception. Buber is aware that the susceptibility of the consciousness to such illusions is problematic, for by means of them a person "is hiding from himself."[66] He refers to "the uncanny game of hide-and-seek in the obscurity of the soul, in which it, the single human soul, evades itself, avoids itself, hides from itself."[67] He grasps the tangles of self-deception as the outcome of the spiritual vortex.[68]

Buber states again, in a work of his later years, that "one cannot do evil with the whole soul, i.e., one can only do it through holding down forcibly the forces striving against it—they are not to be stifled."[69] Here as in his anthropology in general is expressed deep faith in the positive value inherent in man.

It should be noted that a straight line leads back from these late embodiments of his thinking to their root in the foundation of his dialogical thought. In *I and Thou* he had stated: "The basic word I-You can only be spoken with one's whole being. The basic word I-It can never be spoken with one's whole being."[70] In the Bible the joy of making an offering to God is already identified with "a whole heart": "The people rejoiced over the freewill offerings they made, for with a whole heart they made freewill offerings to the Lord" (1 Chron. 29:9).[71] This deep faith, which fastens upon, as we have seen, the anthropology of the rabbis and also of the Hasidism of the BESHT, is far from naive optimism. It addresses not what is assured and self-evident, but looks toward the possibility open to every person, *if he chooses*; the uniqueness of man among all the products of Creation derives from his being created in the image of God. And he must actualize this image in his way of life, in his "direction." No predetermined path is incumbent upon him—Buber does not believe in predestination or fate.[72] "Man is the sole living creature known to us," he says, "in whom the category of possibility is so to speak embodied, and whose reality is incessantly enveloped by possibilities. . . . [By contrast,] every animal is fixed in its this-being, its modifications are preordained."[73]

It is important to note that Buber speaks of "possibility" and not of "ability." He notes the tension, occasionally tragic, between these two. This is the tension between the fateful dimension in a person's world and his spiritual goal—which awaits its realization—between the "person" and the "cause."[74]

"The category of possibility" indicates free will rather than determinism. The human being's powers of will permit him, according to

Buber, to chart his course for himself. Option is given to man; in Buber's writings fundamental discussions are devoted to choice, to free will. Generally the term "decision" does not appear in this context. But there are passages, also in his discussion in "Images of Good and Evil," where he evokes choice and decision together. In one of these passages, the acts embodied in these concepts are identified with each other: he speaks there of "the power of decision" that "was entrusted to man" as equivalent to the personal vocation "to choose between good and evil."[75] This decision opens the way before a person to the self-actualization embodied in a life of relationship, and not only with one's fellow man, but also with "the eternal Thou"—God.[76]

The decision bridges the duality of "vortex" and "direction," opening the possibility for a person's *way*, the actualization of his *vocation* in *direction* he has formed by himself. These three elements—"direction," "way," and "vocation"—are one.

In "Images of Good and Evil," Buber does not extend the discussion to the essence of "direction," and it should be examined against the background of the context of discussion in his other anthropological works. In them he clarifies and emphasizes that every person must give shape to "his direction," according to the uniqueness of his personality, and from it to actualize the virtues of his characteristics. Choice and decision endow every creature with "the chance to become the being that this created person was designed to become through his highest disposition."[77] In most of Buber's references to "destiny," he repeatedly emphasizes the fact that most human beings do not pass the test of confronting their destiny. He asserts that there is "a fundamental awareness inherent in all men, though in the most varied strengths and degrees of consciousness. . . . It is the individual's awareness . . . of what in his unique and non-repeatable created existence he is intended to be." But for the most part this inner knowledge is "stifled" by them.[78] He expresses this more sharply in stating that "each man in some measure had been called to something, which, to be sure, he in general successfully avoids."[79]

Buber connects vocation to a "court within the soul which concerns itself with the distinction between the right and the wrong." This is what he calls "conscience."[80]

He designated a special place for conscience in his anthropological philosophy. Among other things, he refers to the relation between conscience and belief in God. Sometimes he indicates the unequivocal connection between the two. Referring to a rabbinic saying that truth is the seal of the Holy One, blessed be He, Buber states: "[A]nd if His seal is [truth], where is the varied wax in which He presses His seal? To be good—means to be quick and ready like wax. The conscience is living knowledge, knowing when there is coordination between the seal and ourselves, and when there is none. When a person turns away from the hand that seals, it departs, and the light departs from our world."[81] In another work from that year, 1943, he refers more extensively to the connection between conscience and faith.[82]

Shortly afterward he consolidates the formula, from which it emerges that the conscience must draw upon an absolute authority that is not necessarily to be identified with God:

> Conscience is something found within us . . . only a tool, indeed imperfect, but capable to some degree of heeding the absolute demand that comes to me from time to time. The believer calls that absolute authority God; for someone who does not believe, who knows the absolute quality of that authority, something stands in place of God, something that can be named but little in general terms, though its dominion is evident over his soul as well. As opposed to that authority, every collectivity, even the highest, even nation and homeland, has only relative value; and that authority, as it judges me, judges nations and homelands; before it I am absolutely responsible, for no collectivity is fit to take it from me.[83]

Buber sharpens and emphasizes the distinction between personal conscience and collective conscience, about which he is very skeptical:

> The more or less hidden criteria that the conscience employs in its acceptances and rejections only rarely coincide with a standard received from the society or community. . . .
> The vulgar conscience that knows admirably well how to torment and harass, but cannot arrive at the ground and abyss of guilt, is incapable, to be sure, of summoning to such responsibility. For this summoning a greater conscience is needed, one that has become wholly personal, one that does not shy away from the glance into the depths and that already in admonishing envisages the way that leads across it. . . .
> This conscience is possessed by every simple man who gathers himself into himself in order to venture the breakthrough out of the entanglement in guilt.[84]

Buber conceives the conscience as the kernel of what distinguishes man, his humanity, his being created in the image of God. In it is the source of the ability "for personal decision and personal responsibility," for "that which distinguishes man as a human being" is his ability "to judge by himself what he does and refrains from doing."[85] "Decision" and "responsibility" are, as has already been noted from the above discussion, central value concepts in Buber's thought. People without conscience are, in his view, "without constraints and without reflection." Two prominent examples of mortals of this kind are evoked in his writing: Jacob Frank and Adolf Hitler.[86]

When a person tries to evade his vocation, to "silence it," a twisting and turning confrontation takes place between himself and his conscience:

> Each one who has not fulfilled a *task* which he knows to be his own, each who did not remain faithful to his *vocation* which he had become certain of—each such person knows what it means to say that "his conscience smites him." . . . *He who has a vocation* hears at times an inner voice of an entirely different kind. This is *just the voice of conscience*, which compares that which he is with that which he was called to become.[87]

"The connection between conscience and vocation is biographical and not abstract," Buber declared in a conversation with this writer. He made additional remarks in response to my questions, stating:

> *Conscience* is the "inner voice," that rouses and speaks to the individual. It is a certain force inherent in man, it is not something that a person can attain, it is in his possession. *Vocation* [by contrast] is an objective fact, and it can be attained. Contrary to conscience, which is always the product of a certain moment, vocation is permanent. Conscience is the force that rouses and directs one toward vocation. It assists the human vocation, but it is not sufficient.[88]

CONCLUSION

In his article "The Way of Man According to the Teachings of Hasidism," in which the structure "distance – relationship" comprises the latent foundation for the presentation of the ideas,[89] the "vortex –

direction" structure also plays an important role. The reference to individualization in its first chapter is based on the opposition between "no way" (vortex) and "way" (direction).[90] The second member of the structure, represented by the term "way," reverberates even in the title of the second chapter: "The Particular Way."[91] The personal character of the "direction" is emphasized by means of the Hasidic source, which is consistent with Buber's conception, and he states: "It is impossible to tell man what way he should take."[92]

In the third chapter, "Resolution," Buber deals with the process of unifying the forces of the soul, after overcoming inner chaos. There are, he says, two ways of aspiring to a hoped-for purpose: false and true. The first he calls, in Hasidic terms, "patchwork,"[93] meaning action while straddling the fence. He calls the second way "all of a piece,"[94] saying of it that it can be taken "only with a united soul." It can be seen that he presents these two ways of unifying the soul on the armature of the "vortex – direction" structure.

The aforementioned article was completed a few years before the publication of his work, "Images of Good and Evil," and in some ways it can serve not only as a means of illustration but also as a vital supplement to the ideas presented in the latter work. Among other things it is clarified there that

> unification of the soul is never final. Just as a soul most unitary from birth is sometimes beset by inner difficulties, so even a soul most powerfully struggling for unity can never completely achieve it. But any work that I do with a united soul reacts upon my soul in the direction of new and greater unification, leads me, though by all sorts of detours, to a *steadier* unity than was the preceding one. Thus man ultimately reaches a point where he can rely upon his soul, because its unity is not so great that it overcomes contradiction with effortless ease. Vigilance, of course, is necessary even then, but it is a relaxed vigilance.[95]

From this it can be learned, too, that a basic decision that opens up a path is not sufficient, and it does not exempt one from further decisions in new existential situations.

It seems that reference to Buber's conception of good and evil from a viewpoint that combines "Images of Good and Evil" with the three first chapters of "The Way of Man According to the Teachings of Hasidism," permits one to extract his abstract, theoretical ideas and transform the contemplative distance in them into a sense of their human and existential dimension.

In the course of the discussion in the previous section, it emerged that Buber tends not to emphasize that "the impulse of a man's heart is evil from his youth" (Gen. 8:21), but rather "sin lieth at the door" (Gen. 4:7) of him who does not gather strength to make a decision. But an overall view of his dialogical writings shows that he is aware of the limitations of decision. "The soul's freedom of decision" is not "being free of destiny or nature or men but the union and covenant with them."[96] Man is free to choose his destiny, implying that he can free himself from determinism, from predestined doom: "[T]o gain freedom from the belief in unfreedom is to gain freedom."[97] This does not mean that one can erase the element of destiny in one's life: "[F]reedom and fate belong together."[98]

Buber's concepts of "vortex" and "direction," like those of "evil" and "good," are almost never discussed in isolation in his writings, but as two members of a single structure. This structure cannot be defined by any theoretical boundary; even when he presents his view of ethics by means of it, for example, he does not intend to restrict himself to the dimensions of a single discipline.

By means of this structure he represents and expresses, with the various extensions of his spiritual enterprise, his approach to the opposition between "fortune and misfortune or order and disorder,"[99] and, at the same time, between truth and falsehood,[100] right and wrong.[101] All of these instances of polar tensions are, according to Buber, essential states of human reality; they are latent in the depths of the soul and they exist in common human reality.[102] This duality, in its various forms, is essentially useful to him in presenting his dialogical anthropology.

9
MOMENT – ETERNITY

now – NOW [handwritten]

One of the fundamental problems in Buber's thought from the first
was how to reconcile the subjectivity of his lived experience *(Erlebnis)*
with his Jewish-historical identity (and with his Zionist worldview).
From the start of his intellectual activity, his insistence on lived experience was unable to express his entire approach. Even when he focused
on his own personal-existential situation, he was not actually satisfied
with it. Along with his mystical penchant, he tried, on other levels of
his spiritual world, to respond to the "here and now" on the basis of
the values of the past (mythical-archaic and also historical). At the
same time, he also sought to relate the "moment"—the temporal situation—to the horizon of future or eternal orientation.

Structures based on the duality of the momentary-unique and of
the monumental-eternal occupied a place in Buber's articles as early as
the beginning of the century. From then on, they were presented in his
writings in various guises, both explicit (or implied) and latent.

Two opposing tendencies vied within the representations of this
structure in his writings in the early stage of his career, from the beginning of the century until the first years of World War I: (1) a tendency
with Jewish-historical connotations, having its origin and basis in an
existential situation and oriented toward the monumental, eternal;
(2) an anarchical tendency embodied in an urge to transcend belong-
ing and any spiritual identification entailing obligation.

179

These two tendencies bore the clear signs of the early, mystical stage in Buber's thought. He was then deeply interested in "creation" as a realization of the human potentiality. Objects or entities beyond the individual in his individuality exercised no essential function for him. Even the super-human was included within human innerness, in his view (and in his early writings it is difficult to find an expression of a clear relationship to a transcendental God).[1]

One of the first expressions of the Jewish aspect of the "Moment-Eternity" structure is found in "The Way to Zionism" (1901), which is indicative of the spirit of Buber's thought in those years. The Zionist, declared Buber there, creates new values and projects while drawing from "the depths of his primordial self-essence" as a member of his people. The heritage of his people is embodied in his "power of blood." This refers to an individual who, by his creative action, erects "monuments of his essence" in the face of "infinity," and it is as though he makes a "new star" shine in "the enchanted firmament of eternity."[2] These remarks do not attribute independent significance to the concept "eternity," which mainly serves as an echo and a witness to human creativity.

In presenting the other aspect, the anarchical-mystical, he again expresses an aspiration to integrate "the moment" and "eternity" by means of immersion in otherworldly or prehistorical reality. The most extreme expression of these tendencies will be expressed in an article entitled "Buddha," which develops the distinction between Buddha as a mythical entity and the abstract approach to him, an approach embodied in the term "Buddhism." Buddha is for him an expression of a yearned-for reality, entirely different from earthly existence, that which is chained to scientific-logical thinking; "the act [of Buddha] is very distant from the causality of worldly activity [*Weltgetriebe*]. It is not caused by action, it grew from the blink of an eye, from eternity."[3] A similar mystical combination resonates in the rest of this article, which states in the first-person plural: "Such are we, small and great, slaves of time and blood brothers of the high and exalted."[4]

These two tendencies were already consolidated in a structure in his article "Lesser Uri," written in early 1901. With his marvelous linguistic artistry, Buber presents two tendencies there, which probably cannot be reconciled. The Jewish connotations of this structure were presented there by means of the duality of "the Jewish past" and "the Jewish eternity."[5] On the basis of this dual structure, Buber interpreted Uri's work *Jerusalem* (1896), in which he finds an expression of the path "from the historical to the monumental."[6] In his view, the first member of this duality represented the moment of occurrence, "finiteness," and the other member, "eternity within the instant."[7]

Another variant of the same structure is represented in this article by the figure of an old man in Uri's *Jerusalem* as a link in the long chain of Jews who were, except for Spinoza (as he states), almost all anonymous. "They leave the ghetto and their steps are directed directly toward the cosmos, without any transition."[8] The "ghetto" represented the first member of the structure, and the "cosmos" represented the other one.

Along with the phrase "eternity within the instant" (quoted above), in the same context Buber coined the expression, "this instant [is] an eternity."[9] We have before us here the fusion of eternity with the instant, the instant and eternity—as expressed several years later in the context of the article, "Buddha." The Jewish and anarchical-mystic aspects were fused with each other. Expressions of this second aspect seem to have homed in on interpretations of the decidedly Jewish work of Uri. Similarly, Buber's remarks on Uri's work *Jerusalem* contain the following sentence, in relation to "the monumental" (eternal): "the one and only human soul that utters its sound to the end once and never again."[10] It appears that this expresses the yearning of the individual in his individuality to merge his one-time existence with eternity (which has no Jewish-historical connotations).

These two contradictory conceptions had only just begun to seethe in Buber's restless spirit at that time, and he was later to struggle with them in his efforts to relate these poles of his existence to each other.[11]

The tendency that was bound up with Jewish concepts occupied an important place in one of his early "Speeches on Judaism." He speaks of the transitory and relative existence of the Jewish people, within which the constant rebirth of "absolute life" takes place. "The internal history of the Jewish people" is described as a "spiritual process" that aspires from "relative life" toward the absolute, that is, the divine.[12]

Presentations of the path from the relative to the absolute are found in the "Early Speeches" (1909–10), which are based on the model described in "Lesser Uri." They were further developed a number of years later in his book *Daniel*. In presenting this model, *Daniel* expresses yearning to overcome the duality of moment and eternity, and to be encompassed in "the eternity within the moment." Thus, for example, the main protagonist of this philosophical work addresses the "woman" who accompanies him on his excursion in the mountains:

> Certainly, what I experienced as I stood uplifted between heaven and earth was still space and had to remain such; but reflected therein was a kingdom in which there is nothing except my self and over it its completion. For no breadth was there that intersected my uplifting. The torch of my tension burnt unflickering to the zenith; undiverted, the lightning of the heights hurled down on my head, and earthly fire mixed itself with heavenly fire. The scaffolding of my directions had caved in; I, the one set upright, was alone with my direction. And at that time the grace appeared to me which makes one who is borne into one who bears.[13]

In the same work, the structure with which we are dealing also provides the hidden framework for a mystical context with a different nuance: "Each word of a poet is single; and yet there lies around each a ring of ungraspable material which represents the sphere of infinite vanishing."[14]

The moment living in its unique continent continued to be the basis of Buber's Zionist articles in those years. One of them even bore the title "The Blink of an Eye," and the subject concerning us here resonates throughout it. A paragraph of that article opens with a cry of admiration, "How great are the force and splendor of the instant!"[15] In those years Buber's Zionism did not help him to free himself of his mystical inclinations, and it even seems that it was frequently integrated with them. The early fruits of his Hasidic project were also gripped by this tendency, and at the same time they show glimmers of a tendency toward reservations regarding mystical unity, which were expressed in the distinction between the human and historical versus the divine or infinite. Thus, for example, at the end of the introduction to his book *The Legend of the Baal-Shem*, he stated that the Hasidic legend is a myth "of the finite which enters into the infinite and the infinite which has need of the finite."[16]

EMBODIMENTS OF THE STRUCTURE FROM THE END OF
WORLD WAR I TO THE "DIALOGICAL STAGE"

The concepts "absolute," "infinity," and "eternity" are not generally endowed with transcendental connotations in Buber's early writings.

Only with the maturation of his dialogical thought was he to pass beyond the areas of personal-mystical experience. But even a few years before the publication of *I and Thou* (1923), the Moment – Eternity structure permitted him to hint clearly at a new concept of divinity. He abandoned the trend toward the mystical fusion of the momentary-historical with the eternal-monumental, and as early as his work "My Way to Hasidism" (1917) he was groping toward the link between these two elements.

In discussing the essence of the zaddik in the Hasidism of the BESHT, Buber presents him as "the perfected man in whom the immortal finds its mortal fulfillment."[17] Buber states that of him it is said in the Talmud, in the name of Rabbi Eliezer, "that the world was created for the sake of the perfected man."[18] The first quotation above begins with the divine element ("eternity") as the first member of the structure, whereas the other version, added to this work, is more in keeping with the dialogical conception that Buber was later to elaborate: the first member, the point of departure, is the "moment," and from it one strives toward "eternity." The zaddik is depicted there as "the teacher of world-meaning, the conveyor to the divine sparks."[19] In all these representations, "eternity" embodies a transcendental essence.

Though it is clear from the context that Buber is referring to the God of Israel here, five years were to pass before he consolidated his approach and entirely rejected the absorption of the transhuman within the human or the blurring of the boundary between the divine and the human. This is presented in *I and Thou* and in the preface to his collected speeches on Judaism, most of which date from before the First World War.[20] Both books were published in 1923.

In *I and Thou*, the divine element became an essence present to men and coming into contact with them. The eternal is henceforth clearly grasped as "Thou," called "das ewige Du" (the eternal Thou),[21] the "eternal utterance,"[22] and the like. It is noteworthy that this work is formulated in entirely universal concepts, without any connotations identifying the author's Jewish origins. The preface can be seen as complementing *I and Thou* by distinguishing the new concept of "eternity" from the meanings that characterized the concepts of the "absolute" and the "eternal" in Buber's writings in the first fifteen years of the century. He declares there: "I have already stated that by the term 'God' I mean not a metaphysical idea, nor a novel idea, nor a projection of a psychic or a social image, nor anything at all created by, or developed within, man."²³ Those familiar with the development of his thought will understand that Buber is struggling here against the tendencies that characterized him earlier, though it is doubtful whether he freed himself from them.

Most of the expressions Buber used in presenting the structure "Moment – Eternity" at the beginning of the century are also present in the dialogical stage of his career. However, changes and reversals in meaning took place in them. This is true mainly regarding the second member of the structure. Henceforth it is endowed with concrete meaning, and it is no longer possible to combine the two members in mystical union.

Among other things, because of the assumptions of his dialogical worldview, Buber's attitude toward Spinoza's doctrine changed. Formerly he had championed it;²⁴ now he condemns its "objectivity," which lacks connection with "the lived life of the human person." He is no longer able to accept the "impersonal, unaddressable 'purity' of [a] God" like that of Spinoza. Since for Buber, God is "*also* a person," one may call out to Him and speak to Him.²⁵

The existential situation of the individual as the embodiment of the Moment is now stamped with dialogical responsibility: "I know no fullness but each mortal hour's fullness of claim and responsibility."²⁶ But he is not content with this in itself as expressed in the interpersonal realm. The fullness of the momentary in its self-transcendence is presented in the contexts of Buber's Jewish writings in formulations such as this: "[I]n the wavering fraction of time, the fullness of time announces itself—not as a happening in the soul, but as a bodily happening in the world."²⁷ In the same context this view is also expressed in Jewish-historical terms, when he states that "the lived moment of man stands in truth between creation and redemption; it is joined to his being acted upon in creation, but also to his power to work for redemption."²⁸ In different terms, in another work, we are told that the transitory existential situation is nourished by (historical) "remembering faith," on the one hand, and that it draws a productive urge from the (eschatological) "language of expecting," on the other hand.²⁹ Expectant faith there represents yearnings for redemption, which are directed toward "the completion of God's creation to the kingdom of God."³⁰ Representations of the notion of redemption in Buber's writing are consistent with the term "Eternity" in the structure under discussion here.

It is important to distinguish between manifestations of this structure within the system of concepts or expressions from the historical literature of Judaism and their representation in universal meaning (such as that which characterizes his work, *I and Thou*).

In the beginning of his work *Dialogue*, published in 1932, Buber writes in the dedication to his wife, "To Paula—This was and is dialogue with you." In the second and expanded edition of the book, which appeared two years later, the dedication is enlarged and enriched on the latent matrix of the structure we are dealing with here:

> Der Abgrund und das Weltenlicht
> Zeitnot und Ewigkeitsbegier,
> Vision, Ereignis und Gedicht:
> Zwiesprache wars und ists mit dir.

> [The abyss and the light of the World
> The distress of the time and desire for eternity,
> Vision, event, and poem:
> This was and is dialogue with you.][31]

It should be noted that the two members of this structure are subject to polar tension in this representation.[32]

The desire to embody the connection between transhuman experience and historical reality in terms devoid of Jewish-historical identity is notable in Buber's writings even on occasions when one might expect he would appear as a Jew. Thus, for example, when he appeared in the Copernicus Ceremony in Jerusalem, at the height of the Holocaust, he spoke of the "spirit that stands firm against destruction"[33] in a general and opaque manner, lacking all reference to "the eternal Israel" (or to "the spirit of Judaism") or to the identity of those being destroyed.

Many years later, when Buber spoke about the essence of what he calls "eternal values," he presented them only in the light of their universal meaning. They are defined as

> those values, whose origins are not found in specific historical societies, not in their injunctions and not in their prohibitions, but in all of these societies it is best to say: their spiritual leaders saw the general rules set by people as interpretations of eternal values, which superior forces taught to the human race. I said: as interpretations, for one does not impose a single formulation on eternal values; man can only interpret them.[34]

He contrasts these values to "group values, social or national values," which people tried to substitute for absolute values linked to a divine commandment. Faith in "eternal values" is identified by him with "faith in the true absolute," of which he says in the present tense, that it "is revealed to individuals and groups and calls out to them."[35]

In another work where he expresses yearning for universality of belief that will take the place of religions, these eternal values are also identified with the revelation of the divinities of all the historical religions:

> Each religion is a human truth. That means it represents the relationship of a particular human community as such to the absolute. Each religion is a house of the human soul longing for God, a house with windows and without a door. . . . Each religion is an exile into which man is driven. . . . And no sooner than in the redemption of the world can we be liberated from the exiles and brought into the common world of God.[36]

The divine revelation "common to all" is the subject of this work. It is defined in it as "the human elaboration of the divine message."[37] There he presents a duality of "the will of God" and "the present reality of the world" (which must be resolved in its light), and this duality is founded upon that of Moment – Eternity.

The identity of "God" with "Eternity" arises and resonates within his writings from various times; generally it must be deduced, for Buber does not state it explicitly. For example, in one presentation of his belief Buber speaks of the reciprocal conditionality of speech with people and speech with God; in one of his sentences there he uses the term "the divinity" once, and elsewhere, instead of it, the expression, "the eternal Partner."[38] He sometimes makes alternate use of the concepts "absolute" and "eternal," both of them referring to God.[39]

The concept of the eternal, declares Buber, is "man's boldest concept." He identifies it with "One who does not dwell in time but only appears in it," a concept "of eternity set in judgment above the whole course of history."[40] In this context "time" and "history" are figures of the term "Moment." In another work, written close to the time of the one cited above, the mutual connection between the eternal and the momentary is emphasized. The relation between them is described as "the dramatic conflict between limited and unlimited being."[41] There the dialogical expression "Moment – Eternity" is also distinguished from this structure in its earlier manifestations: "I am constitutionally incapable of conceiving of myself as the ultimate source of moral approval or disapproval of myself. . . . The encounter with the original voice, the original source of yes or no, cannot be replaced by any self-encounter."[42] In another article written at the same time as these, we find a direct and clear identification of the divine, the eternal ("the eternally nameless"), and "transcendent beings."[43]

Along with the salient line of thought in which the embodiment of the "Moment" constitutes the first member of the structure under discussion here, and embodiments of the "Eternal" constitute the second one, we find in Buber's writings of the dialogical stage a different tendency, in which representations of the Eternal constitute the first member of the structure. The point of departure in this tendency is the *persistent* versus the *transitory*, the *atemporal* versus the *historical*. A series of such references appear in Buber's introductions to his biblical works. In the beginning of *The Kingship of God* this tendency is interpreted by means of the duality of "the eternal folk-kingship of JHWH" and "historical reconstruction."[44] These expressions also resonate in the beginning of his book, *The Prophetic Faith*, where he develops a discussion of principles based on the structure Moment – Eternity: he presents it as the connection between "the persistent kernel in its existence" and "transitory historical situations."[45]

Representations of the structure under discussion here, where the point of origin is the manifestation of the concept "Eternity," constitute the underpinning of an idea repeatedly expressed in Buber's writings and formulated as dialogue between God and man. "This dialogue between God and Man, God and the world, is the historical hour."[46] On the basis of it, according to his view, the processes of Jewish history take place."[47] Buber is well aware that contact between God and His people over the twisting path of its history is not necessarily a dialogical contact: "but man does not listen with faithful ears to what is spoken to him. Already in hearing he blends together command of heaven and stature of earth." There is also human heedfulness that does not imply the reception of a divine word, and it is accompanied by tension between religious revelation and human understanding. For example, there is the polar tension of which Buber speaks: "Always when I have to translate or to interpret a biblical text, I do so with fear and trembling, in an inescapable tension between the world of God and the words of men."[48] This is done by heeding the concrete human condition. Buber says:

The significance of community in Israelite law is a dynamic and not a static one. But that holds for all peoples, for God is not only the God of Israel. There is no religious and social program, but there is this not-to-be-misunderstood indication of what is right and wrong in the society. There is no firmly established law, formulated once and for all, but only the word of God, and our current situation which we have to learn by listening. We do not have codified principles that we can consult. But we must understand the situation and the moment.[49]

Primacy and centrality are bestowed upon the *human* condition, in which Buber conceives, according to his understanding, the word of God, his God.

Constant, repeated, reiterated examination of the relation between historical reality and absolute values shaped Buber's Zionist conception and also his positions on political issues. It guided him more than anything else in his determinations in the Jewish-Arab conflict.[50] In his opinion, the choice confronting Zionism is whether to be seduced by the lie of "success" of the interests of the historical "Moment," which can lead the Zionist enterprise into desolation or to choose the path of "loyalty." Buber depicts the Moment, freed of ethical obligations beyond it, as absolutely negative. Shortsighted politicians and so-called successes try, according to him, to "react to the moment" only "from the moment." This is a "tactical response," not accompanied by understanding "that deliberating tactically always provides us with the wrong means, sacrifices the future for the sake of the moment." These are the words with which he sums up a kind of short anthology of selections from his speeches and articles on Zionist issues and on Jewish-Arab cooperation, which he assembled a short time after his arrival in the Land of Israel.[51] In contrast to the Moment, he presents the Future, and similarly he confronts the "tactical response" with "the yoke of the truth," and "success" with "faith." And, through all these pairs of concepts, there emerges the Moment – Eternity structure.[52]

These words of Buber from 1939 express a basic attitude that resonates throughout his Zionist career, over all the vicissitudes of time, beyond the changing historical circumstances. It is fascinating to note how a person's truth stands the test of more than sixty years of creativity and active involvement, in struggling with the "questions of the hour" of the nation and of the Zionist movement.

There has been conspicuous tension between two basic tendencies in the history of Zionism from its beginnings in the late nineteenth century: the political tendency and the spiritual-cultural tendency. Theodor Herzl (1860-1904), the prophet of the Jewish state, was regarded as the most striking embodiment of the former tendency; and Asher Ginzberg (1856-1927), who wrote under the nom de plume of "Ahad Ha-Am" (One of the People), became one of the central spokesmen for the latter one. The central aim of the tendency represented by Herzl was to resolve "the affliction of the Jews," whereas Ahad Ha-Am and, similarly, Buber maintained that it was impossible to contend with the problems of Jewish existence in the present without resolving "the affliction of Judaism."

Buber identified with the path of Ahad Ha-Am from the time that he first joined the Zionist movement at the age of twenty in 1898. His disputes with Herzl at the beginning of the twentieth century continued later on, over decades, with spokesmen for the political tendency, which was the central and dominant orientation in Zionist history. Against the background of this opposition between the political and the social-utopian trends, one can also understand the roots of Buber's argument with David Ben-Gurion after the establishment of the State of Israel.

The essence of this opposition is presented from Buber's point of view in a short article by him, published in 1940, where he compares the political-solid approach to "an asphalt road between a bad present and its improved continuation." In contrast he presents the visionary-utopian view, with which he identifies, as "a rope stretched between the secret of the past and the secret of the distant or near future."[53] For him Zionism is not only a tool for solving the pressing problems of the Jewish people's existence, but also a present and obligatory expression of historical Jewish identity, of responsibility to Jewish collective memory, on the basis of which he depicts a Zionist utopia. He does not regard Jewish sovereignty as the ultimate purpose, but as a means, a framework, the meaning of which is the ethical essence that is cast within it. He maintains that "the 'political' is a precondition for the realization of the ideal, no less but no more. . . . For the lover of Zion like Ahad-Ha'am the state is merely the way to the goal called Zion."[54]

Various linguistic guises of the structure whose members are "the reality of the moment" and "eternal reality" repeatedly resonate in the lecture entitled "On Eternity and the Moment," which Buber gave upon receiving the Bialik Prize in 1961. Only then, as an elderly man, did he lay bare and explicitly present his Moment – Eternity structure, making it the title of his lecture-article. The first member of the structure is represented by the expressions "the problems and tasks of [that] hour," "that hour of Israel and that hour of the world," "the situation," "now and here," "transitory reality," and "the doctrine of work in concreteness." His presentations of the second member are "the Eternal," "vital, exalted truth," "the absolute commandment," "spirit" (or "the eternal spirit"), and "the eternal aspect." Incidentally, regarding the variety of God's names, we are told that "this is not the main point, by what name we call the absolute, but the main point is whether we serve it in reality." In that lecture we also find a use of the foregoing structure to explain the way poems come into being; Buber sees in them the fruit of dialogue between "the impenetrable darkness of eternity" and "the bright concreteness of the moment."[55]

*   *   *

Buber apparently uses ambiguous formulations intentionally when, in the field of his Jewish writings as well, he differentiates between "what is conditioned by times and what is timeless."[56] For him eternity seems to be the outcome of a monological encounter (in which he sees the "concretization" of the moment); every single person can grasp it in accordance with the existing givens of his personality and situation. Walter Kaufmann says that Buber finds in his encounter with the Thou what the poet William Blake finds in a grain of sand or a wildflower: infinity and eternity—here and now.[57] Every single person will find his own eternity, if only he has an object of yearnings, an ideal constituting "authority above life of the present."[58] One can have no hold on human reality without the spiritual world beyond and above it, which is not conditioned by it. The duality of "Spirit – Reality" has an important place in Buber's writings, for it, too, is an embodiment of this fundamental structure. The spirit cannot be understood, declares Buber, "as one of the active forces of man, but *as his concentrated fulfillment and wholeness.*"[59]

Just as Buber was to change his conception of the individual spirit, he also changed his conception of the spirit of the nation, "the spirit of Israel." They are distinct from each other in their fulfillment: "fulfillment of the simple truth, that man has been created for purpose,"[60] fulfillment binding the spirit with reality, the eternal with the moment. *Ha-Ruah veha-Metziut* (Spirit and historical reality) is what Buber called a collection of articles on current issues that he published a few years after settling in Jerusalem. The subtitle of the collection is: "Nine Chapters to Clarify the Relation between Them."[61] Most of the contexts of the discussion in which he deals with "spirit" permit us to understand it both in connotations of faith and also of anthropology (which convey meaning even without any direct or obligatory faith connection).

Sometimes the Absolute is identified by Buber with "faith in reality, in the verities of existence." To believe in the absolute (or in Eternity) means to believe "that life will afford some aim for me and existence will have some meaning."[62] He places religiosity of this kind in contrast with formal religion based on liturgy and ceremonies—a normative religious structure. Here we have an expression of the conception that took root in Buber's spiritual world after being presented comprehensively in his early article, "Jewish Religiosity" (1913).[63] He strove to endow the context of man's concrete life with a religious dimension. From the first stirrings of his dialogical thought, one notes in his writings a progressively clearer intention to invoke a life of faith and a life of meaning on an equal basis, without indicating an unequivocal identity between the two.

*   *   *

By means of his concept "Eternity," Buber also presents his approach to death and immortality. The concept of immortality is not common in the presentations of his structure "Moment – Eternity." It is interesting to note that, particularly in the relatively early expression of this structure, where God is already conceived of as a transhuman entity, the concept "Eternity" is identified with that of "Immortality."[64]

Buber could not reconcile his anchoring of himself in "the abundance of every passing hour with demand and responsibility in it" with his efforts at mystical elevation toward other realities. Against this background must be understood, among other things, his reluctance to deal with death. "The genuine faith speaks: I know nothing of death, but I know that God is eternity."[65] Similarly he condemns identification of Eternity (or God) with the immortal. He states that "we are God's, who is not immortal, but eternal."[66]

Seymour Siegal quotes a similar statement by Buber in answer to a question:

> I think death is the end of everything that we are able to imagine. Therefore, this means that we cannot, and we should not, imagine life after death merely as a going on in time. . . . I don't even imagine a going on in time, but I am certain of entering eternity. And though I cannot imagine it, I know I shall enter it, and this means that one can be more certain of God's existence than of his own existence.[67]

This opposition in Buber's spiritual world was preceded by another oppositional distinction, that between "eternity" and "infinity." It "flickered in his thought" even when he was fifteen years old, in the throes of perplexity regarding the essence of the eternal. He recounts this nearly fifty years later in the personal testimony with which his work *What is Man?* (1938) is imbued.[68]

The distinction between eternity and infinity and between eternity and immortality has basic importance in the world of Buber's belief, although he does not discuss them comprehensively in any of his writings. In a conversation that he held with Herbert Wiener about a year before his death, he returned to them, binding them together and presenting them as a single unit:

> I believe in eternity. . . . Eternity is not infinity. What it is I cannot understand. I cannot understand infinite numbers either. But I believe in them. All I know is that nothing is more certain than death. I do not believe in immortality. But I do believe in eternity. With death I can enter into eternity. Do you understand? That is faith.[69]

The reciprocal connection that Buber asserts between the moment and eternity means not only the negation of the possibility of enclosing the human situation within itself but also the assumption that the transhuman has no meaning in itself, lacking all contact with the world and with humanity.

10
CONCLUDING REMARKS

REGARDING THE METHODOLOGY OF THE
DUAL APPROACH TO BUBER'S THOUGHT

Polar duality, as we have seen, occupies a central place in all of Buber's writings. Although extensive, Buber scholarship has hardly taken note of the rootedness and wide application of polar duality, which is more comprehensive than that of his dialogical thought (in all the variety of its expressions). The dialogical theme is only a partial, though prominent, aspect of the representations of polarity in his writings.

In order to test the methodological aspect of the dual approach, one must take note of the distinction embedded in Buber's thought between two binary orders: Dualism[1] and Duality. Buber rebelled against the former and developed the latter.

His opposition to dualism in modern thought is mainly directed against specific instances of it, such as *religious dualism* (found in the thought of Thomas Hyde, one of the first to coin the term "dualism" in the early eighteenth century), according to which religion is founded on the opposition between light and darkness, between divinity and Satan; *ontological or metaphysical dualism*, according to which the world is founded on the opposition between being and becoming, between spirit and matter, and even between the living and the inanimate, seen as essences that stand by themselves, in opposition to each other; *anthropological dualism*, which also has ontological status, according to which the cosmos is built on the opposition between thought and extension, and human existence is based on the contrast between soul and body, as articulated by Descartes in the early development of dualism in the modern age; and *critical dualism*, as expounded by Kant, according to which there are divisions between intuition and understanding, understanding and reason, the finite and infinity, man and God, inclination and duty, and others. In every area of Kant's philosophizing stood a dualism, the oppositions of which could not be bridged.

The rejection of these kinds of dualism was formulated as early as the beginning of the nineteenth century by F. W. Schelling. Among other things, in his highly influential "Philosophische Untersuchungen über das Wesen der menschlichen Freiheit," in volume one of his *Philosophische Schriften* (1809), he rejected thinking based on "two different principles absolutely independent of each other." The principle dualisms in the doctrine of Kant resonate in the writings of Schelling as well as those of Fichte, who sought to unify understanding and sensibility, pure reason and practical reason, spirit and nature. With the aforementioned work Schelling opened the way toward the irrational doctrines of the nineteenth century that were developed by Schopenhauer, Hartmann, and Nietzsche.[2]

These doctrines provided the basis for Duality, a different binary form, the essence of which is not opposition but rather mutual complementarity, the meeting between two contraries that includes the aspiration toward *experiential unity*. Buber concretized his dual approach as a continuation of this tradition, just as he drew upon the romantic "polar doctrine" that strove toward synthesis and renewal that would grow out of tension between opposites. The emphasis in the expressions of this "doctrine of polarity," as well as in the polarity underlying Buber's view, is placed upon becoming and not on being, on action and not on its completion.

On the basis of polar tensions between opposites, Buber forms a duality that is a product of basic existential experiences. I propose calling it "existential duality." One of its most complete expressions may be found in the following statement by Buber:

> The process in the human soul becomes a process in the world: through the recognition of oppositeness, the opposites which are always latently present in creation break out into actuality, they become existent.[3]

The dualities within creation are grasped here as part of a dynamic process of becoming, and human creation is presented as a result of the experience of its opposites. The creative, dynamic process of becoming, which is formed in its encounter with the roughness of lived reality, typifies Buber's dual structures.[4]

ON THE CHARACTER OF THE UNITY THAT BINDS
TOGETHER THE AREAS OF HIS THOUGHT

The study of the history of Buber's ideas reveals lines of continuity and trends of development. The latter are made clear to us by laying bare the conceptual foci and by locating the dual structures upon which his thought is based.

Buber endowed the concepts and structures both with a decided *value orientation* (to be guiding principles marked by drives for concretization) and also with a *formal* purpose (to combine and organize the "events" or "situations" into some systematic order).[5] These two dimensions are connected with each other: so, for example, when Buber tells about the period of "Vortex" and describes it as lacking a "center" and a "growing substance," it is clear that he means not only the lack of order and direction in their spiritual-values meaning.[6]

Reference to the signs of unity of the structures and indication of the relations between their members does not mean that each of the structures forms a separate tendency in Buber's philosophizing. From my discussion above, it is clear that on occasion various structures act jointly, just as their manifestations may overlap partially.

Just as the structures do not indicate the lines of unification or division in his thought, so too it is not ultimately possible to sort and classify them on the basis of the various disciplines to which one tries to assign Buber's writings in various fields. It is doubtful whether it is possible to isolate one branch or discipline within the ensemble of his worldview and to understand it by itself. Anthropological and psychological topics arise in his writings, and philosophical questions are discussed, as well as ethics, education, art, and social and political issues. Some of his writings are called "biblical," "Hasidic," "sociological," "philosophical," "theological," "sociopolitical," etc. But the majority of them do not have a disciplinary or professional character. Buber does not intend to be a "man of science" free of value judgments.[7]

All the areas of knowledge, experience, and thought to which he refers in his writings are decidedly marked with his personal stamp. The spiritual and ethical purpose is joined with the effort to reach a personal truth derived from life, from the special way in which a particular human life is lived. His personal experience is refracted into various aspects. The *personal* point of view is what ties together all of them, and their ensemble functions as a living, organic unity.

The features of this unity are those with which he characterizes the "inner truthfulness of a culture." He sees in it "the active unity of the spirit in all the disciplines of existence, both in the areas of organizing life and also in the areas of exalting life. . . . It is impossible to grasp its essence without grasping its contradictions. . . . The unity of a culture is a unity created by a *polar* process, by means of polar processes."[8] "The double nature of man,"[9] he says, is characterized by "a double dynamics of true movement."[10] The contradictions in Buber's world are not divisive contradictions;[11] the oppositions and rifts that characterize this world are bridged or combined within its organic unity.

Active, living unity like this does not correspond to the definitions that determine lawfulness in a philosophical or scientific system, for "the [organic] whole," in his opinion, "is not made, it grows. He who tries to force it loses it while he appears to be winning it."[12] This growth is based on "a dynamic in which we find the metamorphosis of the first in the second,"[13] and in any event it is impossible to make it compatible with recognition of concepts according to the logical laws characterized by systematic philosophical inquiry. Hence it is understandable that Buber's value concepts lack static, unequivocal persistence.

Buber's writings should be examined in the manner in which he says that one should approach biblical writings: "as a *unity*, which, although it has been formed, combines many and various elements, complete and partial, a true organic unity."[14]

The structures to which separate chapters of the present study have been devoted reached their *mature* crystallization only from the 1930s on. And only from that decade—rather, only after the appearance of the first of Buber's anthropological-philosophical works, *What is Man?*—do the organic features mentioned above apply to his writings as a whole. It then becomes possible to apply to them the phrase with which he expresses the task of philosophical anthropology: only through "recognition of the dynamic that exerts power within every particular reality and between them, and from the constantly new proof of the one in the many, can it come to see the wholeness of man."[15] All of the central structures serving as the foundation of the edifice of Buber's creation came into being as organic extensions of the outgrowths of his thought.

The dialogical worldview was for Buber, in his life, a demand made upon himself and the object of longings more than a lived experience. His spiritual biography was a drama with many episodes, at the bottom of which was tension "between is and ought."[16] Its image is reflected in its binary nature, in expressions of duality that characterize the central structures that constitute the hidden scaffolding that bears his writing in their entirety.

Notes

Introduction

1. See "Vorbemerkung über F. Werfel," *Der Jude* 2 (1917): 111.
2. See chapter 2.
3. See Buber, "Judaism and Mankind," in *On Judaism*, ed. N. N. Glatzer, trans. E. Jospe (New York, 1967), p. 25.
4. See "Lesser Uri," *Ost und West* 1, no. 2 (February 1901): cols. 113–28.
5. H. Heine, *Gedanken und Einfaelle*.
6. Buber, *The Origin and Meaning of Hasidism*, ed. and trans. by M. Friedman (New York, 1960), p. 117.
˙ 7. See chapter 9.
8. Buber, "Spinoza, Sabbatai Zvi, and the Baal-Shem," in *Origin and Meaning of Hasidism*, p. 100.
9. See the section "Soul Peace and World Peace" in chapter 7.
10. Buber, "Religion and Reality" (1951), in *Eclipse of God,* trans. M. Friedman, E. Kamenka, N. Guterman, and I. M. Lask (New York, 1952), p. 21.
11. Buber, "Teaching and Deed" (1934), in *Israel and the World*, trans. O. Marx (New York, 1963), p. 140, and see below, chap. 10.
12. See Buber, "What is Man?," in *Between Man and Man*, trans. R. G. Smith (New York, 1961), p. 185.
13. Buber, "The Foundation Stone," in *Origin and Meaning of Hasidism*, p. 72.
14. The expression "value concepts" derives from the work of Max Kadushin in the study of rabbinic culture. My discussion in this study of the character of Buber's concepts draws upon Kadushin's approach. See M. Kadushin, *The Rabbinic Mind*, 3d ed. (New York, 1972), pp. 1–25; idem, *Worship and Ethics: A Study in Rabbinic Judaism* (New York, 1963), pp. 3–17; and A. Holtz, *Be-Olam*

199

Ha-Mahshava Shel Hazal Be-Ikvot Mishnat M. Kadushin (Rabbinic thought, following the teaching of M. Kadushin) (Tel Aviv, 1979).
15. Midrash Tanhuma, *Hukat* 52.
16. Jerusalem Talmud, *Rosh Ha-Shana,* chap. 3, hal. 5.
17. Buber, *Paths in Utopia* (in Hebrew), ed. A. Shapira, new ed. (Tel Aviv, 1983), pp. 94–95.

Comments on Buber's Means of Expression

1. Most of those poems by Buber which were published were taken from his literary legacy. He usually wrote poetry in German, and it has been translated into Hebrew from the manuscripts and published in various places. Some of his poetry has also been translated into English. See "Two Poems by M. Buber," trans. G. Hartmann, *Orim* (New Haven, Conn.), Spring 1987, pp. 92–97.
2. See Buber, "On the Essence of Culture" (in Hebrew), in *Pnei Adam* (Jerusalem, 1962), p. 384.
3. See G. Scholem, "Le-Demuto Shel Martin Buber" (Regarding the figure of Martin Buber) (1953), in *Devarim Be-Go,* comp. and ed. A. Shapira (Tel Aviv, 1976), p. 457.
4. See A. Shapira, "Meetings with M. Buber," *Midstream* 24, no. 9 (November 1978): 48–54.
5. Among the difficulties confronting the reader: the distinctive concepts as well as his dual structures, on the basis of which he builds his arguments, are hidden or implicit in the texture of his discussion, and for the most part he does not point them out.
6. B. Kurzweill, "'Shlosha Neumim Al Ha-Yahadut' le-M. Buber" (Buber's "Three Addresses on Judaism"), *Haaretz,* 10 July 1953.

Chapter 1. Polar Duality

1. See chapter 4.
2. See Buber, "Judaism and the Jews" (1909), in *On Judaism,* p. 18.
3. See Buber, "The Spirit of the Orient and Judaism," in *On Judaism,* p. 65. On German Jewish life as the platform for Buber's actions, see N. N. Glatzer, editor's postscript to Buber, *On Judaism,* pp. 237–42; G. Scholem, "Martin Buber's Conception of Judaism," in *On Jews and Judaism in Crisis: Selected Essays,* ed. W. J. Dannhauser (New York, 1976), pp. 126–41.
4. See G. Schaeder, *The Hebrew Humanism of Martin Buber,* trans. N. J. Jacobs (Detroit, 1973), pp. 54–124, 130–31.
5. See the section "Fin de siècle" in A. Shapira, "Dual Structures in the Thought of Martin Buber" (in Hebrew) (Ph.D. diss., Tel Aviv University, 1983).
6. See Buber, "Gustav Landauer," *Die Zeit,* 11 June 1904, p. 127; Link-Salinger (Hyman), R., *Gustav Landauer: Philosopher of Utopia* (Indianapolis, 1977), pp. 99–100.

7. See A. E. Simon, "The Builder of Bridges," trans. D. Silverman, *Judaism* 27, no. 2 (Spring 1978): 148–60.

8. See the section "Concepts and Structures: The Background of Their Reference" in chapter 6 and the section, "The Formation of the Structure" in chapter 8, as well as below.

9. Simon, "The Builder of Bridges," p. 150.

10. An expression of that, among other things, is found in his article, "Buddha" (1907), in *Ereignisse und Begegnungen* (Leipzig, 1917), and see also the section, "Concepts and Structures: The Background of Their Reference" in chapter 6.

11. Buber, *Briefwechsel*, 2:272 (letter no. 232).

12. Buber, introduction to *Tales of the Hasidim: The Later Masters*, trans. O. Marx (New York, 1948), p. 29.

13. It should be mentioned here that: (1) he was separated from his mother from his fourth year of life for thirty consecutive years (see chapter 4); (2) his spiritual doubts brought him to the brink of suicide when he was fifteen years old (see the aforementioned section); (3) he described "one of the first hours that he tread upon the earth, an earth of tragedy" (see chapter 2); (4) the deep change in his personality which he calls "a conversion" (see chapter 5); (5) his meeting with his mother after the protracted separation (see chapter 4).

14. See the extended discussion in chapter 8.

15. See Buber, "The Limits of Advice," in *Tales of the Hasidim: The Early Masters*, trans. O. Marx (New York, 1956), p. 66.

16. See also the fourth section below.

17. See chapter 2.

18. The lecture was entitled "Alte und neue Gemeinschaft" (Old and new community) and was published by P. R. Mendes-Flohr and B. Susser in *AJSR* 1 (1976): 50–59. See the articles by Mendes-Flohr and Susser annotating it at pp. 41–49 of that issue. See the section, "Creative Vitalism" in chapter 7.

19. See ibid., pp. 51–52.

20. See ibid., p. 54

21. See ibid., p. 51.

22. See ibid.

23. See Buber, "Lesser Uri" (early version, 1901, later version, 1903). I cite the early version, from *Ost und West* 1, no. 2 (February 1901): cols. 113–28. English translation of both versions by Gilya G. Schmidt is forthcoming from Syracuse University Press (May 1999).

24. See ibid., cols. 115–16.

25. See ibid., col. 116, and see my reference to it in chapter 7.

26. See ibid., col. 116, and see my reference to it in chapter 9.

27. See ibid., cols. 123–24.

28. See ibid., col. 124.

29. See ibid., cols. 125–26.

30. See the section, "Concepts and Structures: The Background of Their Reference" in chapter 6.

31. See "Lesser Uri" (1901), col. 124.

32. See ibid.

33. See D. D. Runes, *Dictionary of Philosophy*, 15th ed. (New York: Philosophical Library, 1960), p. 241; A. Flew, *A Dictionary of Philosophy* (New York: St. Martin's Press, 1979), p. 259.

34. See the discussion by Walter Kaufmann of what he calls "dubious dichotomies," in *Discovering the Mind*, vol. 3: *Freud versus Adler and Jung* (New York, 1980), p. 457.

35. Buber, "Judaism and Mankind," p. 25.

36. Buber, *Briefwechsel*, 1:286.

37. Letter to Egga von Kohl, 20 May 1912, Buber Archive in the Israel National Library in Jerusalem, file 374/h.

38. See *Daniel* in Buber, *Werke I: Schriften zur Philosophie* (Munich and Heidelberg, 1962), pp. 47–63; 64–76.

39. Ibid., p. 49 and see the discussion at ibid., pp. 49–50. This corresponds to pp. 104–5 in the English version of *Daniel*, trans. M. Friedman (New York, 1965), pp. 104–5.

40. See *Daniel* in Buber, *Werke I: Schriften zur Philosophie*, p. 70 (in *Daniel*, trans. Friedman, p. 136).

41. See the Bubersonderheft of *Neue Blätter* 3 (January–February 1913).

42. G. Landauer, "Martin Buber," *Neue Blätter* 3 (January–February 1913): 20–107. This article was later included in G. Landauer, *Der Werdende Mensch* (Potsdam, 1921), pp. 244–58.

43. See G. Landauer, *Sein Lebensgang in Briefen*, Band I (Frankfurt a M., 1929), pp. 434–35.

44. Buber, *Briefwechsel*, 1:324–25.

45. Ibid., p. 324.

46. Ibid., p. 331.

47. Buber, "Judaism and Mankind," p. 31. In the context of this article of 1910 Buber emphasized that in "every Jew" these contrasts dwell "together." Indeed, the rifts in his being and the divisive contradictions that agitated Buber's world were the background for the growth of many of his contemporaries, born or educated during the fin-de-siècle period; thus one is likely to find that polar attitudes exist in the writings of other Jewish thinkers. Two prominent exemplars are A. J. Heschel and J. D. Soloveitchik.

In Heschel's conception of God, pairs of concepts are prominent, such as "uniqueness and togetherness" and "exclusiveness and inclusiveness." These concepts were also significant in his ontology in general. The first of these pairs of concepts is connected to another pair of polar concepts: "event and process." Another pair which occupies an important place in his thought is "uniqueness and repetitiveness." See the extensive treatment of this topic in the introduction by F. A. Rothschild, the editor of *Between God and Man: From the Writings of A. J. Heschel* (New York, 1959), pp. 18, 19, 20.

A final conceptual structure, besides those mentioned above, is what Heschel called, "the polar character of all human experience" (see *Between God and Man*, p. 32).

Even an Orthodox Jewish thinker such as J. D. Soloveitchik is not immune to the existential crises of his time. He speaks of the two faces of existence, basing his doctrine of human nature on it. See "Halachic Man" (in Hebrew) (1944), in *Besod hayahid vehayahad*, ed. P. Hacohen Peli (Jerusalem, n.d.), pp. 48–55, cf. p. 56. Another expression of this fundamental conception is found in *The Lonely Man of Faith* (in Hebrew) (Jerusalem: The Rav Kook Institute, 1965), where he discusses the tragic isolation of the man of faith, an isolation that is an inseparable part of the vocation from which he can never free himself. Or, in other words, "full redemption . . . is not possible," and the believer is condemned to remain "in constant motion" between the pole of the community of natural splendor and the pole of the community of the covenant (see p. 46). Polarity thus characterizes the human situation today, and "the future unity of creation" or "the full redemption" remain the objects of yearnings, "that cannot be fulfilled." (See p. 51.) There is surprising similarity between Soloveitchik's approach and that of Buber as will be discussed in the section below, "Duality and the Yearning for Unity."

48. See Buber, "On the Essence of Culture," pp. 382–83.

49. See the fourth section below.

50. See the section "A Conversion" included in Buber, "Dialogue," in *Between Man and Man*, pp. 13–14.

51. See chapter 5, below.

52. See Sh. H. Bergmann, "Buber's Philosophy," in *Thinkers of the Generation* (in Hebrew) (Mitzpeh, 1935), p. 179.

53. See idem, "Buber's Dialogical Thinking" (in Hebrew), his introduction to Buber, *Besod Siach* (Jerusalem, 1959, pp. xi–xii.

54. Scholars have not given the polarity at the basis of Buber's thought the attention it merits. This has been true since the book by Kohn, *Martin Buber, Sein Werk und Seine Zeit* (1930; reprint, Cologne, 1961), which does indeed refer to polarity on p. 105 and discusses it on p. 131, also referring to it in the notes, p. 323. However, these references are swallowed up in the discussions of the other issues and concepts in Buber's writings. The term "polarity" does not even appear in *The Philosophy of Martin Buber*, ed. P. A. Schilpp and M. Friedman (La Salle, Ill., 1967), nor in the collection of lectures given at the Beersheba conference (see below). M. Friedman, who, in several contexts, refers to polarity as a theme in "Judaism and Mankind" (1910) and in *Daniel*, does not, however, note the fundamental significance of this conception in Buber's thought. See *M. Buber's Life and Work: The Early Years, 1878–1923* (New York: E. P. Dutton, 1981), pp. 135, 161, 167.

Among the well-known scholars who fail to pay attention to the polar character of the I-Thou, I-It duality, we shall mention Walter Kaufmann, who describes it as a dichotomy. See his "Buber's Failures and his Victory" (in Hebrew) in *Martin Buber: One Hundred Years Since His Birth*, the proceedings of the Beersheba conference edited by Y. Bloch, H. Gordon, M. Dorman (Tel Aviv, 1982), pp. 28, 35. See also the manner in which the participants in the discussion followed Kaufmann's lead, pp. 37, 38.

In contrast, see the important comments on this matter in the work of Paul Mendes-Flohr. Criticizing W. Kaufmann's approach to the duality in *I and Thou*, he presents a distinction between the dualism in Buber's early writings and that in his dialogical writings. See Mendes-Flohr, "From Kulturmystik to Dialogue" (Ph.D. diss., Brandeis University, 1974), p. 279 n. 165.

55. See the reference to the stages in development of this structure in the section "Concepts and Structures: The Background of Their Reference."

56. See Buber, *I and Thou*, trans. W. Kaufmann (New York, 1970), pp. 100–109.

57. See Buber, "Dialogue," pp. 30–33.

58. See Buber, "Religion and Philosophy," in *Eclipse of God*, pp. 25–46.

59. See Buber, "Prophecy, Apocalyptic, and Historical Hour," in *On the Bible*, ed. N. N. Glatzer (New York, 1968), pp. 172–87.

60. Buber, "The Faith of Israel" (1928), in *Israel and the World*, p. 17.

61. Buber, "Abraham the Seer," in *On the Bible*, p. 26.

62. Buber, "The Foundation Stone," pp. 72–73.

63. See the section "His Relation to the Organic-Developmental Approach" in Shapira, "Dual Structures in the Thought of Martin Buber."

64. See chap. 8.

65. See Herzl's letter to Buber, *Briefwechsel*, 1:160 (7 August 1901).

66. Buber, "Theodor Herzl" (23 July 1904), in *Die Jüdische Bewegung: Gesammelte Aufsätze, 1900–1915* (Berlin, 1915), p. 138. English translation by G. G. Schmidt is forthcoming from Syracuse University Press (May, 1999).

67. Ibid., p. 143.

68. Ibid., p. 145.

69. Ibid., pp. 148–50.

70. Ibid., p. 152.

71. "Herzl und die Historie," *Ost und West*, August–September 1904. English translation by G. G. Schmidt is forthcoming from Syracuse University Press (May, 1999).

72. "He and We" (1910) (in Hebrew), *Ha'ollam* 8, no. 25 (9 July 1914): 2–4. English translation by G. G. Schmidt is forthcoming from Syracuse University Press (May, 1999)

73. Ibid., p. 3.

74. See ibid. See my reference to this article in the first section of chapter 7.

75. See the section "Duality and the Yearning for Unity," below.

76. See Buber, "He and We," p. 3.

77. See the reference to "Judaism and Humanity" and to "He and We" in the section "Duality and the Yearning for Unity," below.

78. See Buber, "He and We," p. 4.

79. Ibid., p. 2. Here we have an embryonic expression of the duality of "collective" and "society," of "mechanical society" and "organic society." It could be that the influence of F. Tönnies resonates here.

80. See chapter 2.

81. Again, see chapter 2.

82. Buber, "Ilu Haya Herzl Od Be-Hayim" (If Herzl were alive today), *Ha'arets*, 17 May 1940; reprinted in *Shdemot* 79 (1981): 23–25.

83. See ibid. (1981), p. 23.

84. Ibid. His reference to the primordial soul is apparently connected with his conception that speaks of the "innermost stratum of man's disposition, which yields his type, the basic structure of his personality." See my discussion of this topic in chapter 6. On the primordiality of the Jewish soul see also Buber, "The Two Foci of the Jewish Soul" (1930), in *Israel and the World*, pp. 13–27.

85. Buber, "Ilu Haya Herzl Od Be-Hayim" (1981), p. 25.

86. Ibid., p. 24.

87. See Buber, *On Zion: The History of an Idea,* trans. S. Goodman (London, 1952), pp. 123–47.

88. Echoes of his struggle to write this work are found, among other places, in Buber's letters to Franz Rosenzweig of 18 January 1923 and 10 February 1923. See *Briefwechsel,* 2:153–54, 158.

89. Buber, "Geleitwort," in *Der Grosse Maggid und Seine Nachfolge* (Frankfurt a.M., 1922), p. lxxxvi.

90. See the section "Existential Duality and Its Expressions," above.

91. See G. Scholem, "On Buber's Works in the Field of Hasidism" (in Hebrew) (1948), in *Devarim Be-Go* (Tel Aviv, 1976), p. 453. Scholem repeats this statement in "Le-Demuto Shel Martin Buber," p. 456.

92. Buber, foreword to *For the Sake of Heaven,* trans. L. Lewisohn (New York, 1969), p. x.

93. See Buber, "The Question of the Single One," in *Between Man and Man,* p. 74.

94. Ibid.

95. See my chapters devoted to them.

96. See Buber, "The Teacher of Truth" (in Hebrew), in *Paths in Utopia,* ed. Shapira, p. 250.

97. Buber, "The Field and the Stars" (in Hebrew), in *Paths in Utopia,* ed. Shapira, pp. 254–55.

98. Buber, "A Man Who Realizes the Idea of Zion," in *On Zion,* pp. 154–61.

99. See chapter 3.

100. See chapter 2.

101. See the section above, "Existential Duality and Its Expressions."

102. Buber, "Judaism and Mankind," p. 28.

103. See ibid., pp. 32–33.

104. See the section, "What is 'Polar Duality'?," above.

105. Buber, "Judaism and Mankind," p. 25. See also my discussion in the aforementioned section.

106. See Buber, "He and We," p. 3, and my previous section.

107. Letter to Sh. H. Bergmann dated 7 May 1913 (my emphasis). See my discussion of it in the section above, "What is 'Polar Duality'?"

108. See chapter 8.

109. See, for example, Buber, "The Love of God and the Idea of Deity" (1944), in *Eclipse of God,* p. 60.

110. Buber, "Ekstase und Bekenntnis," in *Ekstatische Konfessionen,* gesammelt von Martin Buber (Jena, 1908), p. xvi.

111. Ibid., p. xx.

112. See *Daniel* in Buber, *Werke I: Schriften zur Philosophie,* p. 73 (in *Daniel,* trans. Friedman, p. 140).
113. *Daniel* in Buber, *Werke I: Schriften zur Philosophie,* p. 63 (in *Daniel,* trans. Friedman, p. 124).
114. Buber, "Herut" (1948), in *On Judaism,* p. 170.
115. See my treatment of this article in the section "Concepts and Structures: The Background of Their Reference" in chapter 6.
116. Buber, "Dialogue," p. 25.
117. See Buber, "The Silent Question" (1951), in *On Judaism,* p. 210. This statement is consistent with the far earlier one, according to which love takes place "between I and Thou" (*I and Thou,* p. 60).

Chapter 2. The Cause and the Person: Destiny and Vocation

1. See chapter 5, below.
2. See Bergmann, "Buber's Dialogical Thinking," pp. xi–xii.
3. G. Scholem, "On Buber's Works in the Field of Hasidism" (in Hebrew) (1948), in *Devarim Bego,* ed. A. Shapira (Tel Aviv, 1976), p. 451.
4. Scholem, "Martin Buber's Conception of Judaism," p. 126.
5. See his various autobiographical writings, most of which were first included in other works, in "Autobiographical Fragments" (1960), in *The Philosophy of Martin Buber,* ed. Schilpp and Friedman.
6. See "Jüdische Wissenschaft," *Die Welt* (Wien), 25 October 1901.
7. "Herzl und die Historie," *Ost und West,* August–September 1904.
8. See Buber, "He and We," p. 4.
9. "Zion and Youth" (in Hebrew) (1918), in *Am ve'Olam* (Jerusalem, 1961), p. 216.
10. "The Cause and the Person" (1929) in Buber, "Autobiographical Fragments," p. 17.
11. Ibid., p. 18.
12. Ibid., p. 17.
13. Ibid., p. 19.
14. Buber, *For the Sake of Heaven,* p. 137.
15. B.-Z. Dinur, "Three Conversations with Buber" (in Hebrew), *Molad* 222 (Tammuz–Av 5727 [1967]): 234.
16. On that concept, see M. Kadushin, *The Rabbinic Mind* (New York, 1972), pp. 297–98.
17. See "Judaism and the Jews" (1909), "Judaism and Mankind" (1910), and "The Renewal of Judaism" (1911), all in Buber, *On Judaism.*
18. See Buber, "In Memory of Arthur Ruppin" (in Hebrew), untitled lecture given on the thirtieth day after his death, the second of Adar I, Jerusalem, 1943, p. 3.
19. Ibid.
20. See Buber, *Briefwechsel,* 2:27–28. Cf. R. Horwitz, "Discoveries Regarding the Origins of M. Buber's *I and Thou*" (in Hebrew), *Proceedings of the Israeli National Academy of Science* (Jerusalem) 5, no. 8 (1975): 8.

21. Buber, "Dialogue," p. 35.
22. Buber, "Autobiographical Fragments," p. 3.
23. Buber, "Replies to my Critics," in *Philosophy of Martin Buber,* ed. Schilpp and Friedman, p. 702.
24. Ibid., p. 693.
25. Buber, "What is Man?," p. 123.
26. Ibid., p. 124.
27. I have made a study of this, two chapters of which are called "The Sieve Approach" and "The Approach of Scientific Intuition" (in manuscript).
28. Buber, "Autobiographical Fragments," p. 18.
29. Buber, "Education and World-View" (1935), in *Pointing the Way,* ed. and trans. M. Friedman (New York, 1957), pp. 100–101.
30. See Buber, "Elements of the Interhuman" (1933), in *The Knowledge of Man,* trans. M. Friedman and R. G. Smith (New York, 1965), pp. 75–78.
31. See Buber, "God and the Spirit of Man," in *Eclipse of God,* p. 127.
32. Buber, *I and Thou,* p. 156.
33. New York: Oxford University Press, 1980.
34. See "Prof. Yishayahu Leibowitz Answers" (in Hebrew), *Koteret Rashit,* 16 January 1985.
35. See A. B. Yehoshua, "An Effort to Purify the Vermin: Another Psycho-analytical Interpretation of Kafka's 'Metamorphosis'" (in Hebrew), *Maoznayim* 58, nos. 7–8 (Kislev–Tevet 1985): 10.

Chapter 3. A Divided Heart and Man's Double

1. See the autobiographical chapter, "A Conversion," and the discussion of it in chapter 5, above.
2. "Spinoza, Sabbatai Zvi, and the Baal-Shem" (1927) in *The Origin and Meaning of Hasidism* (New York, 1960), p. 99.
3. See the section "Polarity and Relation" in chapter 1, above.
4. See Buber's relation with Landauer in Shapira, "Communities Coming into Being and Reform of the World in M. Buber's Social Utopianism" (in Hebrew), in Buber, *Paths in Utopia,* ed. Shapira, pp. 296–99.
5. See Buber, "Recollection of a Death," in *Pointing the Way,* pp. 115–20.
6. Ibid., pp. 119–60.
7. Buber, "An Example: On the Landscapes of L. Krakauer," in *A Believing Humanism,* trans. M. Friedman (New York, 1967), pp. 106–7. The last paragraph of the section quoted does not appear in the English version of this essay and was translated from the Hebrew in "Krakauer," an introduction to a volume of drawings by Krakauer, *Ma'ale Yerushalayim* (Tel Aviv, 1956), n.p.
8. The early roots of the dialogical conception and the processes of consolidating the structure in which the Buberian dialogical way is presented have been discussed in many places in this study. I discuss the characteristics and components of his dialogical philosophy in my "The Dialogical Stage in Buber's Path and his Dialogical Teaching" (forthcoming).

9. Buber, *I and Thou*, p. 119.

10. Ibid.

11. Ibid., p. 120.

12. Ibid., p. 109.

13. Ibid., p. 115.

14. Ibid., p. 61.

15. Ibid., p. 115.

16. See Buber, *The Prophetic Faith* (New York, 1977), p. 191.

17. See the section "Polarity and Relation" in chapter 1.

18. See Buber, foreword to *For the Sake of Heaven*, p. x.

19. Buber, "Right and Wrong," in *Good and Evil*, trans. R. G. Smith (New York, 1952), p. 19.

20. See chapter 2.

21. Buber was a genuine poet, not merely a versifier (alternatively, one might say that his thinking was poetical in quality). Not all his poetry was published in his lifetime. See the poems in the German original with facing English translation in *A Believing Humanism*. Additional poems in English translation are forthcoming in G. G. Schmidt (1999).

22. See his remarks upon receiving the Bialik Prize, "On Eternity and the Moment" (in Hebrew), *Lamerhav* ("Massa"), 12 December 1961.

23. Ibid.

24. See, for example, Buber, "The Paths of Religion in our Land" (in Hebrew), in *Haruah vehametsiut* (Tel Aviv, 1942), esp. pp. 125–26, and see below.

25. See the section "Soul Peace and World Peace" in chapter 7, below.

26. Buber, preface to "Images of Good and Evil," in *Good and Evil*, p. 1.

27. See my commentary on his article "Genuine Dialogue and the Possibilities of Peace" in the section "Soul Peace and World Peace" in chapter 7, below.

28. See *Prophetic Faith*, p. 191.

29. Letter to Franz Rosenzweig, 6 June 1925. See *Briefwechsel*, 2:222. "One abyss calls to another" is taken from Ps. 42:8.

30. See *Prophetic Faith*, p. 191.

31. On the concepts of suppression and repression see Erich Neumann, *Tiefenpsychologie und Neue Ethik* (Zürich, 1949).

32. J. L. Borges, *El libro de Arena* (Buenos Aires, 1975).

33. Otto Rank, "The Double and the Permanence of the Soul" (in Hebrew, translated from French by Yehoshua Kenaz), *Haaretz*, 14 September 1973.

34. Ibid.

35. Lea Goldberg, *Drama of Consciousness: Studies in Dostoevsky* (in Hebrew) (Tel Aviv, 1974), pp. 66–75.

36. See Ben-Ami Scharfstein, "I and All my Shadows" (in Hebrew), *Bamachane*, 19 January 1972.

37. See Kaufmann, *Discovering the Mind*, 3:444.

38. See the section "Polarity and Relation" in chapter 1, above.

39. Buber, *For the Sake of Heaven*, p. 7. This picture derives from a Hasidic source: "People come to me in melancholy. And when they travel from me they

glow, but I myself, perish the thought, am melancholy, and he repeated, black, for I do not glow" (M. A. Walden, *Niflaot Harabi* [Pietrkov, 1911], no. 131).

40. Buber, *For the Sake of Heaven*, p. 76.

41. M. A. Walden, *Niflaot Harabi*, no. 129.

42. Cf. ibid., no. 355.

43. See M. A. Walden, "The Light of Miracles," in *Ohel Harabi* (Pietrkov, 1913), pp. 29–30. See the detailed parallel in the collection by Arieh Mordecai Rabinovitz, *Keter Hayehudi* (Jerusalem, 1929), pp. 47–48. But this version lacks the conclusion cited above regarding the Seer.

44. See Yehiel Moshe, *Likutim Hadashim* (Warsaw, 1889), p. 58.

45. See the section "Soul Peace and World Peace" in chapter 7, below.

46. Shmuel Meshinau, *Ramatayim Tzofim on the Tana debey Eliahu,* new ed. (Jerusalem, 1966), no. 65.

47. *Or haniflaot,* no. 25.

48. Buber, *For the Sake of Heaven* , p. 241, a passage copied by Buber with slight changes from "Documents and Supplements" in the collection of Yo'etz Kim Kadish, *Niflaot Hayehudi* (Ostrawazi, 1908), p. 10.

49. See my *"For the Sake of Heaven* and the Spiritual Biography of Martin Buber" (in Hebrew), a lecture delivered at the Ninth World Congress of Jewish Studies, Jerusalem, 6 August 1985.

50. Buber, *For the Sake of Heaven*, p. 10.

51. See ibid., p. 11.

52. Ibid.

53. Ibid.

54. Ibid., p. 12.

55. Ibid., p. 9.

56. Ibid., p. 12.

57. M. A. Walden, *Niflaot Harabi* , no. 54. See also the almost identical version in Yehiel Moshe, *Likutim Hadashim*, p. 106.

58. Shlomo Gabriel Rozenthal, *Hitgalut hatzadikim,* new ed. (Jerusalem, 1959), pp. 24–27.

59. G. Scholem, *Major Trends in Jewish Mysticism* (New York, 1941), p. 344.

60. Ibid., p. 342. Buber coined this expression in his first book, *Die Geschichten des Rabbi Nachman* (1906).

61. M. A. Walden, *Or Hahochma,* no. 150, included in his *Ohel harabbi* (Pietrkov, 1913). There seems to be little connection between the spiritual personality of the Seer as painted in the stories of his disciples and written Hasidic sources in general, and the image arising from his sermons (which are collected in *Zot Zikaron, Zikaron Zot, Divrey Emet, Divrey Emet 'al ha Torah*) or from the *Likutim yekarim beshem hahozeh.*

62. Buber, *For the Sake of Heaven*, p. 91. In the opinion of A. E. Simon, the conversation in which this remark occurred is a kind of preliminary effort at a response to F. Rosenzweig's appeal to Buber in an open letter, "Habonim." See Simon, "M. Buber and Israel's Faith" (in Hebrew), in *Ya'adim, Tzematim, Netivim: Haguto shel M. Buber* (Tel Aviv, 1985), p. 121.

63. Buber, *For the Sake of Heaven*, p. 307.
64. Ibid., p. 73.
65. Ibid.
66. Ibid., p. 234.
67. Ibid., p. 64.
68. Ibid., p. 234.
69. Ibid., p. 258. The "Yehudi" was Rabbi David's son-in-law.
70. Ibid., p. 235.
71. Yo'etz Kim Kadish, *Tiferet Hayehudi* (Pietrkov, 1912), p. 16. See an echo of this story in a collection by the same author, *Siach sarfey kodesh* I, no. 308. See also Y. Alfasi, *Hahozeh miLublin* (Jerusalem, 1969), pp. 94–95.
72. See E. A. Poe, "William Wilson," in *Edgar Allan Poe*, ed. P. Van Doren Stern (New York, 1957), pp. 57–81.
73. Poe's story was already well known in Europe when Dostoyevski published his novel *The Double* (a revised, second edition was published in 1866). He might have been influenced by Poe, for in his letters of those years he expresses admiration for Poe's stories.
74. I discuss this in the section "His Affinity with the Organic-Developmental Approach," in Shapira, "Dual Structures in the Thought of Martin Buber."
75. See "A Conversion," in Buber, "Dialogue."
76. See M. Friedman's introduction to his translation of *Daniel*, p. 15.
77. Buber, *Knowledge of Man*. I am presently working on a study of the reciprocal relations among the subjects of the double, conversion, and guilt feelings in Buber's thought.
78. See "Ilu Haya Herzl Od Be-Hayim" and the discussion of that article in the section "Polarity and Relation" in chapter 1, above.
79. See Buber, "The Way of Man According to the Teachings of Hasidism," in *Hasidism and Modern Man,* ed. and trans. M. Friedman (New York, 1958), p. 159.
80. See Buber, "The Elements of the Interpersonal" (in Hebrew) (1953), in *Besod Siach,* pp. 224–25.

Chapter 4. Existential Tensions and Early Struggles

1. See Buber, "Autobiographical Fragments," p. 3.
2. See ibid., p. 4.
3. Ibid., pp. 3–4.
4. Buber, *Briefwechsel,* 1:169.
5. See Buber, "Autobiographical Fragments," p. 4.
6. Ibid.
7. See Hans Kohn, "Martin Buber's Youth" (in Hebrew), *Ha-Po'el Ha-Tza'ir* 21, nos. 16–17 (1928): 6.
8. Buber, "Autobiographical Fragments," p. 4.
9. See the remarks of his eldest son, Raphael Buber, "Die Buber-Familie: Erinnerungen," in *Dialog mit Martin Buber* (Frankfurt a.M., 1982), p. 352.

10. See "Languages," in Buber, "Autobiographical Fragments," pp. 5–6.
11. See "The School," in Buber, "Autobiographical Fragments," p. 8.
12. Buber Archive, file A1.
13. See A. E. Simon, "Martin Buber and German Jewry" (in Hebrew), *Ya'adim* (Tel Aviv, 1985), p. 10.
14. See Buber, "Autobiographical Fragments," pp. 8, 6–7.
15. See Buber, "My Way to Hasidism" (1917), in *Hasidism and Modern Man,* p. 57.
16. Ibid.
17. See Buber, "What is Man?," pp. 135–36.
18. See chapter 9.
19. See Buber, "Philosophers," in "Autobiographical Fragments," p. 11. Also see the discussion of Buber and Nietzsche in G. G. Schmidt, *Martin Buber's Formative Years: From German Culture to Jewish Renewal, 1897–1909* (Tuscaloosa and London, 1995), pp. 23–29.
20. See the appendix giving Buber's course of study in Schmidt, *Martin Buber's Formative Years,* pp. 127–30.
21. On his dissertation, see Schaeder, *Hebrew Humanism of Martin Buber,* pp. 54–60.
22. See J. L. Magnes, "The Seer of Full Reality" (in Hebrew), *Ner* (Jerusalem) 15, nos. 9–10 (1965): 20.
23. See "Gebet," *Die Welt,* 28 June 1901, p. 13.
24. See Buber, *Briefwechsel,* 1:153.
25. See the opening sections of chapters 7 and 8, below.
26. See Scholem, "Martin Buber's Conception of Judaism," p. 142 n. 21.
27. See Buber, "My Way to Hasidism," p. 59.
28. See P. Winkler, "Betrachtungen einer Philozionistin," *Die Welt,* 6 September 1921.
29. Kohn, "Martin Buber's Youth," p. 8.
30. See Schaeder, *Hebrew Humanism of Martin Buber,* pp. 66, 84–87.

Chapter 5. A Conversion

1. See P. R. Mendes-Flohr, *From Mysticism to Dialogue: Martin Buber's Transformation of German Social Thought* (Detroit, 1989), pp. 131–32.
2. Sh. H. Bergmann, "M. Buber and Mysticism," in *Philosophy of Martin Buber,* ed. Schilpp and Friedman, p. 302.
3. See Buber, foreword to *Pointing the Way,* p. xv.
4. Buber, "What is Man?," pp. 184–85.
5. See especially chapters 1 and 2, above.
6. Buber, "Dialogue," pp. 24–25. As mentioned, "A Conversion," to be discussed below, is included in that work.
7. Buber, "God and the Soul," in *Origin and Meaning of Hasidism,* p. 186.
8. This testimony regarding himself is a subchapter of "Dialogue," pp. 13–14.

9. Ibid., p. 13.

10. Ibid., p. 14.

11. The Buber Archive (file 812B) contains a letter written by Buber on 26 January 1962 to "Mrs. Tilman," from which we learn that his correspondent also believed, on the basis of the passage above, that the young visitor had committed suicide. She apparently translated a section of Buber's writings, including "A Conversion," into English, the language in which Buber writes to her. He writes to her: "First of all, your words on p. . . . , 'The young man killed himself,' are not at all consistent with the actual event which I am telling (in my chapter, "A Conversion," where you will find the words: 'He himself was no longer among the living'). In fact the young man found his death during the First World War." On this issue see also M. Friedman, *M. Buber's Life and Work: The Early Years, 1878–1923* (New York, 1981), p. 396.

12. Buber, "Dialogue," p. 14.

13. G. Scholem, *On the Kabbalah and its Symbolism* (New York, 1969), pp. 49–50.

14. Buber, "Dialogue," pp. 13–14. See also the connotations of "A Conversion" in the context of the later discussion in which Buber argues against the positive view of Aldous Huxley about the astonishing effects of mescaline intoxication. See below.

15. See *Encyclopedia of Religion,* ed. V. Ferm (Paterson, N.J.: Littlefield, Adams, 1959), pp. 200–203.

16. Ibid., p. 202.

17. William James, *The Varieties of Religious Experience,* in *The Works of William James* (Cambridge, Mass., 1985), preface.

18. Ibid., chap. 9.

19. Ibid.

20. The terms of Buber's approach to guilt quoted here come from his "Guilt and Guilt Feelings" (1957), in *Knowledge of Man,* pp. 121–48, where he develops his attitude to guilt. I discuss this in an unpublished study.

21. Babylonian Talmud, *Sanhedrin,* 101a. Translation by Nathan Ausubel from his *A Treasury of Jewish Folklore* (New York, 1948), pp. 135–36.

22. For the problematics of purifying feelings of guilt by means of physical torments, see Sh. H. Bergmann, "Suffering and the Consciousness of Guilt," in *Dialogical Philosophy from Kierkegaard to Buber* (in Hebrew) (Jerusalem, 1974), pp. 159–63.

23. L. H. Farber, "Martin Buber and Psychotherapy," in *Philosophy of Martin Buber,* ed. Schilpp and Friedman, pp. 580–82, attempts to show that the "conversion" Buber recounts is parallel to the experience of H. S. Sullivan; and see "A Conversion" in J. Drever, *A Dictionary of Psychology* (Harmondsworth, U.K.: Penguin Books, 1952), p. 51. For ways in which psychotherapy deals with conversion, see J. C. Nemia, "The Dynamic Bases of Psychopathology," in *The Harvard Guide to Modern Psychiatry,* ed. A. M. Nicholi (Cambridge, Mass., 1978), pp. 160–61.

24. See Buber, "Preface to the 1923 Edition," in *On Judaism,* pp. 3–10.

25. Ibid.

26. Buber, "Translation of Bible, its Intentions and Paths" (in Hebrew, 1940), in *Darko shel mikra* (Jerusalem, 1964), p. 349.

27. See Buber, foreword to *Pointing the Way*.

28. In his dialogical thought as consolidated systematically there are "three . . . spheres in which the world of relation arises. The first: life with nature. . . . The second: life with men. . . . The third: life with spiritual beings." See Buber, *I and Thou*, pp. 56–57.

29. See Buber, "What is Man?," p. 184.

30. This sentence is found only in the Hebrew original of this work and was not translated into English.

31. See Buber, "Replies to my Critics," pp. 689–90.

32. Ibid.

33. Ibid., p. 702. "Aesthetic tendencies" has a pejorative connotation here. See also G. Landauer's criticism of Buber in his letter of 12 May 1916 with regard to his "aestheticism," below.

34. "Hope for this Hour" (in Hebrew) (1952), in *Am ve'Olam*, p. 83.

35. The conversation was published in *Psychologia: An International Journal* (Kyoto), December 1960; and later in Buber, *Knowledge of Man*, pp. 166–84.

36. He is referring here to the murder of Gustav Landauer.

37. See Buber, *Knowledge of Man*, pp. 167–68.

38. See chap. 3 of Mendes-Flohr, *From Mysticism to Dialogue*.

39. See Buber, *Briefwechsel*, 1:378.

40. For the distinction between secular mysticism and that which grows up in the framework of a traditional historical authority, see G. Scholem, "Religious Authority and Mysticism," in *On Kabbalah and its Symbolism*, pp. 16–17.

41. See G. L. Mosse, *The Jews and the German War Experience, 1914–1918*, Leo Baeck Memorial Lecture 21 (New York, 1977).

42. See Buber, *Briefwechsel*, 1:370 (the two men whom he mentions were members of the Stefan George circle). For the critical attitude toward Buber's position and those who followed it at that time, see Tzur and Shapira, "With G. Scholem: An Interview Conducted by M. Tzur and A. Shapira," in Scholem, *On Jews and Judaism in Crisis*, pp. 13–15.

43. Ibid., pp. 388–89.

44. See Sh. H. Bergmann, "Three Sermons on Judaism [by Martin Buber]" (in Hebrew), *Hashiloach* (Odessa) 26 (Shevet–Tammuz, 5672 [January–June, 1912]): 555.

45. See Buber, *Briefwechsel*, 1:61–68.

46. See P. R. Mendes-Flohr, "The Road to *I and Thou*: An Inquiry into Buber's Transition from Mysticism to Dialogue," in *Texts and Responses*, ed. M. Fishbane and P. R. Mendes-Flohr (Leiden, 1975), pp. 200–225.

47. On the expression of identification with Landauer's spiritual world, see Buber's article, "Gustav Landauer" (1904) in the section "Existential Duality and Its Expressions" in chapter 1. For Landauer's influence on Buber, see my "Communities Coming into Being and Reform of the World in M. Buber's Social Utopianism," in Buber, *Paths in Utopia*, ed. Shapira, pp. 292, 296–300; and Schaeder, *Hebrew Humanism of Martin Buber*, pp. 257–68.

48. See Mendes-Flohr, "The Road to *I and Thou*," pp. 211–16.

49. See Buber, *Briefwechsel*, 1:433–38.

50. Mendes-Flohr, "The Road to *I and Thou*," p. 217.

51. Ibid.

52. Ibid., pp. 217–18.

53. In response to my query, Sh. H. Bergmann wrote to me on 7 March 1973, "Regarding the quarrel between Gustav Landauer and Buber I must disappoint you. Indeed, it does appear to me that Buber mentioned those matters once, but now I would have to open his *Briefwechsel* I, p. 64, etc. [in the German original] to recall. . . . I can tell nothing about Landauer's relation with Buber."

54. These words are directed to his introductory essay to *Am ve'Olam*, "Buber's Political Path and his National Conception" (included in A. E. Simon, *Ya'adim* [Tel Aviv, 1985]), which does not refer to the years 1914–16. In his book *Kav Hatichum* (Nationalism, Zionism, and the Jewish-Arab conflict in the thought and actions of M. Buber) (Givat Haviva, 1973) there is a short reference to Landauer and mention (in a note) of Buber's works that were dedicated to the memory of Landauer, as well as his activity in publishing Landauer's writings; see *Kav Hatichum*, pp. 46–47, 130. "M. Buber and German Jews," in *Leo Baeck Institute Year Book* (London) 3 (1958), which also lacks reference to the years 1914–16, mentions Landauer twice, but without speaking of the quarrel between him and Buber.

55. *Entziklopedia 'Ivrit*, 1954 ed., s.v. "Buber, Mordecai Martin" (written by Sh. H. Bergmann). See also the additions to that article in the supplementary volume of 1967; "Buber, Martin" (written by A. E. Simon), *Encyclopedia Britannica*, 1974 ed., s.v. "Buber, Mordecai Martin" (written by Sh. H. Bergmann); *International Encyclopedia of Social Sciences*, 1962 ed., s.v. "Buber Martin" (written by S. N. Eisenstadt). Both Sh. H. Bergmann in his two articles in the *Entziklopedia 'Ivrit* and A. E. Simon mention the biography by Hans Kohn in their respective source lists. Simon also calls it "the authoritative biography." Perhaps their dependence upon that source caused this omission or forgetfulness.

56. See Mendes-Flohr, "The Road to *I and Thou*," pp. 281–22.

57. Ibid., p. 203.

58. Ibid., p. 218.

59. See A. E. Simon, "The Living Heritage of M. M. Buber: One Hundred Years Since his Birth" (in Hebrew), in *Ya'adim*, pp. 300–301. This article was written after the publication of the *Briefwechsel* and contains references to Landauer's letter there as well as to the long comment by G. Schaeder.

60. See Buber, *Ich und Du* (Leipzig, 1923) p. 137.

61. See the reference to my discussion of the series of articles by Buber from 1918 in my "Communities Coming Into Being and Reform of the World," in Buber, *Paths in Utopia*, ed. Shapira.

62. See R. Horwitz, *Buber's Way to "I and Thou": The Development of Martin Buber's Thought and his "Religion as Presence" Lectures* (Philadelphia, 1988), and see my reference to this book in the section "Concepts and Structures: The Background of Their Reference" in chapter 6.

63. On the traumatic experiences and tragic spiritual struggles that marked his life, see the section "Existential Duality and Its Expressions" in chapter 1. The conversion under discussion here is mentioned among these.

64. Buber, *Briefwechsel,* 2:273 (letter no. 32). See the text of this letter below in the first section of chapter 1.

65. Buber, *The Prophetic Faith,* p. 183. It is noteworthy that this book appeared in the midst of the Second World War.

66. See Buber, "Thou shalt love thy neighbor as thyself" (in Hebrew), in *Darko shel mikra* (Jerusalem, 1964), pp. 103–5.

67. See T. Dreyfus, "Understanding the Term 'Umkehr' in the Philosophy of M. Buber" (in Hebrew), *Daat* (Ramat Gan), no. 9 (Summer 1982): 71–74.

68. See Buber, "The Renewal of National Life" (in Hebrew), in *Am ve'Olam,* p. 180.

69. See Dreyfus, "Understanding the Term 'Umkehr'," p. 72, and see also his mention of related terms.

70. Buber, *Nachlese,* 3d. ed. (Gerlingen, 1993), p. 235. Poem translated by G. Schmidt.

71. Buber, *Origin and Meaning of Hasidism,* p. 99.

72. See the section "A Divided Heart and Self-Contradiction" in chapter 3.

73. See Buber, *For the Sake of Heaven,* pp. 131–34.

74. Ibid., p. 134.

75. Yo'etz Kim Kadish, "Niflaot ha-Yehudi," in *Mikhtavei te'uda 'im tosafot* (Ostrawazi, 1908), p. 14. For another story with a similar foundation, see *Mikhtavei te'uda 'im tosafot,* pp. 16–17.

76. Buber, "Prophecy, Apocalyptic, and Historical Hour," p. 173.

77. Buber, "What is Common to All," in *Knowledge of Man,* p. 99.

78. See A. Huxley, *The Doors of Perception* (New York, 1954). A continuation of this book appeared as the article "Heaven and Hell, Visionary Experience, Visionary Art, and the Other World," *Tomorrow* (New York), Summer 1955. Buber's "What is Common to All" first appeared in German in January 1955, after the publication of Huxley's book.

79. Buber, "What is Common to All," p. 100.

80. See Buber, *Pointing the Way,* p. xvi.

81. Buber, "What is Common to All," p. 100.

82. Ibid.

83. Ibid., pp. 101–2.

84. See Buber, "Dialogue," p. 31.

85. Amos Oz, *Black Box* (in Hebrew) (Tel Aviv, 1987), p. 157.

Chapter 6. Duality and Its Structures

1. See K. Levin, *Resolving Social Conflicts* (New York, 1948), p. 57.

2. See P. Berger, "Identity as a Problem of the Sociology of Knowledge," in *The Sociology of Knowledge,* ed. J. E. Curtis and J. W. Petras (New York, 1972), pp. 375, 378. On personal identity see also the new definition of E. Erickson, "Crisis of the Identity Crisis," in *Identity, Youth, and Crisis* (New York, 1968), pp. 99–111.

3. See C. Geertz, *The Interpretation of Cultures* (New York, 1973), p. 52.

4. Concerning problems of tradition in Jewish culture since the beginning of

the modern period, see J. Katz, *Tradition and Crisis* (New York, 1961); N. Rotenstreich, "Tradition," in *Contemporary Jewish Religious Thought*, ed. A. Cohen and P. R. Mendes-Flohr (New York, 1987), pp. 1007–15.

5. See A. Flew, *A Dictionary of Philosophy* (New York, 1987); and A. Bullock and O. Stallybrass, *The Fontana Dictionary of Modern Thought* (New York, 1977).

6. See the section, "The Quality of His Utilization of 'Purified Conceptualism'," below.

7. See M. Kadushin, *The Rabbinic Mind* (New York, 1972), p. 4; J. Goldin, "The Thinking of the Rabbis," *Judaism* 5, no. 1 (Winter 1956): 3–12, esp. 5–10.

8. See Geertz, *Interpretation of Cultures*, pp. 46, 50.

9. See W. M. Johnston, *The Austrian Mind: An Intellectual and Social History, 1848–1938* (Los Angeles, 1972); and S. Beller, *Vienna and the Jews, 1867–1938* (Cambridge, 1989).

10. See Buber's accompanying essay to the collected writings of Richard Beer-Hofmann, *Olalot* (in Hebrew) (Jerusalem, 1966), pp. 35–43.

11. H. von Hofmannsthal, "Der Brief des Lord Chandos," in H. Glaser, F. Lehmann, and A. Lubos, *Wege der deutschen Literatur* (Frankfurt a.M., 1961), p. 429.

12. See ibid.

13. See ibid., p. 430.

14. See G. D. Cohen, "German Jewry as Mirror of Modernity," *Leo Baeck Institute Year Book* (London) 20 (1975): ix–xxxi. See also R. J. Z. Werblowsky, *Beyond Tradition and Modernity* (London, 1976); S. N. Eisenstadt, "Historical Traditions and Patterns of Modernization (Introduction)," *Jerusalem Quarterly*, no. 38 (1986): 3–4; and J. Katz, "The Jewish Response to Modernity in Western Europe," *Jerusalem Quarterly*, no. 38 (1986): 5–13.

15. Buber, "Judaism and the Jews," pp. 15, 17.

16. Ibid., p. 16.

17. Ibid., p, 14. On the biological line and the birth of the spirit, see Buber, "Teaching and Deed," p. 137.

18. Buber, "Judaism and the Jews," p. 18.

19. See Buber, "Shalosh Tachanot," in *Am ve'Olam* (Tel Aviv, 1929), p. 211.

20. See the section "Creative Vitalism" in chapter 7.

21. See "Ein Wort über Nietzsche und die Lebenswerte," *Die Kunst im Leben* 1, no. 2 (1900): 13.

22. See Buber, "Renewal of Judaism" (1910), in *On Judaism*, p. 43; "Jewish Religiosity" (1913), in *On Judaism*, p. 93.

23. Buber, "Lesser Uri," cols. 113–28.

24. Ibid., col. 114.

25. Ibid.

26. Ibid. See my reference to this quotation in chapter 8.

27. He took this as a Jewish trait; at the end of his article he writes, "Lesser Uri is a Jew. The truth is that he is a Jewish artist. His struggle, filled with great yearnings, to break barriers; his feeling of the unity of creation, which alone has

no boundaries; these have been the basic forces of the Jewish people from time immemorial. Infinity without rest, the kingdom of the Lord which entails neither the annihilation of the personality nor of movement" (ibid., cols. 127–28).

28. See chapter 1 and see my interpretation of this source in the section of that chapter entitled "Duality and the Yearning for Unity."

29. See Buber, "Judaism and Mankind," pp. 27–30.

30. See the quotation from his article, "Judaism and the Jews," p. 18, referred to in the previous section (n. 18, above).

31. See the previous section and the section below entitled "The Change in the Character of His Concepts and its Embodiment in a Structure of Ideas in the Articles of 1918."

32. See chapter 9.

33. See chapters 7 and 8.

34. See chapter 1.

35. See Buber, "Renewal of Judaism," in *On Judaism*, p. 42.

36. Buber, *I and Thou*, pp. 119–20.

37. "Jüdische Wissenschaft," *Die Welt* 5, no. 41 (11 October 1901) and 5, no. 43 (25 October 1901).

38. "Jüdische Wissenschaft," *Die Welt* 5, no. 41 (11 October 1901).

39. "Jüdische Wissenschaft," *Die Welt* 5, no. 43 (25 October 1901).

40. See ibid.

41. Buber, "Lesser Uri," col. 114.

42. On the term "Erlebnis," see chapter 5.

43. For the first time in a special issue of the magazine *Neue Blätter* (1913) that was devoted to Buber, and afterward in a collection of his articles (from which I quote) *Ereignisse und Begegnungen* (Leipzig, 1917), pp. 3–9.

44. Buber, *Ereignisse und Begegnungen*, p. 3.

45. Ibid., pp. 4–5.

46. As he testifies of himself in "A Conversion" in Buber, "Dialogue," p. 13. For more detail, see chapter 5.

47. See Buber, "Buddha," pp. 7–8 and, in more detail, chapter 9.

48. See the chapters "Polar Duality," and "Vortex – Direction."

49. See Buber, "With a Monist" (1914), in *Pointing the Way*, pp. 25–30.

50. Ibid., p. 27.

51. Ibid., p. 28.

52. Ibid.

53. Ibid.

54. Buber, "Elements of the Interhuman," p. 81.

55. Preface to *Kalewala: Das Nationalepos der Finnen* (Munich, 1914).

56. See references to the distinction between the Mystical Stage and the Dialogical Stage in chapter 5.

57. See Buber, *I and Thou*.

58. Buber, "The History of the Dialogical Principle," in *Between Man and Man*, p. 216.

59. See Buber, *On Judaism*, pp. 60, 61, 65.

60. See ibid., pp. 81–82, 93–94.

61. On value concepts see the sections "The Problem of Personal Identity in a Period of Cultural Disintegration" and "The Character of His Concepts."

62. See the section "(Personal) Creativity and 'Fellowship' as Members of a Structure in Formation" in chapter 7.

63. See my essay, "Communities Coming into Being and Reform of the World in M. Buber's Social Utopianism," pp. 276–314.

64. See Buber, "The Holy Way," in *On Judaism*, pp. 146–47.

65. See ibid., p. 122.

66. Ibid., pp. 145–46.

67. See Buber, *Die Jüdische Bewegung: Gesammelte Aufsätze, 1916–1920* (Berlin, 1920).

68. See Horwitz, *Buber's Way*, pp. 133–43.

69. Ibid., pp. 203–4.

70. The concept of Responsibility is already mentioned in a number of Buber's early works, written prior to those that reflect the turning point in his thought. For example, the introduction to the magazine *Der Jude*, which began to be published under his editorship in March 1916, mentions the responsible *(verantwortlich)* man several times. See Buber, "Die Losung," in *Die Jüdische Bewegung: Gesammelte Aufsätze, 1916–1920*, p. 11. There is also a short reference to Responsibility in a Zionist article of 1917. See "Ein politischer Faktor" (August 1917), in *Die Jüdische Bewegung: Gesammelte Aufsätze, 1916–1920*, p. 116. In none of these contexts, nor in other such brief references to this concept, does it have a developmental history. This comes into being only in the stage of his dialogical thought.

71. Buber, *I and Thou*, p. 157.

72. Ibid., p. 66.

73. Buber, "Dialogue," p. 14.

74. Buber, "Hebrew Humanism," in *Israel and the World*, p. 244.

75. See Buber, "Dialogue," pp. 16–17.

76. See Buber, "The Question of the Single One," pp. 65–71.

77. See Buber, "The Prejudices of Youth," in *Israel and the World*, pp. 46–48.

78. Buber, "Verantwortung," *Berliner Tageblatt*, 1 January 1929.

79. Buber, "Zwiesprache," *Die Kreatur* (Berlin) 3, no. 3 (1929–30): 201–22.

80. Buber, "The Way of Man According to the Teachings of Hasidism," pp. 125, 127. See the discussion of the nature of decision and of conscience in the section "Images of Good and Evil" in chapter 8. On responsibility in Buber's doctrine, see N. Rotenstreich, "Immediacy and Dialogue," *Revue Internationale de Philosophie*, no. 126 (1978): 467–68.

81. Buber, "The Question of the Single One," p. 45.

82. See Buber, "Dialogue," p. 16, and idem, "Replies to my Critics," p. 698.

83. See Buber, "Dialogue," p. 17.

84. See "Education and Worldview" (in Hebrew) (1935), in *Am ve'Olam* (1961), p. 419.

85. Buber, *I and Thou*, pp. 143–44.

86. Ibid., p. 84.

87. Buber, "The Heart Determines," in *On the Bible*, p. 199.

88. See his testimony from a distance in time regarding his susceptibility to mystical experiences, as quoted in the chapter "A Conversion."

89. Buber, "Spirit and Body of the Hasidic Movement," in *Origin and Meaning of Hasidism*, p. 127.

90. "State and Culture" (in Hebrew) (remarks made upon receiving the Israel Prize), *Haaretz*, 30 April 1953.

91. Buber, "Gershom Scholem: At Sixty" (in Hebrew), *Haaretz*, 6 December 1957.

92. Foreword (in Hebrew) to *Be-Fardes Ha-Hasidut* (Tel Aviv, 1945), p. 5. This foreword does not appear in the English version, *Origin and Meaning of Hasidism*.

93. Ibid.

94. Buber, *Briefwechsel*, 1:482. This letter provided the basis for the chapter, "To Create New Words?" in the collection, *A Believing Humanism*, p. 31.

95. From his remarks at a seminar devoted to popular education given by the Culture Committee of the Histadrut in Jerusalem, which were presented under the title, "Martin Buber on Popular Education" (in Hebrew), *Davar*, 13 April 1927.

96. See Buber, "Adult Education" (in Hebrew), (1950) in *Am ve'Olam* (1961), p. 410.

97. Buber, "Herut," p. 161.

98. See "Interrogation of M. Buber," conducted by M. Friedman, *Philosophical Interrogations*, S. and B. Rome (eds.), (New York: Harper Torchbooks, 1970), pp. 46–47.

99. See N. N. Glatzer, "Reflections on Buber's Impact on German Jewry," *Leo Baeck Institute Year Book* 25 (1980), pp. 308–9.

100. Buber, "What is Man?" p. 188.

101. See the section "Concepts and Structures: The Background of Their Reference," above.

102. See ibid. and see also the matter of value concepts in the section, "Major Milestones in the Consolidation of Concepts in the Mystical Stage."

103. Buber, "Education and Worldview" (in Hebrew) (1935), in *Am ve'Olam* (1961), p. 415.

104. See chapter 2.

105. Buber, "Preface to the First Edition," in *Kingship of God*, trans. R. Scheimann (New York, 1967),.p. 20.

106. Max Weber maintained that the social sciences must be objective, that metaphysical assumptions and value judgments have no place in them. In his opinion, "the scientific ethos" necessitates a value-free approach, and research, being a theoretical activity, must not be guided by any value terms or values. On Weber's approach, see H. S. Hughes, *Consciousness and Society* (New York, 1958), pp. 323–31; A. Mitzman, *Sociology and Estrangement* (New York, 1973), pp. 33–34; and K. H. Wolff, *Trying Sociology* (New York, 1974), pp. 251–52, 268, 285, 307–8.

107. Buber, "Preface to First Edition," pp. 19–20.

108. "On Thinking," in Buber, "Dialogue," p. 27.
109. Ibid.
110. See Buber, "Hebrew Humanism," p. 244.
111. Buber, "On the Essence of Culture," p. 392.
112. See Buber, "Religion and Philosophy," in *Knowledge of Man*, p. 39.
113. Ibid., p. 43.
114. In the symposium "Popular Education in Israel and Jewish Education in the Diaspora," held at the Hebrew University, Jerusalem, in 1949, Buber used these expressions to indicate the nature of "culture." See Buber, "Religion and Philosophy," pp. 48–49. I find in them a suitable indication of the dynamic formative powers of his concepts.
115. A. N. Whitehead, *The Aims of Education* (New York, 1929), p. 6. Buber's attitude on this topic is also consistent with that of Geertz and his colleagues regarding human learning by means of the formative powers of the society, based on "the attainment of concepts, the apprehension and application of specific systems of symbolic meaning." The consolidations of ways of behavior, judgment, and values of a certain society are embodied in concepts and conceptual structures; Geertz calls them "conceptual structures molding formless talents." See C. Geertz, *The Interpretation of Cultures* (New York, 1973), pp. 49–50.
116. See the section "Concepts and Structures: The Background of Their Reference," above.
117. Again, see the section "Concepts and Structures: The Background of Their Reference," above.
118. Thus it is understood why he points out his own conceptual neologism, "The Between," as a name for "the oscillating sphere between the persons" (Buber, "The Word that is Spoken," in *Knowledge of Man*, p. 112).
119. See Buber, "Religion and Philosophy," p. 52.
120. Buber, "Replies to my Critics," pp. 691–92.
121. Ibid., p. 693.
122. See "Interrogation of M. Buber," conducted by M. Friedman, *Philosophical Interrogations* (New York 1970), p. 20.
123. Buber, *I and Thou*, p. 53.
124. See "Distance and Relation" (1950), in *Knowledge of Man*, p. 60.
125. Ibid.
126. This formulation appears in the introduction to the German version of "Distance and Relation." See Buber, "Vorwort" to *Urdistanz und Beziehung* (Heidelberg, 1960).
127. On the meaning of Direction, see chapter 8.

Chapter 7. Distance – Relation

1. See Buber, *Briefwechsel*, 1:148.
2. See the subchapter "His Relation to the Organic-Developmental Approach" in Shapira, "Dual Structures in the Thought of Martin Buber."
3. See Bergmann, "Three Sermons on Judaism [by M. Buber]," p. 555.

4. See Buber, *Briefwechsel,* 1:254.

5. Buber, "Judaism and the Jews," p. 17. These formulations were not only influenced by Dilthey, Buber's teacher, but they might also have been directly related to his language: "All human creativity springs from the life of the soul and from its relations with the outer world" (my translation). W. Dilthey, "Das Wesen der Philosophie" (1907), in *Gesammelte Schriften* (Stuttgart, 1958), 5:372. Dilthey, whose point of departure was the individual's inner life, assumes a reciprocal action between it and the external environment. He states that "the basic form of spiritual bonding is determined by the fact that all psychic life is shown to be contingent upon its environment and influences it in turn, in accordance with its goal" (ibid., p. 373). Dilthey was one of Buber's professors at the university in Berlin in the summer of 1898 and the autumn of 1899. He is the only one whom Buber felt the need of mentioning, many years later, as his "teacher." See Buber, "What is Man?," p. 126. In his old age Buber tried to shake off the influence of Dilthey's philosophy of life (Buber, "Replies to my Critics," p. 702). However, it remains powerful in his writing. Some commentators even maintain that Dilthey's influence was decisive on Buber's views. See also J. Habermas, "Dilthey's Theory of Understanding . . . ," in *Knowledge and Human Interests* (Boston, 1971).

6. "Judaism and the Jews," p. 14. This duality is basic in the structure of "Vortex – Direction." See chapter 8, below.

7. On the loss of "cosmological security" and "sociological security," cf. Buber, "What is Man?," p. 157.

8. Mendes-Flohr and Susser, "Alte und neue Gemeinschaft," pp. 41–56.

9. Ibid., p. 50.

10. Ibid., p. 53.

11. Ibid., p. 55.

12. Buber, "Lesser Uri," cols. 115–16.

13. Ibid., col. 118.

14. Ibid., col. 119.

15. Buber, "Wege zum Zionismus" (1901), in *Die Jüdische Bewegung: Gesammelte Aufsätze, 1900–1915,* p. 42.

16. Ibid.

17. See Kohn, *Martin Buber,* p. 295; Buber, *Briefwechsel,* 1:254.

18. Buber, "Renewal of Judaism," p. 34–35.

19. Buber, "Hu ve-Anahnu" (He and we), *Ha'Olam* 8, no. 25 (9 July 1914): 3.

20. Ibid., p. 4.

21. Ibid.

22. See Buber, "Jewish Religiosity," p. 80.

23. Buber, "Teaching and Deed," p. 139. For the denial of "religion" from the standpoint of this conception of faith, see, among other writings, Buber, "The Question of the Single One," pp. 57–58.

24. M. Buber, "Me-ha-Rishonim" (Among the first ones) is included in *Berthold Feiwel: ha-Ish u-Foalo* (Jerusalem, 1959), pp. 48–49.

25. Sh. H. Bergmann, "Berthold Feiwel ve-'avodat ha-hoveh'" in *Berthold Feiwel: ha-Ish u-Foalo,* p. 64.

26. See Buber, *Briefwechsel,* 1:320.

27. See *Daniel* (1913) in Buber, *Werke I: Schriften zur Philosophie*, pp. 27–29.

28. Buber, "Die Eroberung Palästinas," *Der Jude* 10–11 (January–February 1918): 633–34. References to this article below use the page numbers in the collection in which it is found: Buber, *Die Jüdische Bewegung: Gesammelte Aufsätze, 1916–1920.*

29. The draft is dated 5 February 1918. See Horwitz, *Buber's Way*, pp. 155–65.

30. Buber, *Die Jüdische Bewegung: Gesammelte Aufsätze, 1916–1920*, p. 135.

31. Ibid., p. 137.

32. See Buber, "Vor der Entscheidung" (1919), in ibid., p. 197.

33. The first of them was also published that year (1918), and the other two were published in 1919. See my discussion of the notable change apparent in Buber's thinking in his articles of 1918 in the section "Concepts and Structures: The Background of Their Reference" in chapter 6.

34. See Buber, "The Holy Way," pp. 145–48.

35. See "Zion and Youth," *Avukah Annual* (New York), 1930, pp. 45–53.

36. See Buber, "Herut," p. 152.

37. See ibid., p. 169.

38. Buber, "'Al ha-Hevra ve-'al ha-Tzibbur" (On society and on the public), *Ma'abarot* (Jaffa), May 1920, p. 215.

39. Buber, "Ha-Ra'ayon ve-Hagshamato" (The idea and its realization), *Ha-Po'el ha-Tza'ir* (Jaffa) 14, (16 October 1921): 13. This speech was, in many respects, an expanded and enriched version of the previously cited article, "Die Eroberung Palästinas" (see n. 28, above); ideas that were first expressed in early 1918 here assume a programmatic guise.

40. See *Ha-Ra'ayon ve-Hagshamato*, p. 11.

41. Ibid., p. 13.

42. See Buber, "The Holy Way," p. 146.

43. See Buber "Die Revolution und Wir" (1918), in *Die Jüdische Bewegung: Gesammelte Aufsätze, 1916–20*, p. 187.

44. Ibid., p. 183.

45. See *A. D. Gordon: A Bibliography, 1904–1972* (in Hebrew) (Degania A, 1979), pp. 22, 42.

46. See B. Ben Avram, "The German Hapoel Hatzair: The History of an Intellectual Group (1917–1920)" (in Hebrew) *Zionism* (Tel Aviv) 6 (1981): 49–95.

47. See A. Shapira, "A. D. Gordon and the Second Aliyah, Realization of Utopia," in *Communal Life*, ed. Y. Gorni, Y. Oved, and I. Paz (New Brunswick, N.J., 1968), pp. 130–41; and G. D. Cohen, "Aliyah" (New York, 1968), pp. 11–14 (offprint).

48. See S. Tzemah, "Beyn Shney Ofakim" (Between two horizons), *Ha-Po'el Ha-Tza'ir*, Sixtieth Anniversary Issue, 26 September 1967, p. 10; idem, *Shanah Rishona* (First year) (Tel Aviv, 1961).

49. See S. Tzemah, *Bimey Masah* (In times of examination) (Jerusalem, 1945), p. 20.

50. See his poem, "Birkat 'Am" (The people's blessing) (1894).

51. See Buber, "The Holy Way."

52. See chapter 2.

53. A. D. Gordon, *Collected Writings* (in Hebrew), ed. Sh. H. Bergmann and Eliezer Shochat (Jerusalem, 1951), 2:326.

54. Ibid., 1:225.

55. Ibid., 1:142.

56. For more detail, see chapter 5.

57. See G. Scholem, "Martin Buber's Interpretation of Hasidism" (1961), in *The Messianic Idea in Judaism* (New York, 1971), p. 245.

58. See my discussion of "The Way of Man According to the Teachings of Hasidism" in the summary of chapter 8.

59. See chapter 8.

60. An Address to the Third International Educational Conference, Heidelberg, August 1925.

61. And cf. my reference to this structure below as well as in other chapters of this work.

62. Buber, "Education," in *Between Man and Man*, p. 75.

63. Ibid., p. 88

64. Ibid., pp. 85–86.

65. Ibid., p. 83.

66. Ibid., p. 85.

67. Ibid.

68. Ibid., p. 87.

69. See Buber, *Briefwechsel*, 1:320.

70. Buber, "Man and his Image-Work," in *Knowledge of Man*, p. 150.

71. See Buber, "Education," p. 86.

72. See Buber, "The Power of the Spirit" (1934), in *Israel and the World*, p. 178.

73. See Buber, "Education," pp. 93–94, 95.

74. Ibid., p. 86.

75. See Buber, *I and Thou*, p. 79.

76. Ibid.

77. Ibid.

78. Ibid., p. 128.

79. Ibid., p. 78.

80. See Buber, "Education," p. 91, and, at more length, the summary of chapter 8.

81. See Buber, *I and Thou*, pp. 97–98. Cf. my discussion in chapter 8 of manifestations of the "Vortex – Direction" structure in the dialogical stage.

82. See Buber, "What is Man?," pp. 186–87.

83. Ibid., p. 186.

84. See ibid., pp. 189–90.

85. See ibid., p. 196. See also, regarding Buber's attitude towards Freud, G. Schaeder, "Martin Buber: Ein biographischer Abriss," in Buber, *Briefwechsel*, 1:94.

86. Buber, "What is Man?," p. 190.

87. Ibid., p. 193.

88. Ibid., p. 197.
89. Ibid., pp. 197–98.
90. See ibid., p. 193.
91. See ibid.
92. Ibid., p. 197.
93. See Buber, "The Way of Man According to the Teachings of Hasidism," p. 142.
94. See Buber, "On the Essence of Culture," p. 384.
95. Ibid.
96. See the first section of this chapter above and the references in notes 5 and 6.
97. See the second section above.
98. Buber, "The Holy Way," p. 110.
99. See about "the soul may become one" in Buber, *I and Thou*, p. 134.
100. See Buber, "Spinoza, Sabbatai Zvi, and the Baal-Shem," p. 94.
101. Buber, "Dialogue," p. 21.
102. See chapter 2.
103. Buber refers here to what he calls the "three spheres of relation," in *I and Thou*, pp. 56, 149.
104. See Buber, "What is Man?," p. 179.
105. See ibid., pp. 176–77.
106. See Buber, "The Education of Character" (1939), in *Between Man and Man*, pp. 110–11.
107. Ibid., p. 104.
108. See, Buber, "The Way of Man According to the Teachings of Hasidism," pp. 130–37, 138–44, 146–51.
109. Ibid., pp. 154–59.
110. Ibid., pp. 162–67.
111. Ibid., pp. 170–76.
112. Ibid., p. 163.
113. See Buber, "Distance and Relation," pp. 59–71.
114. See ibid., p. 64.
115. Ibid., p. 60.
116. See Buber, "The Way of Man According to the Teachings of Hasidism," pp. 165–66.
117. Buber, "'Al ha-Mashber ha-Gadol" (On the great crisis), in *Am ve'Olam* (1961), pp. 75–76.
118. Ibid., p. 77.
119. See Buber, "The Word that is Spoken," p. 117.
120. See Buber, "Man and his Image-Work," p. 163.
121. See ibid., pp. 164–65.
122. Buber, "Guilt and Guilt Feelings," p. 125.
123. Ibid., p. 137.
124. Ibid., p. 147.
125. See the first section, above.
126. See chapter 1.
127. See Buber, "Judaism and Mankind," p. 29.

128. See Buber, "The Spirit of the Orient and Judaism," p. 65.

129. See Buber, "Judaism and the Jews," p. 20.

130. See Buber, "Judaism and Mankind," p. 27.

131. Buber, "Renewal of Judaism," pp. 41–42.

132. See Buber, "Ha-Bayit ha-Leumi u-Mediniut Leumit be-Eretz Yisrael" (The national home and national policy in the Land of Israel), in *Am ve'Olam* (1929), p. 311.

133. See the explanation and analysis of the ramifications of this process in Buber, "The Holy Way," pp. 145–46.

134. See my "Time and Eternity in Buber's Conception of Redemption: The Meeting of Utopia and Eschatology," a paper delivered at the international conference at the University of Frankfurt, 15 May 1985.

135. Buber, "Landauer and the Revolution" (in Hebrew) in *Paths in Utopia*, ed. Shapira, pp. 237–38. This is the text of a lecture given in Frankfurt shortly after Landauer was murdered.

136. Buber, "A Conversation with Tagore" (1950), in *A Believing Humanism*, p. 184.

137. Ibid., and see P. R. Mendes-Flohr, "Fin-de-siècle Orientalism, the Ostjuden and the Aesthetics of Jewish Self-Affirmation," in *Studies in Contemporary Jewry*, ed. J. Frankel (Bloomington, 1984).

138. See Buber, "At this Late Hour" (1920), in *A Land of Two Peoples: Martin Buber on Jews and Arabs*, ed. P. R. Mendes-Flohr (New York, 1983), p. 46.

139. Buber, "Vorwort," in *Die Jüdische Bewegung: Gesammelte Aufsätze, 1916–1920*, p. 5.

140. See Buber, *A Land of Two Peoples*.

141. Buber, "Genuine Dialogue and the Possibilities of Peace" (1953), in *A Believing Humanism*, p. 198.

142. Ibid., p. 196.

143. Buber, "Fragments on Revelation," in *A Believing Humanism*, p. 115.

144. See his development of this idea in *Paths in Utopia* (Boston, 1958).

145. See Buber, "The Silent Question" (1951), in *At the Turning* (New York, 1952), pp. 37–38.

146. Ibid., p. 39.

147. See Buber, "Politics Born of Faith" (1933), in *A Believing Humanism*, p. 175.

148. See Buber, *Origin and Meaning of Hasidism*, p. 239.

149. See the fourth section above and my reference to Buber's "What is Man?" and "The Education of Character."

150. See Buber, *Tales of the Hasidim: Later Masters*, p. 264.

151. See Buber, "The Way of Man According to the Teachings of Hasidism," p. 156. The view that the root of the problems of external life (the macrocosm) is to be found within the problems of inner life (the microcosm) was brought into Hasidic literature from the Kabbalah. See G. Scholem, "The Idea of the Golem," in *On the Kabbalah and its Symbolism* (New York, 1965), p. 168.

Interestingly, this very worldview guided the leaders of the Second Aliyah in the Land of Israel. They too were well versed in the Bible, and many of them drew

NOTES TO CHAPTER EIGHT

upon the world of Hasidism (this applies especially to A. D. Gordon). In the midst of their own personal renewal, the people of the Second Aliyah felt the burden of Jewish history on their shoulders. In carrying out their task, which was based on "The Day of Small Things," they saw the opening and commencement of the renewal of their people. In A. D. Gordon's writings, this feeling of heavy personal responsibility was also expressed in reflections that transcend the specific time and place: "There can be no renewal of mankind, of human nature," stated Gordon, like Buber, "as long as there is no renewal of the individual, every individual, every human soul, without exception." "Le-Berur Ra'ayonenu mi-Yesodo" (Toward a clarification of our idea from its foundation), in Gordon, *Collected Writings*, 2:194.

Gordon held that "the primary characteristic of our [Zionist] creation is comprised in the fact that each one of us must first of all create himself anew. And this is the essential point. Every one of us must look deep within his 'self' and clarify for himself that his entire concern for the existence of his national soul is not in fact concern for his own soul, for deepening its life—concern for his private "self," for his own life and creation. . . . It will become clear to him that the rift within the nation begins with a rift in the soul of each individual among us." "The Fourth Letter to the Diaspora," in Gordon, *Collected Writings*, 1:534.

Chapter 8. Vortex – Direction

1. See the beginning of chapter 7 and my references in the notes there.
2. See chapter 1.
3. See Buber, "Lesser Uri" (1901), cols. 113–28.
4. Buber, "Gustav Landauer," *Die Zeit*, 11 June 1904, p. 127.
5. See Buber, "Judaism and the Jews," pp. 14–15. This duality serves as the background for the structure to which this chapter is devoted as well as for the "Distance – Relation" structure; see the discussion of it in the beginning of chapter 7.
6. Ibid., p. 18.
7. Buber, "Judaism and Mankind," p. 33.
8. Buber, "Er und Wir," *Die Welt*, 20 May 1910, p. 445. See also the discussion of that article in chapter 1.
9. Ibid.
10. Buber, "Zwiefache Zukunft" (1912), in *Die Jüdische Bewegung: Gesammelte Aufsätze, 1916–1920*, p. 220.
11. Ibid., p. 221. See the duality of "culture" and "religiosity" there, at the beginning of the article.
12. Buber, "The Spirit of the Orient and Judaism," p. 65.
13. See the fifth section of chapter 7.
14. See the second section of chapter 6.
15. See Buber, "The Spirit of the Orient and Judaism," p. 66.
16. Ibid., p. 67.
17. On the sources of this conception, see chapter 1, above. The quotation

comes from "Das Epos des Zauberers," Buber's introductory essay to *Kalewala: Das Nationalepos der Finnen* (Munich, 1914).
18. See Buber, "Gespräch von der Richtung," *Neue Blätter* 2, no. 1 (1912): 5–20.
19. *Daniel*, in Buber, *Werke I: Schriften zur Philosophie*, p. 17.
20. See ibid., pp. 22–25. Sh. H. Bergmann expands the discussion on the nature of this opposition and in doing so presents it in a manner overlapping with the duality with which the present chapter is concerned:

Man is subject to a whirlpool of directions, tendencies, tendencies ad infinitum, tensions ad infinitum, and feelings ad infinitum that seduce a person. A person is lost in this infinity of proposals, of trends, if he has no direction of his own. . . . It seems that this is an important autobiographical moment. Buber himself hints at it here and there in his writings, and in private conversation he openly declared that he had undergone a period of aesthetization like that. He was in Vienna at that time, where he was studying and editing the Zionist newspaper *Die Welt*, and he was subject to many influences from life and literature; . . . when Buber speaks of evil, he defines it as lack of direction—there is no good or evil in the regular sense, but evil is lack of direction, that whirlpool of possibilities. If a person finds his direction and the power to impose his direction upon the chaos of temptations with which the world seduces him, then a kind of metamorphosis takes place within one, and the whole world is open before one.

Sh. H. Bergmann, *Ha-Pilosofia Ha-Dialogit Mi-Kierkegaard ad Buber* (Dialogical philosophy from Kierkegaard to Buber) (Jerusalem, 1974), p. 249.
21. See "Die Losung," *Der Jude*, April 1916, reprinted in Buber, *Die Jüdische Bewegung: Gesammelte Aufsätze, 1916–1920*, p. 15.
22. See chapter 5.
23. Buber, "My Way to Hasidism," pp. 56–57. Buber states that he had been preoccupied with the problem of evil since his youth, "but not until the year following the first World War" did he develop an independent conception of it. See Buber, preface to "Images of Good and Evil," p. 63.
24. Buber, "Zion ve-ha-No'ar" (Zion and youth) (1918), in *Am ve-'Olam* (1961), p. 215.
25. Buber, *I and Thou*, pp. 97–98. On this idea see the following section.
26. See chapter 7.
27. See Buber, *I and Thou*, p. 134.
28. Buber, "Spinoza, Sabbatai Zvi, and the Baal-Shem," pp. 98–99.
29. Ibid., p. 102.
30. Buber, "Emunat Yisrael" (The faith of Israel) (1928) in *Te'udah ve-Ye'ud* (Jerusalem, 1959), p. 184. The contrast with the ancient Iranian view is already found in "Religion as Presence," his lecture series of 1922. See the text in Horwitz, *Buber's Way*, p. 38.
31. Ibid., p. 185.

32. Ibid., p. 184.

33. Ibid., p. 185.

34. See Buber, "The Question of the Single One," pp. 78–79.

35. See ibid., pp. 69, 70.

36. "Unser Bildungsziel" (June 1933), in *Die Stunde und die Erkenntnis: Reden und Aufsätze, 1933–1935* (Berlin, 1936), p. 91.

37. See Buber, "Zion ve-ha-No'ar," p. 217.

38. See Buber, "And Today?" (March 1939), in *A Land of Two Peoples*, p. 135. And see also in chapter 9, below.

39. Buber, "Davar el Bnei Shlosh-'Esreh" (A word to thirteen-year-olds"), *Ba'ayat Ha-Yom* (Jerusalem), 16 March 1941.

40. "A Conversion," in Buber, "Dialogue," p. 14.

41. See Buber, preface to "Images of Good and Evil," p. 63.

42. See Buber, foreword to *Good and Evil*, p. v.

43. See Buber, "Images of Good and Evil," in *Good and Evil*, p. 121.

44. See Buber, "Religion and Ethics" (1952), in *Eclipse of God*, p. 95.

45. See Buber, "Images of Good and Evil," p. 64.

46. Ibid., p. 88.

47. See ibid., p. 64.

48. See ibid., p. 91.

49. See ibid., p. 93.

50. Ibid.

51. See Buber, "The Foundation Stone," p. 78.

52. See Buber, "'Am U-Manhig" (Nation and leader) (1942), in *Am ve'Olam* (1961), p. 65.

53. Buber, "Man and His Image-Work," p. 159.

54. See Buber, "Images of Good and Evil," p. 95.

55. Ibid.

56. Ibid., p. 97.

57. See chapter 7.

58. See the first section above and the reference to the article, "Gustav Landauer" (1904).

59. Buber, "The Way of Man According to the Teachings of Hasidism," p. 142.

60. See chapter 7.

61. See the series of lectures from 1922, "Religion as Presence," in Horwitz, *Buber's Way*, p. 37.

62. See Buber, "Ha-Bayit Ha-Leumi u-Mediniut Leumit be-Eretz Yisrael" (The national home and national policy in the Land of Israel) (1929), in *Am ve'Olam* (1929), p. 311.

63. See Buber, "Ahavat Elohim ve-Ahavat Ha-Briot" (The love of God and the love of men) (1945), in *Ba-Fardes He-Hasidut*, p. 109. See below the discussion of Buber's concept of the essence of the conscience.

64. See Buber, "Images of Good and Evil," pp. 104, 130.

65. Ibid., pp. 130–31.

66. Buber, "The Way of Man According to the Teachings of Hasidism," p. 134.

67. See Buber, "Images of Good and Evil," p. 111.
68. See Buber, "The Way of Man According to the Teachings of Hasidism," pp. 135–36.
69. See Buber, "Replies to my Critics," p. 720. Here he replies to Marvin Fox's criticism of his ethical views. See M. Fox, "Problems in Buber's Moral Philosophy," (1963), in *Philosophy of Martin Buber,* ed. Schilpp and Friedman, pp. 161–68. Fox discusses Buber's ethics again, as well as Buber's reply to his criticism, in "Translating Jewish Thought into Curriculum," in *From the Scholar to the Classroom* (New York, 1977), pp. 76–81.
70. Buber, *I and Thou,* p. 54.
71. See the reference to this verse in Muffs's discussion of the joy of giving as an expression of the fullness of a person's abilities and desires: Y. Muffs, "The Joy of Giving," part 2 of "Love and Joy as Metaphors of Volition in Hebrew and Related Literatures," *Journal of Ancient Near Eastern Society of Columbia University* 11 (1979): 108–11.
72. Buber, "Prophecy, Apocalyptic, and the Historical Hour," pp. 172–87.
73. Buber, "Images of Good and Evil," p. 135.
74. See chapter 2.
75. See Buber, "Images of Good and Evil," p. 101.
76. See, for example, ibid., p. 135.
77. See Buber, "Guilt and Guilt Feeling," p. 129.
78. See Buber, "Religion and Ethics," pp. 95–96.
79. See Buber, "Religion and Modern Thinking," in *Eclipse of God*, p. 87.
80. Ibid., p. 86.
81. "Ha-Mashber ve-ha-Emet" (The crisis and the truth) (1945), in *Am ve'Olam* (1961), p. 81.
82. See Buber, "Ahavat Elohim ve-Ahavat Ha-Briot" (n. 63 above).
83. Buber, "Achrayut Li-Shma" (Responsibility for its own sake), *Maoznayim* 22, no. 2 (1946): 103.
84. Buber "Guilt and Guilt Feeling," pp. 134–35.
85. Buber, "'Am U-Manhig" (n. 52 above), p. 67.
86. Ibid., p. 70. Before these two were associated in Buber's writing, he compared Sabbatai Zvi to Jacob Frank; Sabbatai Zvi was "a man who had taken the fateful step from the hiddenness of the servants of the Lord to Messianic self-consciousness." See Buber, "Spinoza, Sabbatai Zvi and the Baal-Shem," p. 111. That is to say, he became a false messiah. Buber emphasizes that Sabbatai Zvi first believed in God and only afterward came to nihilism and to a "zero point." From this verge of destruction it is possible to continue, as did Jacob Frank, into the area of self-messianism, which is all lie. See "The Beginnings" (1940), in *Be-Fardes Ha-Hasidut,* pp. 32–33. Frank's path was from the beginning that of the "perfect lie":

> He cannot believe genuinely even in himself, but only in the manner of the lie, through filling the space of nothing with himself. . . . Actually he relies on nothing but himself, and he manages to hold to himself without having any sort of foothold in reality. Therefore he no longer has

any restraint, and his absence of restraint is his magic with which he works on the men on whom he wants to work.

Frank's very nature precludes the question of whether he was mentally ill or healthy. He has a real delusion, the delusion that produces absence of restraint, but he utilizes this real delusion in order to work magically on men—and he needs the magically compelling effect on them not merely for his current aims; he needs it ever more because the nihilistic belief in himself, threatened by the crisis of self-awareness, must nourish itself from the belief of others to be able to continue to exist. (Ibid., p. 34)

It must be remembered that this was written during the Second World War.

Another extreme image of disintegration is, in Buber's view, that of Hitler. Two years after he distinguished between Sabbatai Zvi and Jacob Frank, he asserted the parallel between Hitler and Frank in his article, "'Am U-Manhig" (n. 85, above). He no longer maintains, as he had when he wrote the aforementioned chapter "The Beginnings," that Frank was totally devoid of a conscience, just as he does not believe that Hitler was entirely devoid of humanity.

87. Buber, "Religion and Modern Thinking," p. 87 (my emphasis). Regarding the interaction between conscience and decision, cf. N. Rotenstreich, "Conscience and Norm," *Journal of Value Inquiry* 27 (1993): 34.

88. According to my notes from a conversation with Buber in his home in Jerusalem in the winter of 1962.

89. See chapter 7.

90. See Buber, "The Way of Man According to the Teachings of Hasidism," pp. 134–35.

91. Ibid., p. 138.

92. Ibid. This is based on the version in the collection of Hasidic sayings and stories entitled *Ohel Ha-Rebbi* (Pyetrekov, 1913). See also the formulation of this conception in an article by Buber, written at the same time as the work "The Way of Man According to the Teachings of Hasidism":

As for me, I have no "Torah." I have only a finger extended and pointing at realities. . . . Anyone who expects to hear Torah from me, which means some instruction, will always be disappointed. But it seems to me that at this critical moment, there can be no bestowal of solid Torah, but only recognition of the eternal reality and realization of its power in the face of the present reality. . . . In this desert night one cannot point the way; one can help people maintain an erect soul, until the dawn breaks and lights the path—where no person will light it.

"Le-'Inyan 'Gog U-Magog'" (Regarding "Gog and Magog"), *Ha-Aretz,* 8 December 1944.

93. Buber, "The Way of Man According to the Teachings of Hasidism," p. 146.

94. Ibid., p. 148.

95. Ibid., p. 150.
96. See Buber, "Education," pp. 90–91.
97. See Buber, *I and Thou*, p. 107.
98. Ibid., p. 108.
99. Buber, "Images of Good and Evil," p. 73.
100. See the second section, above.
101. See Buber, "Right and Wrong," pp. 3–60.
102. See Buber, "Images of Good and Evil," p. 76.

Chapter 9. Moment – Eternity

1. See references in the section "Creative Vitalism" in chapter 7.
2. "Wege zum Zionismus," *Die Welt* (Berlin), 20 December 1901, pp. 5–6.
3. Buber, "Buddha," pp. 7–8.
4. Ibid., p. 8. On "Buddha," see the section "Concepts and Structures: The Background of Their Reference" in chapter 6.
5. See "Lesser Uri" (1901), col. 117.
6. Ibid., col. 116.
7. Ibid.
8. See ibid., col. 119. The importance of the uniqueness here attributed to Spinoza is not a one-time occurrence. About ten years later, he is presented again as being exceptional: "The Jew was denied immediate unity, . . . original experience of unity within the I and within nature." These were available to Spinoza, for "Spinoza's 'I' had become one; thus, he could posit unity for the world." See Buber, "Judaism and Mankind," pp. 39–41.
9. Buber, "Lesser Uri" (1901), col. 117.
10. Ibid., p. 116.
11. See chapter 1.
12. See Buber, "Renewal of Judaism," pp. 39–41.
13. *Daniel*, trans. Friedman, p. 51. The concept "direction" in the citation means the basic tendency of the human soul to choose a potential possibility from its infinite possibilities and to realize it. See chapter 8.
14. Ibid., p. 123.
15. "Der Augenblick," *Die Welt* (Berlin), 9 January 1914, p. 31.
16. Buber, introduction to *The Legend of the Baal-Shem* (New York, 1969), p. 31.
17. Buber, "My Way to Hasidism," p. 51.
18. See ibid., p. 52.
19. Ibid.
20. See Buber, "Preface to the 1923 Edition," pp. 3–10.
21. See Buber, *I and Thou*, pp. 57, 123.
22. Ibid., p. 168.
23. Buber, "Preface to the 1923 Edition," p. 4.
24. See n. 8, above.
25. See Buber, "Spinoza, Sabbetai Zvi, and the Baal-Shem," pp. 92, 96.

26. Buber, "Dialogue," p. 14, and on the entire context, see chapter 5, above.
27. Buber, "Spinoza, Sabbetai Zvi, and the Baal-Shem," p. 107.
28. Ibid., pp. 105–6.
29. See Buber, "Preface to the First Edition," p. 14.
30. Buber, "Politics Born of Faith," p. 175.
31. See Buber, *Zwiesprache* (Berlin, 1934), p. 5.
32. See chapter 1 on its place in Buber's spiritual world.
33. "The Place of Copernicus in Philosophy" (in Hebrew), remarks presented at the Copernicus Ceremony at the Hebrew University in Jerusalem, 26 May 1944, p. 5.
34. Buber, "On A. E. Simon the Educator" (in Hebrew), in *Adam Mul Arakhav* (Man confronting his values), p. 5. Remarks presented at the Hebrew University in Jerusalem on 15 March 1959, in honor of Professor A. E. Simon's sixtieth birthday, Jerusalem 1959.
35. Ibid.
36. Buber, "Fragments on Revelation," in *A Believing Humanism*, p. 115.
37. Ibid.
38. From a manuscript note of Buber's in the book of the student organization of Basel, 5 May 1929. In 1983 a photocopy of it was sent to Raphael Buber, who made it available to me.
39. In his article "Gordon and the Land," *Arakhim* (Tel Aviv, 1942), p. 24, he speaks of "contact with the absolute." This article was included in Buber's book *Bein Am Le-Artzo* as a chapter entitled "Ha-Magshim" (A man who realizes the idea of Zionism). In translation (*On Zion*, p. 159) the title was changed to "Intercourse with Eternity."
40. See Buber, "The Validity and Limitation of the Political Principle" (1953), in *Pointing the Way* (New York, 1957), p. 215.
41. Buber, "Religion and Reality," p. 20.
42. Ibid., p. 18.
43. Buber, "Religion and Modern Thinking," p. 76.
44. Buber, "Preface to the First Edition," p. 15.
45. See "Hakdama La-Mahadora Ha-Rishona" (Introduction to the first edition) (1942), in *The Prophetic Faith* (Hebrew edition). This introduction is not included in the English translation of the book.
46. Buber, "Politics Born of Faith," p. 177.
47. See Buber, "The Dialogue Between Heaven and Earth" (1951), in *On Judaism*, pp. 214–25.
48. See Buber, "Autobiographical Fragments," pp. 32–33.
49. Buber, "Politics Born of Faith," p. 178.
50. For his way of handling questions like this, see Buber, *A Land of Two Peoples*, p. 319.
51. See M. Buber, "Din ve-Cheshbon" (Accounting), in *Al Parashat Derakhim* (Jerusalem, March 1939), pp. 135–36a. The volume is a collection of articles related to problems of Zionist policy and Jewish-Arab cooperation. See the English version of "Din ve-Heshbon," entitled "And Today?," pp. 136–37.

52. Ibid., p. 136.
53. Buber, "Ilu Haya Herzl Od Be-Hayim" (1940).
54. Buber, *On Judaism*, p. 144.
55. See Buber, "Al Ha-Netzach ve-ha-Rega" (On Eternity and the moment), *Lamerchav*, 22 December 1961.
56. See Buber, "Hebrew Humanism," p. 244.
57. W. Kaufmann, "I and Thou: Prologue," in Buber, *I and Thou*, p. 30.
58. Buber, "Hebrew Humanism," p. 244.
59. See Buber, "Teviot ha-Ruach ve-ha-Metziut ha-Historit" (The demands of the spirit and historical reality) (1938), in *Am ve'Olam* (1961), p. 51.
60. "The Spirit of Israel and the World of Today" (1939), in *Israel and the World*, p. 185.
61. Published in 1943 in Hebrew in Tel Aviv.
62. Buber, "The Silent Question," in *On Judaism*, p. 202.
63. See Buber, "Jewish Religiosity," 79–94. The duality of "Religiosity – Religion" underlies this article. See the discussion of its expressions throughout Buber's spiritual biography in the section "Creative Vitalism" in chapter 7.
64. See the discussion of his work "My Way to Hasidism" earlier in this section.
65. See Buber, "After Death," in *A Believing Humanism*, p. 231.
66. Ibid.
67. From a memorial ceremony held thirty days after Buber's death and included in *Martin Buber (1878–1965), An Appreciation of His Life and Thought*, Proceedings of a Memorial Meeting Held at the Park Avenue Synagogue, New York City, July 1965 (New York, 1965), p. 10.
68. See Buber, "What is Man?," p. 136.
69. See H. Weiner, "Hasidism and M. Buber," *9 1/2 Mystics: The Kabbalah Today* (New York, 1969), p. 134.

Chapter 10. Concluding Remarks

1. See V. Bianchi, "Dualism in Religious Ethnology," in *Gilgul: Essays on the History of Religions, Dedicated to R. J. Z. Werblowsky* (Leiden, 1987), pp. 45–49.
2. See the reference to Schelling in section entitled "What is Polar Duality" in chapter 1.
3. Buber, "Images of Good and Evil," p. 76.
4. An important place is attributed to "becoming" in the worldview of Gustav Landauer, Buber's close friend and a very significant figure in his spiritual biography (see chapter 5). The dynamic purpose of Buber's conceptual structures is similar and very close to the processes that Landauer attributes to what he called "exact science." "The meaning" of this, says Landauer, is "the gathering and description of all the givens of the senses, criticism of the generalizations renewed at regular intervals, and, on the basis of these: general criticism of the world of experience, the creation of becoming, which will explain the assumption regarding the substance of

our sensible intelligence and will bring it into concord with our inner experience" (Landauer, "The Revolution" [in Hebrew] [1907], in *Ha-Kria Le-Sozialism, Ha-Mahapakha*, trans. I. Cohen [Tel Aviv, 1951], p. 150). It is no coincidence that the title of Landauer's collected writings, edited by Buber after Landauer was murdered, was *Der Werdende Mensch* (Potsdam, 1921).

5. See the section "The Character of His Concepts" in chapter 6.

6. See Buber, "My Way to Hasidism," pp. 56–57.

7. In the section "Duality and the Yearning for Unity" in chapter 1 and the summary of the section "Concepts and Structures: The Background of Their Reference" in chapter 6.

8. See Buber, "On the Essence of Culture," pp. 382–83.

9. Buber, "God and the Spirit of Man," p. 127.

10. See Buber, "On Two Hebrew Books" (in Hebrew) (1928), in *Paths in Utopia*, ed. Shapira, p. 256.

11. Cf. the remarks of Max Kadushin on the place of contradiction in the organic thinking of the rabbis. M. Kadushin, *The Rabbinic Mind* (New York, 1965), pp. x–xi, 5, 14ff., 22, 24.

12. Buber, "Education and World-View," p. 102.

13. Buber, "Tziunim le-Chugei Tanakh" (Points for Bible circles), in *Darko shel Mikra* (Jerusalem, 1964), p. 365.

14. Ibid., p. 364.

15. Buber, "What is Man?," p. 123.

16. See Buber, *I and Thou*, p. 156.

Bibliography

Alfasi, Y. *Hahozeh miLublin.* Jerusalem, 1969.

Ausubel, Nathan. *A Treasury of Jewish Folklore.* New York, 1948.

Beller, S. *Vienna and the Jews, 1867–1938.* Cambridge, 1989.

Ben Avram, B. "The German Hapoel Hatzair: The History of an Intellectual Group (1917–1920)" (in Hebrew). *Zionism* (Tel Aviv) 6 (1981): 49–95.

Berger, P. "Identity as a Problem of the Sociology of Knowledge." In *The Sociology of Knowledge,* edited by J. E. Curtis and J. W. Petras. New York, 1972.

Bergmann, Sh. H. "Berthold Feiwel ve-'avodat ha-hoveh'." In *Berthold Feiwel: ha-Ish u-Foalo.* Jerusalem, 1959.

———. "Buber's Dialogical Thought" (in Hebrew). Introduction to *Besod Siach,* by Martin Buber. Jerusalem, 1959.

———. "Buber's Philosophy." In *Thinkers of the Generation* (in Hebrew). Mitzpeh, 1935.

———. *Ha-Pilosofia Ha-Dialogit Mi-Kierkegaard ad Buber* (Dialogical philosophy from Kierkegaard to Buber). Jerusalem, 1974.

———. "M. Buber and Mysticism." In *Philosophy of Martin Buber,* edited by P. A. Schilpp and M. Friedman. La Salle, Ill., 1967.

———. "Suffering and the Consciousness of Guilt." In *Dialogical Philosophy from Kierkegaard to Buber* (in Hebrew). Jerusalem, 1974.

———. "'Three Sermons on Judaism' [by Martin Buber]" (in Hebrew), *Hashiloach* (Odessa) 26 (Shevet-Tammuz, 5672 [January–June, 1912]).

Bergmann, Sh. H., and Eliezer Shochat, eds. *Collected Writings* (in Hebrew), by A. D. Gordon. Jerusalem, 1951.

Berlin, I. *The Age of Enlightenment.* New York, 1960.

Biale, D. *Gershom Scholem, Kabbalah and Counter-History.* Cambridge, Mass., 1979.

———. "Gershom Scholem and Anarchism as a Jewish Philosophy." *Judaism,* Winter 1983.

Bianchi, V. "Dualism in Religious Ethnology." In *Gilgul: Essays on the History of Religions, Dedicated to R. J. Z. Werblowsky.* Leiden, 1987.

Borges, J. L. *El libro de Arena.* Buenos Aires, 1975.

Borowitz, E. B. "Humanism and Religious Belief in M. Buber's Thought." *Fordham University Quarterly,* no. 210 (September 1978).

Buber, M. "Abraham the Seer." In *On the Bible,* edited by N. N. Glatzer. New York, 1968

———. "Adult Education" (1950, in Hebrew). In *Am ve'Olam.* Jerusalem, 1961.

———. "After Death." In *A Believing Humanism,* translated by M. Friedman. New York, 1967.

———. "Ahavat Elohim ve-Ahavat Ha-Briot" (The love of God and the love of men) (1945). In *Be-Fardes He-Hasidut.* Tel Aviv, 1945.

———. "Achrayut Li-Shma" (Responsibility for its own sake). *Maoznayim* 22, no. 2 (1946): 103.

———. "Al ha-Hevra ve-al ha Tzibbur" (On society and on the public). *Ma'abarot* (Jaffa), May 1920, p. 215.

———. "Al ha-Mashber ha-Gadol" (On the great crisis). In *Am ve'Olam.* Jerusalem, 1961.

———. "Al Ha-Netzach ve-ha-Rega" (On Eternity and the moment). *Lamerchav,* 22 December 1961.

———. "Alte und neue Gemeinschaft" (1900), *AJS Review* (Cambridge, Mass.) 1 (1976).

———. " 'Am U-Manhig" (Nation and leader) (1942). In *Am ve'Olam.* Jerusalem, 1961.

———. "And Today?" In *A Land of Two Peoples: Martin Buber on Jews and Arabs,* edited by P. R. Mendes-Flohr. New York, 1983.

———. "At this Late Hour" (1920). In *A Land of Two Peoples: Martin Buber on Jews and Arabs,* edited by P. R. Mendes-Flohr. New York, 1983.

———. "Der Augenblick." *Die Welt* (Berlin) 9, no. 1 (1914).

———. "Autobiographical Fragments." In *The Philosophy of Martin Buber,* edited by P. A. Schilpp and M. Friedman. La Salle, Ill., 1967.

———. *A Believing Humanism.* Translated by M. Friedman. New York, 1967.

———. *Between Man and Man.* Translated by R. G. Smith. New York, 1961.

———. *Briefwechsel aus sieben Jahrzehnten.* Herausgegeben G. Schaeder. Band I: *1897–1918.* Heidelberg: 1972.

———. *Briefwechsel aus sieben Jahrzehnten.* Herausgegeben G. Schaeder. Band II: *1918–1938.* Heidelberg, 1973.

———. *Briefwechsel aus sieben Jahrzehnten.* Herausgegeben G. Schaeder. Band III: *1938–1965.* Heidelberg, 1975.

———. "Buddha" (1907). In *Ereignisse und Begegnungen.* Leipzig, 1917.

———. "A Conversion." In *Between Man and Man,* translated by R. G. Smith. New York, 1961.

———. "A Conversation with Tagore" (1950). In *A Believing Humanism,* translated by M. Friedman. New York, 1967.

———. *Daniel.* Leipzig, 1913.

———. "Davar el Bnei Shlosh-Esreh" (A word to thirteen-year-olds). *Ba'ayat Ha-Yom* (Jerusalem), 16 March 1941.

———. "Dialogue" (1932). In *Between Man and Man,* translated by R. G. Smith. New York, 1961.

———. "Din ve-Cheshbon" (Accounting). In *Al Parashat Derakhim.* Jerusalem, 1939.

———. "Distance and Relation." In *The Knowledge of Man,* translated by M. Friedman and R. G. Smith, edited with an introduction by M. Friedman. New York, 1965.

———. *Drei Reden über das Judentum.* Frankfurt a.M., 1911.

———. "Drei Sätze eines religiösen Sozialismus." *Neue Wege* 22, nos. 7–8 (1928).

———. *Eclipse of God.* Translated by M. Friedman, E. Kamenka, N. Guterman, and I. M. Lask. New York, 1952.

———. *Ecstatic Confessions.* Edited by P. R. Mendes-Flohr. Translated by E. Cameron (New York, 1985).

———. "Education." In *Between Man and Man,* translated by R. G. Smith. New York, 1961.

———. "Education and World-View" (1935). In *Pointing the Way,* edited and translated by M. Friedman. New York, 1957.

———. "The Education of Character" (1939). In *Between Man and Man,* translated by R. G. Smith. New York, 1961.

———. "Ekstase und Bekenntnis." In *Ekstatische Konfessionen,* gesammelt von Martin Buber. Jena, 1908.

———. *Ekstatische Konfessionen.* Jena, 1908.

———. "Elements of the Interhuman." In *The Knowledge of Man,* translated by M. Friedman and R. G. Smith, edited with an introduction by M. Friedman. New York, 1965.

———. "Emunat Yisrael" (The faith of Israel) (1928), in *Te'udah ve-Ye'ud.* Jerusalem, 1959.

———. *Ereignisse und Begegnungen.* Leipzig, 1917.

———. "Die Eroberung Palästinas." *Der Jude* 10-11 (January–February 1918).

———. "Er und Wir." *Die Welt* 14, no. 20 (May 1910).

———. "An Example: On the Landscapes of L. Krakauer." In *A Believing Humanism*, translated by M. Friedman. New York, 1967.

———. "The Field and the Stars" (in Hebrew). In *Paths in Utopia*, ed. A. Shapira. New ed. with supplement. Tel Aviv, 1983.

———. *For the Sake of Heaven*. Translated by L. Lewisohn. New York, 1969.

———. "The Foundation Stone." In *The Origin and Meaning of Hasidism*, edited and translated by M. Friedman. New York, 1960.

———. "Fragments on Revelation." In *A Believing Humanism*, translated by M. Friedman. New York, 1967.

———. "Geleitwort." In *Der Grosse Maggid und Seine Nachfolge*. Frankfurt a.M., 1922.

———. "Geltung und Grenze des politischen Prinzips" (1953). In *Hinweise: Gesammelte Essays (1909-1953)*. Zurich, 1953.

———. "Genuine Dialogue and the Possibilities of Peace" (1953). In *A Believing Humanism*, translated by M. Friedman. New York, 1967.

———. "Gershom Scholem: At Sixty" (in Hebrew). *Haaretz*, 6 December 1957.

———. *Die Geschichten des Rabbi Nachman*. Frankfurt a.M., 1906.

———. *Die Gesellschaft: Sammlung sozialpsychologischer Monographien*. Edited by M. Buber. 40 vols. Frankfurt a.M., 1906-12.

———. "Gespräch von der Richtung." *Neue Blätter* 2, no. 1 (1912).

———. "God and the Soul." In *Origin and Meaning of Hasidism*, edited and translated by M. Friedman. New York, 1960.

———. "God and the Spirit of Man" (1952). In *Eclipse of God*, translated by M. Friedman, E. Kamenka, N. Guterman, and I. M. Lask. New York, 1952.

———. *Good and Evil*. Translated by G. Smith. New York, 1952.

———. "Gordon and the Land." In *Arakhim*. Tel Aviv, 1942.

———. "Guilt and Guilt Feelings." In *The Knowledge of Man*, translated by M. Friedman and R. G. Smith, edited with an introduction by M. Friedman. New York, 1965.

———. "Gustav Landauer." *Die Zeit* (Vienna) 39, no. 506 (November 1904).

———. "Ha-Bayit ha-Leumi u-Mediniut Leumit be-Eretz Yisrael" (The national home and national policy in the Land of Israel). *Am ve'Olam*. Tel Aviv, 1929.

———. "Hakdama La-Mahadora Ha-Rishona" (Introduction to the first edition) (1942). In *The Prophetic Faith*, Hebrew ed. Tel Aviv, 1942.

———. *Hasidism and Modern Man*. Edited and translated by M. Friedman. New York, 1958.

———. "He and We" (1910) (in Hebrew). *Ha'Olam* 8, no. 25 (9 July 1914).

———. "The Heart Determines." In *On the Bible*, edited by N. N. Glatzer. New York, 1968.

———. "Hebrew Humanism" (1941). In *Israel and the World*, translated by O. Marx. New York, 1963.

———. *Der heilige Weg*. Frankfurt a.M., 1919.

———. "Herut." In *On Judaism*, translated by E. Jospe, edited by N. N. Glatzer. New York, 1967.

———. "Herzl und die Historie." *Ost und West* 4, nos. 8–9 (1904).

———. "The Holy Way." In *On Judaism*, translated by E. Jospe, edited by N. N. Glatzer. New York, 1967.

———. "Hope for this Hour" (in Hebrew) (1952). In *Am ve'Olam*. Jerusalem, 1961.

———. *I and Thou*. Translated by W. Kaufmann. New York, 1970.

———. *Ich und Du*. Leipzig, 1923.

———. "Ilu Haya Herzl Od Be-Hayim" (If Herzl were alive today). *Ha'aretz*, 17 May 1940. Reprinted in *Shdemot* 79 (1981).

———. "Images of Good and Evil." In *Good and Evil*. New York, 1952.

———. *Israel and the World*. Translated by O. Marx. New York, 1963.

———. "Jewish Religiosity." In *On Judaism*, edited by N. N. Glatzer, translated by E. Jospe. New York, 1967.

———. "Judaism and Mankind." In *On Judaism*, edited by N. N. Glatzer, translated by E. Jospe. New York, 1967.

———. "Judaism and the Jews." In *On Judaism*, edited by N. N. Glatzer, translated by E. Jospe. New York, 1967.

———. *Die Jüdische Bewegung: Gesammelte Aufsätze und Ansprachen*. Band I: *1900–1915*. Berlin, 1916.

———. *Die Jüdische Bewegung: Gesammelte Aufsätze und Ansprachen*. Band II: *1916–1920*. Berlin, 1920.

———. "Jüdische Künstler." Introduction to *Jüdische Künstler*, edited by M. Buber. Berlin, 1903.

———. "Jüdische Wissenschaft." *Die Welt* 5, no. 41 (11 October 1901) and 5 no. 43 (25 October 1901).

———. *Kingship of God*. Translated by R. Scheimann. New York, 1967.

———. *The Knowledge of Man*. Translated by M. Friedman and R. G. Smith. Edited with an introduction by M. Friedman. New York, 1965.

———. *A Land of Two Peoples: Martin Buber on Jews and Arabs*. Edited by P. R. Mendes-Flohr. New York, 1983.

———. *Die Legende des Baal Schem*. Frankfurt a.M., 1908.

——. *The Legend of the Baal-Shem.* Translated by M. Friedman. New York, 1969.

——. "Die Lehre und die Tat." *Jüdische Rundschau* 39, no. 40 (18 May 1934).

——. "Lesser Uri." *Ost und West* 1, no. 2 (February 1901).

——. "Die Losung." *Der Jude* 1 (1 April 1916).

——. "The Love of God and the Idea of Deity" (1914). In *The Eclipse of God,* translated by M. Friedman, E. Kamenka, N. Guterman, and I. M. Lask. New York, 1952.

——. "Man and his Image-Work." In *The Knowledge of Man,* translated by M. Friedman and R. G. Smith, edited with an introduction by M. Friedman. New York, 1965.

——. "Me-ha-Rishonim" (Among the first ones). In *Berthold Feiwel: ha-Ish u-Foalo.* Jerusalem, 1959.

——. *Mein Weg zum Chassidismus.* Frankfurt a.M., 1918.

——. "Mit einem Monisten" (1914). *Ereignisse und Begegnungen.* Leipzig, 1917.

——. "My Way to Hasidism." In *Hasidism and Modern Man,* edited and translated by M. Friedman. New York, 1958.

——. *Nachlese.*3d ed. Gerlingen, 1993.

——. "On A. E. Simon the Educator" (in Hebrew). In *Adam Mul Arakhav* (Man confronting his values). Remarks presented at the Hebrew University in Jerusalem on 15 March 1959, in honor of Prof. A. E. Simon's sixtieth birthday.

——. "On Eternity and the Moment" (in Hebrew). *Lamerchav,* 12 December 1961.

——. *On Judaism.* Translated by E. Jospe. Edited by N. N. Glatzer. New York, 1967.

——. *On the Bible.* Edited by N. N. Glatzer. New York, 1968.

——. "On the Essence of Culture" (in Hebrew). In *Pnei Adam.* Jerusalem, 1962.

——. "On Two Hebrew Books" (in Hebrew). In *Paths in Utopia,* edited by A. Shapira. Tel Aviv, 1983.

——. *On Zion: The History of an Idea.* Translated by S. Goodman. London, 1952.

——. *The Origin and Meaning of Hasidism.* Edited and translated by M. Friedman. New York, 1960.

——. *Paths in Utopia.* Translated by R. F. C. Hull. Boston, 1958.

——. *Paths in Utopia* (in Hebrew). Edited by A. Shapira. New ed. with supplement. Tel Aviv, 1983.

———. "The Paths of Religion in our Land" (in Hebrew). In *Haruach vehametziut*. Tel Aviv, 1942.

———. *Pointing the Way*. Translated and edited by M. Friedman. New York, 1957.

———. "Politics Born of Faith" (1933). In *A Believing Humanism*, translated by M. Friedman. New York, 1967.

———. "The Power of the Spirit" (1934). In *Israel and the World*, translated by O. Marx. New York, 1963.

———. Preface to "Images of Good and Evil." In *Good and Evil*. New York, 1952.

———. Preface to *Kalewala: Das Nationalepos der Finnen*. Munich, 1914.

———. "Preface to the First Edition." In *Kingship of God*, translated by R. Scheimann. New York, 1967.

———. "Preface to the 1923 Edition." In *On Judaism*, edited by N. N. Glatzer, translated by E. Jospe. New York, 1967.

———. "The Prejudices of Youth." In *Israel and the World*, translated by O. Marx. New York, 1963.

———. "Prophecy, Apocalyptic, and the Historical Hour." In *On the Bible*, ed. N. N. Glatzer. New York, 1968.

———. *The Prophetic Faith*. New York, 1977.

———. "The Question of the Single One." In *Between Man and Man*, translated by R. G. Smith. New York, 1961.

———. "Recollection of a Death." In *Pointing the Way*, translated and edited by M. Friedman. New York, 1957.

———. *Rede über das Erzieherische*. Berlin, 1926.

———. *Reden über das Judentum*. Frankfurt a.M., 1923.

———. "Religion and Ethics." In *Eclipse of God*, translated by M. Friedman, E. Kamenka, N. Guterman, and I. M. Lask. New York, 1952.

———. "Religion and Modern Thinking." In *Eclipse of God*, translated by M. Friedman, E. Kamenka, N. Guterman, and I. M. Lask. New York, 1952.

———. "Religion and Philosophy." In *The Knowledge of Man*, translated by M. Friedman and R. G. Smith, edited with an introduction by M. Friedman. New York, 1965.

———. "Religion and Reality" (1951). In *Eclipse of God*, translated by M. Friedman, E. Kamenka, N. Guterman, and I. M. Lask. New York, 1952.

———. "Renewal of Judaism" (1910). In *On Judaism*, translated by E. Jospe, edited by N. N. Glatzer. New York, 1967.

———. "The Renewal of National Life" (in Hebrew). In *Am ve'Olam*. Jerusalem, 1961.

———. "Replies to my Critics." In *The Philosophy of Martin Buber*, edited by P. A. Schilpp and M. Friedman. The Library of Living Philosophers, vol. 12. La Salle, Ill., 1967.

———. "Die Revolution und Wir." *Der Jude* 3, nos. 8-9 (November–December 1918).

———. "Right and Wrong." In *Good and Evil*. New York, 1952.

———. "Shalosh Tachanot." In *Am ve'Olam*. Tel Aviv, 1961.

———. "The Silent Question" (1951). In *On Judaism*, translated by E. Jospe, edited by N. N. Glatzer. New York, 1967.

———. "Spinoza, Sabbatai Zvi, and the Baal-Shem." In *The Origin and Meaning of Hasidism*, edited and translated by M. Friedman. New York, 1960.

———. "The Spirit of the Orient and Judaism." In *On Judaism*, edited by N. N. Glatzer, translated by E. Jospe. New York, 1967.

———. "State and Culture" (in Hebrew). *Haaretz*, 30 April 1953. Remarks made upon receiving the Israel Prize.

———. *Die Stunde und die Erkenntnis: Reden und Aufsätze*. Berlin, 1936.

———. *Tales of the Hasidim: The Early Masters*. Translated by O. Marx. New York, 1956.

———. *Tales of the Hasidim: The Later Masters*. Translated by O. Marx. New York, 1948.

———. "The Teacher of Truth" (in Hebrew). In *Paths in Utopia*, edited by A. Shapira. New ed. with supplement. Tel Aviv, 1983.

———. "Teaching and Deed." In *Israel and the World*, translated by O. Marx. New York, 1963.

———. "Teviot ha-Ruach ve-ha-Metziut ha-Historit" (The demands of the spirit and historical reality) (1938). In *Am ve'Olam*. Jerusalem, 1961.

———. "Theodor Herzl." *Freistatt* 6, no. 29 (23 July 1904).

———. "Translation of Bible, its Intentions and Paths" (in Hebrew) (1940). In *Darko shel mikra*. Jerusalem, 1964.

———. "The Two Foci of the Jewish Soul." In *Israel and the World*, translated by O. Marx. New York, 1963.

———. "Two Poems by M. Buber." Translated by G. Hartman. Commentary by M. Idel. *Orim* (New Haven, Conn.), Spring 1987.

———. *Two Types of Faith*. Translated by N. P. Goldhawk. New York, 1951.

———. "Tziunim le-Chugei Tanakh" (Points for Bible circles). In *Darko shel Mikra*. Jerusalem, 1964.

———. "Über Jacob Böhme." *Wiener Rundschau* 5, no. 12 (15 June 1901).

———. "Unser Bildungsziel." *Jüdische Rundschau* 38, no. 54 (7 July 1933).

———. *Urdistanz und Beziehung*. Zweite Ausgabe. Heidelberg, 1960.

———. "The Validity and Limitation of the Political Principle" (1953). In *Pointing the Way*. New York, 1957.

———. "Verantwortung." *Berliner Tageblatt*, 1 January 1929.

————. "Vorbemerkung über Franz Werfel." *Der Jude* 2, nos. 1–2 (April–May 1917).

————. "Vor der Entscheidung." *Der Jude* 3 (12 March 1919).

————. "Vorwort." In *Urdistanz und Beziehung.* Heidelberg, 1960.

————. "The Way of Man According to the Teachings of Hasidism." In *Hasidism and Modern Man,* edited and translated by M. Friedman. New York, 1958.

————. "Wege zum Zionismus." *Die Welt* 5, no. 51 (20 December 1901).

————. *Werke I: Schriften zur Philosophie.* Munich and Heidelberg, 1962.

————. "What is Common to All." In *Knowledge of Man,* translated by M. Friedman and R. G. Smith, edited with an introduction by M. Friedman. New York, 1965.

————. "What is Man?" In *Between Man and Man,* translated by R. G. Smith. New York, 1961.

————. "With a Monist." In *Pointing the Way,* translated and edited by M. Friedman. New York, 1957.

————. "The Word that is Spoken." In *The Knowledge of Man,* translated by M. Friedman and R. G. Smith, edited with an introduction by M. Friedman. New York, 1965.

————. *Worte an die Zeit . . . 2. Heft: Gemeinschaft.* Munich, 1919.

————. "Ein Wort über Nietzsche und die Lebenswerte." In vol. 1 of *Die Kunst im Leben.* Berlin, 1900.

————. "Zion and Youth" (in Hebrew) (1918). In *Am ve'Olam.* Jerusalem, 1961.

————. "Zwiesprache." *Die Kreatur* (Berlin) 3, no. 3 (1929–30).

Buber, R. "Die Buberfamilie. Erinnerungen." In *Dialog mit Martin Buber.* Frankfurt a.M., 1982.

Casper, B. *Das dialogische Denken: Eine Untersuchung der religions-philosophischen Bedeutung F. Rosenzweigs, F. Ebners und M. Bubers.* Freiburg, 1967.

Cohen, Arthur A., ed. *The Jew: Essays from Martin Buber's Journal "Der Jude" (1916-1928).* Tuscaloosa, Ala., 1980.

Cohen, G. D. "Aliyah." New York, 1968. Offprint.

————. "German Jewry as Mirror of Modernity." *Leo Baeck Institute Year Book* 20 (1975).

Cohen, M., and R. Buber, comps. *Martin Buber: Bibliography of his Writings, 1897–1978.* Jerusalem, 1980.

Dilthey, W. *The Essence of Philosophy.* Translated by S. A. Emery and W. T. Emery (Chapel Hill, N.C., 1954.

————. *Patterns and Meaning in History.* Edited by H. P. Rickman. New York, 1962.

————. "Das Wesen der Philosophie" (1907). In Band V of *Gesammelte Schriften*. Stuttgart 1958.

Dinur, B.-Z. "Three Conversations with Buber" (in Hebrew). *Molad* 222 (1967).

Dreyfus, T. "Understanding the Term 'Umkehr' in the Philosophy of Martin Buber" (in Hebrew). *Daat* (Ramat Gan), no. 9 (Summer 1982).

Eisenstadt, S. N. "Historical Traditions and Patterns of Modernization (Introduction)." *Jerusalem Quarterly*, no. 38 (1986).

Erickson, E. "Crisis of the Identity Crisis." In *Identity, Youth, and Crisis*. New York, 1968.

Farber, L. H. "Martin Buber and Psychotherapy." In *Philosophy of Martin Buber*, edited by P. A. Schilpp and M. Friedman. La Salle, Ill., 1967.

Fishbane, M., and P. R. Mendes-Flohr, eds. *Texts and Responses*. Leiden, 1975.

Fox, E. "Problems in Buber's Moral Philosophy." In *The Philosophy of Martin Buber*, edited by Philip A. Schilpp and M. Friedman. La Salle, Ill., 1967.

————. "Translating Jewish Thought into Curriculum." In *From the Scholar to the Classroom*. New York, 1977.

Friedman, M. "Interrogation of M. Buber." In *Philosophical Interrogations*, edited by S. and B. Rome. New York, 1970.

————. *Martin Buber's Life and Work: The Early Years, 1878–1923*. New York, 1981.

Friedman, M., trans. Introduction to *Daniel*, by Martin Buber. New York, 1965.

Geertz, C. *The Interpretation of Cultures*. New York, 1973.

Glatzer, N. N. "Aspects of Martin Buber's Thought." *Modern Judaism* 1, no. 1 (May 1981).

————. Editor's postscript to *On Judaism*, by Martin Buber. New York, 1967.

————. *Essays in Jewish Thought*. Tuscaloosa, Ala., 1978.

————. Interview with Prof. N. Glatzer. University of Arizona, April 1978.

————. "Reflections on Buber's Impact on German Jewry." *Leo Baeck Institute Year Book* 25 (1980): 301–9.

————. ed. *On Judaism*, by Martin Buber. New York, 1967.

Goldberg, Lea. *Drama of Consciousness: Studies in Dostoevsky* (in Hebrew). Tel Aviv, 1974.

Goldin, J. "The Thinking of the Rabbis." *Judaism* 5, no. 1 (Winter 1956).

Habermas, J. *Knowledge and Human Interest*. Boston, 1971.

Heine, H. *Gedanken und Einfälle*.

Heschel, A. J. *Between God and Man*. Edited by F. A. Rothschild. New York, 1959.

Herder, J. G. *Sämtliche Werke*. Herausgegeben von B. Supham. Bände I, VIII. Berlin, 1981.

Hodes, A. *Encounter with Martin Buber*. London, 1975.

Hofmannsthal, H. von. "Der Brief des Lord Chandos." In *Wege der deutschen Literatur*, by H. Glaser, F. Lehmann, and A. Lubos. Frankfurt a.M., 1961.

Holtz, A. *Be-Olam Ha-Machshava Shel Hazal Be-Ikvot Mishnat M. Kadushin* (Rabbinic thought, following the teaching of M. Kadushin). Tel Aviv, 1979.

Horwitz, R. "Buber and Ebner." *Judaism* 32 (Spring 1983).

———. *Buber's Way to "I and Thou": The Development of Martin Buber's Thought and his "Religion as Presence" Lectures*. Philadelphia, 1988.

———. "Discoveries Regarding the Origins of M. Buber's *I and Thou*" (in Hebrew). *Proceedings of the Israeli National Academy of Sciences* (Jerusalem) 5, no. 8 (1975).

Hughes, H. S. *Consciousness and Society*. New York, 1958.

Huxley, A. *The Doors of Perception*. New York, 1954.

James, William. *The Varieties of Religious Experience*. In *The Works of William James*. Cambridge, Mass., 1985.

Johnston, W. M. *The Austrian Mind: An Intellectual and Social History, 1848–1938*. Los Angeles, 1972.

———. "Martin Buber's Literary Debut: 'On Viennese Literature' (1897)." *The German Quarterly* 27, no. 4 (November 1974).

Kadish, Yo'etz Kim. *Tiferet Hayehudi*. Pietrkov, 1912.

Kadushin, M. *The Rabbinic Mind*. New York, 1972.

———. *Worship and Ethics*. New York, 1963.

Katz, J. "The Jewish Response to Modernity in Western Europe." *Jerusalem Quarterly*, no. 38 (1986): 5–13.

———. *Tradition and Crisis*. New York, 1961.

Kaufmann, W. "Buber's Failures and his Victory" (in Hebrew). In *Martin Buber: One Hundred Years Since His Birth*, edited by Y. Bloch, H. Gordon, and M. Dorman. Tel Aviv, 1982. Proceedings of the Beersheba conference.

———. *Discovering the Mind*. Vol. 3. New York, 1980.

———. *Existentialism, Religion and Death*. New York, 1976.

———. "I and Thou: Prologue." In *I and Thou*, by M. Buber. New York, 1970.

Kohn, H. *Karl Kraus, Arthur Schnitzler, Otto Weininger: Aus dem Jüdischen Wien der Jahrhundertwende*. Tübingen, 1962.

———. *Living in a World Revolution*. New York, 1965.

———. *Martin Buber: Sein Werk und seine Zeit, 1880–1930*. Afterword by R. Weltsch. Cologne, 1961.

————. "Martin Buber's Youth" (in Hebrew). *Ha-Po'el Ha-Tza'ir* 21, nos. 16–17 (1928).

————. "The Religious Philosophy of Martin Buber." *The Menorah Journal* (New York) 26, no. 2 (April–June 1938).

Kraft, W. *Gespräche mit Martin Buber.* Munich, 1966.

Kurzweill, B. " 'Shlosha Neumim Al Ha-Yahadut' le-M. Buber" (Buber's "Three Addresses on Judaism"). *Haaretz,* 10 July 1953.

Landauer, G. "Martin Buber." *Neue Blätter* 3 (January–February 1913).

————. *Sein Lebensgang in Briefen.* Frankfurt a.M., 1929.

————. *Der Werdende Mensch.* Potsdam, 1921.

Langer, S. K. *Philosophy in a New Key.* 3d ed. Cambridge, Mass., 1978.

Levin, K. *Resolving Social Conflicts.* New York, 1948.

Link-Salinger (Hyman), R. *Gustav Landauer: Philosopher of Utopia.* Indianapolis, 1977.

Magnes, J. L. "The Seer of Full Reality" (in Hebrew). *Ner* (Jerusalem) 15, nos. 9–10 (1965).

M. Buber (1878-1965). Proceedings of the Memorial Meeting Held at the Park Avenue Synagogue, New York City, 13 July 1965.

Mendes-Flohr, P. R. "Fin-de-siècle Orientalism, the Ostjuden and the Aesthetics of Jewish Self-Affirmation." In *Studies in Contemporary Jewry,* ed. J. Frankel. Bloomington, Ind., 1984.

————. "From Kulturmystik to Dialogue: An Inquiry into the Formation of Martin Buber's Philosophy of I and Thou." Ph.D. diss., Brandeis University, 1974.

————. *From Mysticism to Dialogue: M. Buber's Transformation of German Social Thought.* Detroit, 1989.

————. "Martin Buber's Concept of the Centre and Social Renewal." *The Jewish Journal of Sociology* (London) 18, no. 1 (June 1976).

————. "M. Buber and Hebrew Humanism." *Orim* (New Haven, Conn.), Spring 1988.

————. "M. Buber and the Metaphysicians of Contempt." In *Living with Antisemitism: Modern Jewish Responses,* edited by J. Reinharz. Hanover, N.H., 1987.

————. "M. Buber's Reception among Jews." *Modern Judaism,* May 1986.

————. "The Road to *I and Thou:* An Inquiry into Buber's Transition from Mysticism to Dialogue." In *Texts and Responses,* edited by M. Fishbane and P. R. Mendes-Flohr. Leiden, 1975.

Mendes-Flohr, P. R., and B. Susser. "Alte und neue Gemeinschaft: An Unpublished Buber Manuscript." *AJS Review* (Cambridge, Mass.), 1976.

Mendes-Flohr, P. R., and J. Reinharz, eds. *The Jew in the Modern World: A Documentary History.* New York, 1980.

Mitzman, A. *Sociology and Estrangement: Three Sociologists of Imperial Germany*. New York, 1973.

Moser, R. *Gotteserfahrung bei Martin Buber: Eine theologische Untersuchung*. Heidelberg, 1979.

Mosse, G. L. *The Crisis of German Ideology*. New York, 1964.

———. *Germans and Jews*. New York, 1970.

———. *The Jews and German War Experience, 1914–1918*. Leo Baeck Memorial Lecture 21. New York, 1977.

Muffs, Y. "Love and Joy as Metaphors of Volition in Hebrew and Related Literatures. Part 2: The Joy of Giving." *The Journal of Ancient Near Eastern Society of Columbia University* 11 (1979).

Nash, S. "Berdyczewsky and the Jewish Sorrow." *Conservative Judaism* (New York) 29 (Fall 1974).

Nemia, J. C. "The Dynamic Bases of Psychopathology." In *The Harvard Guide to Modern Psychiatry*, edited by A. M. Nicholi. Cambridge, Mass., 1978.

Neumann, Erich. *Tiefenpsychologie und Neue Ethik*. Zürich, 1949.

Otto, R. *The Idea of the Holy*. Translated by J. W. Harvey (Harmondsworth, U.K., 1959.

———. *Mysticism East and West*. Translated by B. L. Bracey and R. C. Payne. New York, 1970.

Oz, Amos. *Black Box* (in Hebrew). Tel Aviv, 1987.

Piaget, Y. *Main Trends in Interdisciplinary Research*. New York, 1973.

Poe, E. A. "William Wilson." In *Edgar Allen Poe*, edited by P. Van Doren Stern. New York, 1957.

Poppel, S. M. *Zionism in Germany, 1897–1933*. Philadelphia, 1977.

Rank, Otto. "The Double and the Permanence of the Soul" (in Hebrew), translated from French by Yehoshua Kenaz. *Haaretz*, 14 September 1973.

Reinharz, J. "Martin Buber's Impact on German Zionism before World War I." *Studies in Zionism* (Tel Aviv), Autumn 1982.

Rosenzweig, F. *On Jewish Learning*. Edited by N. N. Glatzer. New York, 1955.

Rotenstreich, N. "Conscience and the Norm." *Journal of Value Inquiry* 27 (1993).

———. "Convertibility and Alienation." In *Substance and Form in History*, edited by Pompa and Dray. Edinburgh, 1981.

———. "Immediacy and Dialogue." *Revue Internationale de Philosophie*, no. 216 (1978).

———. *Man and his Dignity*. Jerusalem, 1983.

———. "Spontaneity and Alienation." *International Philosophical Quarterly* 11, no. 9 (December 1971).

———. "Tradition." In *Contemporary Jewish Religious Thought*, edited by A. Cohen and P. R. Mendes-Flohr. New York, 1987.

Rothschild, F. A., ed. *Between God and Man: From the Writings of A. J. Heschel.* New York, 1959.

Rozenthal, Shlomo Gabriel. *Hitgalut hatzadikim.* New ed. Jerusalem, 1959.

Schaeder, G. *The Hebrew Humanism of Martin Buber.* Translated by N. J. Jacobs. Detroit, 1973.

———. "Martin Buber: Ein biographischer Abriss." In M. Buber, *Briefwechsel aus sieben Jahrzehnten,* herausgegeben G. Schaeder. Band I: *1897–1918.* Heidelberg, 1972.

Scharfstein, Ben-Ami. "I and All my Shadows" (in Hebrew). *Bamachane,* 19 January 1972.

Schilpp, P. A., and M. Friedman, eds. *The Philosophy of Martin Buber.* Vol. 12 of the Library of Living Philosophers. La Salle, Ill. 1967.

Schmidt, G. G. *Martin Buber's Formative Years: From German Culture to Jewish Renewal, 1897–1909.* Tuscaloosa and London, 1995.

Scholem, G. "Le-Demuto Shel Martin Buber" (Regarding the figure of Martin Buber) (1953). In *Devarim Be-Go,* compiled and edited by A. Shapira. Tel Aviv, 1976.

———. *Major Trends in Jewish Mysticism.* New York, 1941.

———. "Martin Buber's Conception of Judaism." In *On Jews and Judaism in Crisis,* edited by W. J. Dannhauser. New York, 1976.

———. "Martin Buber's Interpretation of Hasidism" (1961). In *The Messianic Idea in Judaism.* New York, 1971.

———. "On Buber's Works in the Field of Hasidism" (in Hebrew) (1948). In *Devarim Be-Go.* Tel Aviv, 1976.

———. *On the Kabbalah and its Symbolism.* New York, 1969.

Schorske, C. E. *Fin-de-Siècle Vienna.* New York, 1980.

Shapira, A. "A. D. Gordon and the Second Aliya Realization of Utopia." In *Kibbutz and Communes: Past and Future,* edited by I. Paz, Y. Gorni, and Y. Oved. New Brunswick, N.J., 1987.

———. "Bubers Platz in der jüdischen Kultur der Gegenwart." *Judaica: Stiftung für Kirche und Judentum* (Basel) 44 (February 1988).

———. "Communities Coming into Being and Reform of the World in M. Buber's Social Utopianism" (in Hebrew). In Martin Buber, *Paths in Utopia,* edited by A. Schapira. (German ed. Heidelberg, 1985).

———. "Dual Structures in the Thought of Martin Buber" (in Hebrew). Ph.D. diss., Tel Aviv University, 1983.

———. "Meetings with Buber." *Midstream* 24, no. 9 (November 1978).

———. "Messianismus und Erlösung." In *Martin Buber: Internationales Symposium, Frankfurt a.M., May 1985.* Frankfurt a.M., 1989.

―――. "Political Messianism in Buber's Conception of Redemption." *Journal of Jewish Studies* (Oxford Center for Hebrew Studies), Summer 1991.

―――. "The Symbolic Plane and its Secularization in the Spiritual World of G. Scholem." *Jewish Thought and Philosophy* (New York) 3 (1994).

―――. "Werdende Gemeinschaft und die Vollendung der Welt." In *Martin Bubers Erbe für unsere Zeit.* Frankfurt a.M., 1985.

―――. "Work [and creative connotations in Jewish history of ideas]." In *Contemporary Jewish Religious Jewish Thought,* edited by A. A. Cohen and P. R. Mendes-Flohr. New York, 1987.

―――, ed. *The Seventh Day: Soldiers' Talk about the Six-Day War.* General editor of the English edition: H. Near. New York, 1970.

Simon, A. E. *Aufbau im Untergang: Jüdische Erwachsenenbildung im nationalsozialistischen Deutschland als geistiger Widerstand.* Tübingen 1959. Translated into English under the title "Jewish Adult Education in Nazi Germany as Spiritual Resistence," *First Yearbook of the Leo Baeck Institute* (London), 1956.

―――. *Bubers Dialogisches Denken.* Frankfurt a.M., 1974.

―――. "The Builder of Bridges." *Judaism* 27, no. 2 (Spring 1978).

―――. "From Dialogue to Peace." *Jerusalem Post,* 18 June 1965.

―――. "G. Scholem and M. Buber." *Neue Züricher Zeitung,* 11 June 1967.

―――. *Kav Hatichum.* Givat Haviva, 1973.

―――. "The Living Heritage of M. M. Buber: One Hundred Years Since his Birth" (in Hebrew). In *Ya'adim Tzematim Netiv'im: Haguto shel M. Buber.* Tel Aviv, 1985.

―――. "Martin Buber and German Jewry" (in Hebrew). In *Ya'adim Tzematim Netiv'im: Haguto shel M. Buber.* Tel Aviv, 1985.

―――. *Ya'adim Tzematim Netiv'im: Haguto shel M. Buber.* Tel Aviv, 1985.

Soloveitchik, J. D. "Halachik Man" (in Hebrew) (1944). In *Besod hayadid vehayahad,* edited by P. Hacohen Peli. Jerusalem, n.d.

―――. *The Lonely Man of Faith* (in Hebrew). Jerusalem: The Rav Kook Institute, 1965.

Susser, B. "Ideological Multivalence: M. Buber and the Völkisch Tradition." *Political Theory* 5, no. 1 (February 1977).

Swart, K. W. *The Sense of Decadence in Nineteenth-Century France.* The Hague, 1964.

Tal, U. "Forms of Pseudo-Religion in the German Kulturbereich prior to the Holocaust." *Immanuel* (Jerusalem) 3 (Winter 1973).

―――. "Man and Society: Hermeneutical Aspects of Social Theology according to Jewish Sources." *Sidic* (Rome) 12, no. 1 (1979).

―――. "Young German Intellectuals on Romanticism and Judaism . . . Early 19th Century." In *Salo Baron Jubilee Volume II,* edited by S. Lieberman. Jerusalem, 1974.

Tzemah, S. "Beyn Shney Ofakim" (Between two horizons). In *Ha-Po'el Ha-Tza'ir*, Sixtieth Anniversary Issue, 26 September 1967.

———. *Bimey Masah* (In times of examination). Jerusalem, 1945.

———. *Shanah Rishona* (First year). Tel Aviv, 1961.

Tzur, M., and A. Shapira. "With Gershom Scholem: An Interview." In *On Jews and Judaism in Crisis*, by G. Scholem. New York, 1976.

Walden, M. A. *Niflaot Harabi*. Pietrkov, 1911.

Weiner, H. "Hasidism and M. Buber." In *9 1/2 Mystics: The Kabbala Today*. New York, 1969.

Werblowsky, R. J. Z. *Beyond Tradition and Modernity*. London, 1976.

Whitehead, A. N. *The Aims of Education*. New York, 1929.

Winkler, P. "Betrachtungen einer Philozionistin." *Die Welt*, 6 September 1901.

Wolff, K. H. *Trying Sociology*. New York, 1974.

Yehoshua, A. B. "An Effort to Purify the Vermin: Another Psychoanalytical Interpretation of Kafka's 'Metamorphosis'" (in Hebrew). *Moznayim 58*, nos. 7–8 (Kislev-Tevet 1985).

Index

260
INDEX

polarity, 2, 23, 24, 25, 26, 27, 28, 29, 39, 193, 203n. 54
a living, existential reality, 2
political realism, 155
political tendency, 189
"Politics Born of Faith," 225n. 147, 232nn. 30, 46, and 49
potentiality, 37
power of decision, 173
"Power of the Spirit, The," 223n. 72
powers, 3
Prague, 42, 90, 138
"Prayer" 77
"Prejudices of Youth, The," 218n. 77
premystical stage of Buber's thought, 112
present – historical, 10, 38
primal dualism, 39
primary creativity, 9
primordial soul, 205n. 84
"problem of man," vii
problematic nature, 39
process of consolidation, 2
Prolegomena to any Future Metaphysics, 76
prophecy and apocalypse, 27
prophecy and destiny, 27
"Prophecy, Apocalyptic, and Historical Hour," 99, 204n. 59, 215n. 76, 229 n. 72
Prophetic Faith, The, 187, 208nn. 16, and 30, 215n. 65
"Pshysha," 56
"purified conceptualism," 120
purpose of Buber's concepts, 6

Question of the Single One, The (1936), 117, 205n. 93, 218nn. 76 and 81, 221n. 23, 228n. 34

Rank, Otto, 59
Raphael [Buber], 78
Realization, 110, 111, 112, 113, 114, 116, 117, 118, 119, 158, 164, 171, 172, 180
Realization – Orientation, 4, 110, 112
rebirth, 95, 181
of "absolute life," 181
"Recollection of a Death," 52, 54, 55, 207n. 5
"reconcilation," 152
redemption, 4, 5, 95, 100, 113, 162

need for, 4
personal, 4
"Regarding Gog and Magog," 230n. 92
"Relation," 11, 12, 26, 27, 126, 128, 151
"relation – distance" structure, 152
"relative life," 181
"Religion and Ethics," 228n. 44, 229n. 78
"Religion and Modern Thinking," 229n. 79, 230n. 87, 232n. 43
"Religion and Philosophy," 204n. 58, 220nn. 112, 114, and 119
"Religion as Presence," 116, 227n. 30, 228n. 61
"Religion and Reality" (1951), 199n. 10, 232n. 41
religiosity, 135, 191
religiosity and philosophy, 27
religious dualism, 193
Renaissance, 103
renewal, 194
renewal of Judaism, 38, 134, 154, 206 n. 17
"Renewal of Judaism" (1910), 113, 216 n. 22, 217n. 35, 221n. 18, 225n. 131, 231n. 12
"Renewal of National Life," 215n. 68
"Replies to my Critics," 207n. 23, 213 n. 31, 218n. 82, 220n. 120, 221n. 5, 229n. 69
response, 117
responsibility, 116, 117, 118, 122, 174, 175, 218n. 70
return (Umkehr), 95
revelation and concealment, 7
Revelation – the Eclipse of God, 12
"Revolution und Wir, Die," 222n. 43
Revolutionary – Soldier, 12
"Right and Wrong," 208n. 19, 231n. 101
Rilke, Rainer Maria, 13, 71
Rogers, Carl, 88, 94
romantic "polar doctrine," 194
rootedness, 3, 21
Rosenzweig, 116
Rubashov-Shazar, Zalman, 140
Ruppin, Arthur, 38, 45

salvation, 4
sanctification of lived reality, 118
"Saul unter den Propheten" (Saul among the Prophets), 71
Schaeder, Grete, 91, 94, 96